THE A TO Z OF

EDI

And itmmerce

n

29th Street PRESS

A Division of
DUKE COMMU
221 E. 29th Stre
(800) 621-1544 •
www.29thstreet

Library of Congress Cataloging-in-Publication Data

Jilovec, Nahid, 1958-
    The A to Z of EDI / by Nahid Jilovec. — 2nd ed.
    p. cm.
Includes index.
ISBN 1-882419-16-2 (pbk.)
1. Electronic data interchange. I. Title.
HF5548.33 .J55 1998
658'.0546—ddc21

                                          98-9045
                                            CIP

Published by 29th Street Press
DUKE COMMUNICATIONS INTERNATIONAL
Loveland, Colorado

This book was printed and bound in Canada.

ISBN 1-882419-16-2

2001 2000 1999 WL 1 10 9 8 7 6 5 4 3 2

This book is dedicated to my parents, A. and B. Malekzadeh,
for years of love and support and for teaching me to believe in myself.

Acknowledgments

Many thanks go to my staff at Whittman-Hart, who have taught me a lot of things about EDI and EC and without whose support I would not have been able to focus on this book.

I am also very grateful to Whittman-Hart for providing a nurturing and mutually respectful work environment. Whittman-Hart's support of my writing and public speaking engagements has given me the ability to be creative and to pursue my passion for e-business.

Finally, I wish to express my great appreciation for the years of support and encouragement from the staff at Duke Communications. They are a joy to work with and have made this a lot of fun!

Table of Contents At a Glance

Table of Contents

Introduction

Electronic data interchange (EDI) is an electronic means for companies to exchange business documents, such as purchase orders and invoices, over telephone lines. Because EDI eliminates the need for sending paper documents through traditional means — including mail, faxes, or telexes — EDI is a major contributor to creating a "paperless" office environment. What sets EDI apart from other electronic tools is that EDI documents are standardized.

Companies that exchange documents via EDI are called *trading partners.* The implementation of EDI requires trading partners to evaluate business procedures and to invest in and learn about special software and hardware as well as communications, standards, audit issues, and legal support necessities. Although EDI implementation requires an investment up front, the benefits generally outweigh the costs.

The concept and technology of EDI have been around for a long time. Many large corporations have long been using EDI, some for as many as 25 years. In recent years, EDI has caught the attention of the world, as governments and private industries strive to become more competitive internationally and increase profitability. Because EDI is a necessary component of such cutting-edge manufacturing and supply strategies as just in time (JIT), demand for EDI solutions has been growing rapidly. Worldwide, companies are realizing that EDI as a technology can help reduce administrative costs, accelerate information processing, and ensure data accuracy. And EDI as a strategic tool can eliminate certain business transactions, streamline business procedures, re-engineer the way business is done, and tighten vendor/customer relations.

Today, most companies have implemented EDI to some extent. Many companies are faced with the challenges involved in further leveraging their existing EDI investment. One of the biggest challenges EDI managers face is convincing noncompliant trading partners to use EDI. Many middle-market companies have initiated EDI activity because of pressure from a larger "hub" company. The hub companies often start with an aggressive trading partner penetration plan, but realize quickly that expanding EDI to trading partners is not as easy as they may have thought.

Although the major hubs are using EDI with their first-tier suppliers, they are struggling to extend EDI to the second tier. Most middle-market organizations cannot provide financial support for EDI projects to their smaller trading partners, but many hubs do. Hubs have been known to penalize those who are not using EDI. Remember, leveraging your investment in EDI requires a long-term perspective and commitment. For example, you can extend your EDI investment by using it with other electronic commerce technologies.

At the outset, many believe that EDI will be easy to implement. However, once you start implementing, you realize how much more you can do with EDI. EDI involves computer hardware and software and requires redefinition of typical business tasks, ranging from keeping paper records in files to accommodating audit procedures. EDI is a strategic tool that reduces expenses, streamlines business procedures, and creates a competitive advantage. Because EDI crosses many boundaries within an organization, you need a sound EDI education for confident decision making. Integration of EDI with other business procedures in a company requires evaluation of current procedures in an effort to define and prioritize EDI applications. It is important to develop a long-term EDI strategy to ensure a successful program.

This book addresses these issues. If you're like most business professionals who are making the move towards EDI, you don't need another general introduction to EDI basics. You need concrete, practical information about what EDI standards are and what standards you need to implement. You need criteria for selecting and prioritizing EDI applications. You want to be prepared for the challenges you face in getting management approval for EDI and in the actual implementation and day-to-day operations. What hardware, software, and communications issues should you prepare for, and what will each component cost you? Because surprises are no fun when you're setting up a new technology, you also need some solid, head-start knowledge about the audit and legal issues EDI will introduce.

Based on years of consulting practice setting up EDI in all types and sizes of business, this book gives you the practical details of EDI implementation. Not only does it show you how to cost justify EDI, but it gives you job descriptions for the EDI team members, detailed criteria and forms for evaluating EDI vendors, considerations for trading partner agreements, an EDI glossary, and lists of EDI organizations (complete with industry information and phone numbers) and publications (complete with subject matter and contact information).

EDI has been around since the late 1960s. The transportation industry was primarily responsible for establishing EDI in an effort to remain competitive in the world market. As EDI gained popularity, it spread to other industries and is now a part of business in all industries around the world. The question is no longer whether your company should use EDI; the question is whether you can afford not to. If you are not using EDI, you will be soon. And if you are using EDI, you may need to implement it more extensively or move to advanced forms of EDI.

Chapter 1

An Overview of EDI

In this chapter, we look at the basics of EDI — its benefits, its applications across industries and around the world, and its challenges.

EDI BASICS

As Figure 1.1 illustrates, in traditional business environments, customers and suppliers have used a variety of nonelectronic and electronic methods for exchanging business documents. The nonelectronic methods include mail, telegram, telephone calls, and personal delivery. Trading business information using these approaches requires considerable turnaround time and incurs expenses. The postal service can take four to six days to deliver mail, and overnight services are costly. Calling in business information requires resource time and a focus on receiving the information accurately.

FIGURE 1.1
Traditional Methods of Exchanging Business Documents

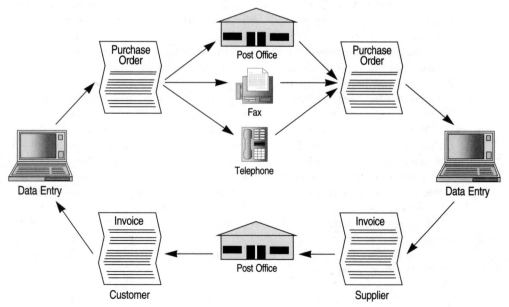

Some electronic forms of information exchange in traditional business environments include telephone, telex, fax, and e-mail. Although these electronic communication methods reduce the delivery time, they do not influence the effectiveness of the data exchange. Like paper documents, information sent via fax, telex, and telephone requires manual entry of the information into the recipient's computer, and data entry errors are inevitable. Faxes and e-mail, although popular for their delivery speed, usually require manual intervention as well. Not only must we read the documents, but someone must rekey the information in the computer systems for necessary action to be taken.

Paper and traditional electronic data exchange take time and involve a lot of data entry and re-entry, manual intervention, interpretation, and manipulation to make them processable. Delays are inherent in manual processing of information, and businesses experience numerous errors from incorrect transcription and entry of information.

An alternative to these traditional methods of information exchange is EDI. EDI is the computer-to-computer exchange of machine-processable business documents in a standard format. With EDI, you send business documents directly from one computer to the other, the documents are in machine-processable form, the exchange is limited to documents rather than data, and the document exchange is governed by standards. Let's look at the implications of these characteristics of EDI.

Computer-to-computer. The data is sent from one computer to another without manual intervention and without re-entry of data, eliminating delays and manual errors.

Machine-processable. The data is in a format that does not require human interpretation. With the proper translation software (i.e., the software that interprets the electronic data into a form your application software can use), each computer can automatically process EDI data and route it to the appropriate files, applications, or other computer platforms for further action.

Business documents. EDI is used for the exchange of business documents, including purchase orders, invoices, and bills of lading. EDI is not intended for the exchange of data, unless it consists of a specific business document.

Standards. EDI requires you to follow standards that define the format and content of business documents, giving sending and receiving computers the ability to "speak the same language." The business documents sent by a company, regardless of that company's industry and regardless of its location in the world, look and feel to the receiving computer like every other business document.

Information Flow Using EDI

To understand what EDI involves and how it works, let's look at the major elements of EDI information flow, which are illustrated in Figure 1.2.

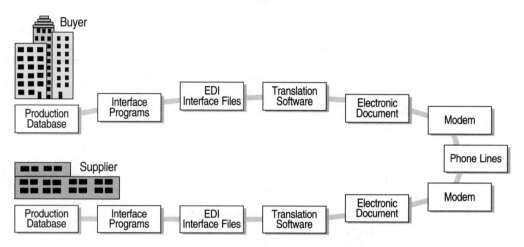

FIGURE 1.2
EDI Data Flow

In Figure 1.2, you see the flow of an electronic document — in this case a purchase order — from a buyer to a supplier. Beginning in the buyer's application database, the document moves through seven steps until it reaches the supplier's application database. After the transaction is completed, the supplier's invoice takes the same route back to the buyer. Let's look at each of these steps:

1. The buyer's production database includes data generated by the application software. The application software may be a vendor-purchased package or custom-developed. The buyer enters order information, generating a purchase order on the computer. The order information then channels through a number of interface programs.

2. The interface programs perform edits and checks on the document and direct the order data into predefined EDI interface files. The EDI interface files contain the order information in a form that can be read by the EDI translation software — a set of programs that translates or maps the interface file data into an electronic document formatted according to EDI standards. The electronic document (in this case, the purchase order) consists of a file (or files) that contains the order data in a predefined, recognizable format.

3. The communications software adds appropriate communications protocols (e.g., asynchronous or bisynchronous) to the EDI document in preparation for transmission over telephone lines.

4. Using a modem and telephone line, the buyer transmits the electronic standard purchase order to the supplier's computer.

5. The communications software on the supplier's computer interprets and/or converts the communications protocols to open the electronic document. The standard EDI purchase order is now in a recognizable format in a file or files and is available on the supplier's computer.

6. The supplier's translation software interprets the file from the EDI format and places the order information in interface file(s). The EDI interface files contain the translated purchase order information in a format predefined by the supplier.

7. The interface programs perform edits and checks before the data is integrated with the supplier's application software and populates the production database. The application software on the supplier's computer can now process the buyer's order.

Upon receipt of the electronic purchase order on its computer, the supplier can verify receipt of the document by automatically generating and sending the buyer an acknowledgment via the same route in reverse. This is a value-added process because in traditional paper environments, the receiver of a business document does not notify the sender or send any form of acknowledgment of receipt.

Advanced EDI

As EDI is rolled out in an organization, more sophisticated applications are often born; EDI can actually modify or eliminate certain business procedures. These forms of advanced EDI are generally employed by organizations that use EDI as an EC tool. Let's look briefly at two advanced EDI applications. Figure 1.3 shows EDI as a paper document replacement technique. In this scenario, existing paper documents, such as the purchase order and the invoice, are replaced by EDI equivalents. The order information the supplier receives is accurate (the supplier does not re-enter it on his/her computer), the data is sent quickly (no mail lag time), and therefore the supplier deals with more reliable information.

Figure 1.4 shows EDI as a business process elimination technique, using EDI strategically to eliminate unnecessary procedures and improve the overall business process. In this scenario, redundant or unnecessary business functions are eliminated. Because the supplier receives the customer's point-of-sale data, (s)he knows exactly what the customer requires to restock shelves. Also, the invoice is no longer exchanged because the customer pays for the goods (s)he has received.

This concept is referred to as vendor-managed inventory (VMI) and continuous replenishment program (CRP). To manage inventory in this way, not only must the vendor be EDI-capable, but the application software must be

FIGURE 1.3
EDI as a Paper Replacement Technique

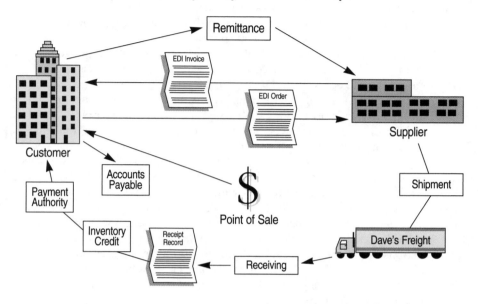

FIGURE 1.4
EDI as a Process Elimination Technique

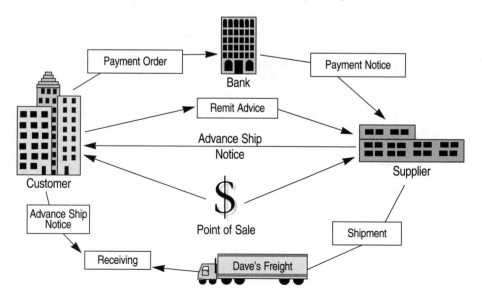

sufficiently sophisticated. More importantly, this type of vendor/customer relationship requires a true trading partnership. A true trading partnership exists when a supplier and a customer work together very closely and rely on one another to conduct business — a relationship that requires a high degree of stability, cooperation, trust, and ongoing support.

The next step in VMI involves EDI application to the settlement cycle. Rather than pay on invoice, many companies with advanced EDI capabilities choose a process called evaluated-receipt settlement (ERS) to pay the supplier with a payment order directly to the bank. The supplier must send the customer an electronic advance ship notice (ASN) when the material is shipped. Often the ASN must be sent within a very short time of the truck's leaving the supplier's dock (within 30 minutes for JIT manufacturing environments). Bar code labels are adhered to the containers or pallets being delivered. These bar codes act as unique license plates for the shipment. The customer scans the bar codes on the containers when they arrive, allowing the computer to automatically track the specific orders received, update inventory levels, and initiate the payment process based on the materials receipt match with the ASN information.

With advanced EDI, retailers and their suppliers can be in what is called a quick response (QR) environment, and grocers and their suppliers in efficient consumer response (ECR). EDI brings companies closer together by requiring them to define their working relationship in more detail. Trading partners increase their reliance on one another.

EDI BENEFITS

Several years ago, companies were deciding whether to implement EDI. Today, being EDI-capable is no longer a decision to be made; it is a business requirement. Although management still often views EDI as a nuisance or as one more necessity for doing business with a customer or two, that view quickly shifts when management gains a better understanding of EDI and its benefits. To give you the information you need to convince management of EDI's strategic business value, let's examine the benefits of EDI in terms of cost savings, improved customer service, enhanced internal processing, and competitive advantage.

Cost Savings

EDI will not make business transactions free, but among its tangible benefits are reduced expenses in several areas. You should have no trouble convincing management that EDI can save money if you point out areas that will show immediate results: paper and postage, labor, inventory, and shipping.

Paper and Postage

By replacing a paper document with an electronic one, you eliminate the expense of preprinted envelopes and forms, including purchase orders, invoices, customer records, and so on. In addition, copies for files and for routing and file cabinets are no longer necessary, saving both paper and copier costs. You can also replace paper correspondence with electronic correspondence, saving not only paper, but the direct expense of postage.

Labor

A further area where you will experience cost savings is in direct labor. EDI will eliminate redundancy in data entry, manual review and reconciliations, sorting, copying, and filing of documents, and error corrections.

It is important to keep in mind that while EDI may not reduce personnel headcount, it has the potential to. EDI may allow for the reassignment of existing personnel to other tasks. You might reassign staff to other, more productive tasks. For example, a salesperson can spend more time searching for new customers and servicing existing customers and less time taking orders.

A final point about labor costs: Documents will no longer require mundane, repetitive handling and, as a result, employees will be happier. Happier employees and a more challenging work environment reduce absenteeism and increase productivity.

Inventory

EDI is noted for saving the cost of carrying inventory. EDI reduces inventory levels by improving several procedures that directly affect required inventory levels.

Inventory levels are aligned with order lead time, demand, and seasonal or environmental changes. EDI reduces the order lead time because a purchase order can reach the supplier within minutes rather than the days required in a traditional paper environment. The order data is received accurately, assuring correct inventory requirements. In addition, seasonal or environmental changes do not require accurate inventory-level estimates. Rather, because you can place an order quickly, the supplier can make the goods to order. The supplier no longer must keep high stock levels to deal with environmental uncertainties. With less stock needed on hand, warehousing costs can be significantly reduced. This situation fits into today's management strategies as companies move toward JIT manufacturing and QR environments.

Shipping

Many companies spend a lot of money on small shipments to customers because the time allocated for transportation planning and management is usually not sufficient. EDI provides accurate data quickly, so better planning of transportation is possible. When you can consolidate shipments, improve routing, and find cost-effective transport alternatives, you can quickly lower shipping-related expenses.

Improved Customer Service

Although good customer service is an intangible benefit of EDI, it is one that serves business objectives and has a positive long-range effect on the bottom line. Studies show that about one half of EDI-capable companies experience better customer relations because EDI improves service.

EDI improves customer service by providing quick and efficient response to customer needs. A tangential benefit of EDI is that it improves communications with business partners and creates strong relationships.

Response to Customer Needs

Due to the reliability and timeliness of the information exchanged with EDI, suppliers are more responsive to customer orders. Order information is available from a customer within minutes, so the supplier can react quickly by initiating the manufacturing and distribution process immediately. In fact, some retailers provide point-of-sale or usage information to their vendors to allow automatic stock reordering and avoid order-processing lead time.

One of the top goals of suppliers in distinguishing themselves from their competition is superior customer service. Improved customer service means letting the customer view your inventory levels or pricing before they make buying decisions. It means letting the customer make changes to an order quickly and with the certainty that the correct goods will be shipped and shipped on time. It also means customers can reduce their administrative overhead in the process of doing business with you electronically. By being EDI-capable, you not only reduce costs for your organization, you reduce the expense for customers who do business with you.

Enhanced Partnership

EDI encourages participants to redefine business partnerships because the business functions of one company depend heavily on those of another. As a result, key people in companies communicate better than before and share the improved results. A dependence on one another requires trust, coordination, and cooperation and thus brings companies into true collaboration. Companies will experience decreased frustration and conflicts stemming from errors, lost documents, and waiting for things to happen.

Enhanced Internal Processing

Not only does your customer service improve when you implement EDI, but your organization's internal processing improves as well. You notice fewer data-entry errors, more and better business information is available for reporting and forecasting, and that information is reliable. Information exchange within your company is more efficient and quicker. Most important, you receive and make payments in a more timely fashion, improving your cash flow.

Accuracy

EDI data is received exactly as transmitted, so you eliminate rekeying errors. The data is accurate and complete (sufficient audit and controls are in place to ensure this). As a result, you will have fewer product returns, lost orders, back-orders, and credit/debit memos. EDI allows better information handling, improving the internal processing of data.

Better Information

EDI makes available new kinds of reliable information that can improve decision-making procedures. Point-of-sale or usage information you share with a supplier reduces order lead time and gives you more reaction time to meet customer demands. Inquiry into the supplier's inventory levels lets customers evaluate stock availability. The ability to look up supplier price lists allows for better buying decisions. The capability to access sales and usage information makes it possible to adjust buying decisions based on changes in factors such as climate changes and fashion trends.

Dependability

The information exchanged via EDI is dependable. The supplier can trust that when the customer order arrives, it is accurate, complete, and timely, allowing the vendor to fill it quickly. As the supplier initiates the manufacturing and distribution processes, (s)he knows (s)he can depend on the internal procedures to follow real requirements.

Streamlined Processes

As a result of instantaneously shared information among departments in a company (minimizing human intervention and eliminating the need to interpret information), EDI streamlines business processes. Processes become smooth and efficient. Departments or divisions within a company can use EDI to exchange information accurately and quickly to respond to customer demand.

Improved Cash Flow

Many companies initially apply EDI to their procurement cycle because that is the most paper- and labor-intensive area of their business. Others take advantage of EDI applications in the financial area to exchange payment and remittance information. With financial EDI, electronic funds transfer (EFT), and EDI, companies can improve cash flow. For example, you can receive your customer's remittance detail electronically and reconcile it with your accounts receivable. If you receive the remittance detail before the electronic payment advice to the bank, you gain time to reconcile the data with your accounts receivable system, correct discrepancies, and make adjustments before the cash transaction between the banks takes place. This significantly improves the speed and accuracy of integration with your applications. Furthermore, advance notice that a customer has initiated the payment process reduces your efforts in collections and avoids an unnecessary and unpleasant call or letter to the customer.

Financial EDI also improves cash forecasting capabilities by providing details of exact monies that will be deposited to a company's account on an exact date. In addition, companies that use financial EDI can sometimes negotiate better terms with their suppliers. In such circumstances, the customer negotiates more favorable payment terms but gives the supplier the advantage and the certainty of receipt of payment per the agreed terms.

Competitive Advantage

An EDI benefit not to be overlooked is the advantage you gain over non-EDI-capable competitors. Companies that use EDI often increase their sales and improve market penetration because efficiency improves and customer or lead response is immediate.

Increased Sales

Many companies experience an increase in their sales volumes with existing customers because EDI lets suppliers respond quickly to customer demand. Therefore, retailers who send point-of-sale information to their suppliers may experience an increase in sales because suppliers can replenish shelves with the right product at the right time. Consider that consumer trends or environmental changes can increase sales for a given item during a limited time. If the shelves are empty, the consumer goes elsewhere.

Competitive Advantage

Some companies implement EDI because their competition is doing it. These companies know they need EDI to remain competitive. Others implement EDI to gain a competitive advantage over a non-EDI-capable competitor.

In an EDI-capable environment, customers and suppliers can exchange key business information quickly to engineer, manufacture, purchase, and sell products more efficiently. These capabilities improve a company's internal procedures and external relations. Thus, for non-EDI competitors, gaining access to an already tough market can be even more difficult. In this way, EDI-capable companies use EDI as a tool to increase market penetration.

What everyone involved in EDI implementation needs to remember is that EDI is a long-term solution to business management, so measuring tangible benefits becomes easier once you've implemented EDI. Then you can measure and quote the increased inventory turns, reduced inventory levels and warehousing costs, the new business you have secured because a competitor is not EDI-capable, and sometimes the personnel head count reduction. Keep in mind that you can further leverage the benefits of EDI by using it along with other EC technologies.

In the next section, we look at industries around the world that are enjoying the benefits of EDI.

INDUSTRY AND WORLDWIDE APPLICATIONS

The EDI initiative began in the 1960s with the transportation industry's desire to reduce operating expenses and become more competitive in the world market. Although at first EDI standards were proprietary, EDI spread to and gained momentum among automotive companies and other industries. Today, EDI is used in all industries, regardless of the size of the company, and it addresses many business functions, including procurement and settlement cycles, transportation, and even government reporting.

EDI in Transportation

The transportation industry was among the first to develop and use EDI. Various carriers developed EDI standard transactions and began using them with their customers. Trucking companies, for example, developed and used standards known as MOTOR to satisfy the demands of their customers using documents such as freight bills.

Let's trace the steps of an EDI application in transportation. A freight forwarder generates and sends an EDI freight bill to its customer when a shipment is made. The customer matches the freight bill against the shipment when it is received, forwarding all matched entries to its accounts-payable system. Due to the timeliness of the receipt of the EDI documents, the customer can electronically accept or reject the contents of the freight bill. For companies that use motor carriers, reducing the administrative effort of keying the freight bill information means a reduction in personnel time and in postage and telephone expenses, and improves cash flow due to the reduced information processing time.

The rail industry uses EDI differently. Most large railroad companies actively use EDI to exchange purchase orders, bills of lading, freight bills, freight claims, and waybills, as well as for car location and tracing. Rail-car location is critical to the rail industry because it provides shippers and receivers with exact information regarding shipment arrival. This information is critical for production line scheduling.

One example of an EDI application for railways relates to the automotive industry. In their effort to maintain a JIT environment, some automotive companies use EDI rail transactions, such as car tracing and waybills, to plan and ensure the arrival of specific parts at the production line within 30 minutes of their installation. Such tight scheduling requires information to be exchanged quickly indeed. Before EDI, an automotive company employed several personnel to gather the same information by telephone, making it a very expensive and error-prone process.

In addition to the rail and trucking industries, other transportation industries that use EDI include air and ocean transport. EDI has been recognized as a means of allowing various carriers to communicate with one another when intermodal transportation is used. EDI allows effective means of communicating necessary information quickly and accurately.

EDI in Automotive

In the early 1980s, the Automotive Industry Action Group (AIAG) was formed to administer EDI standards for the industry and promote EDI's use with suppliers. Automotive companies' suppliers now realize that EDI is an absolute requirement for doing business. EDI has helped automotive companies trim expenses to remain competitive in a tough worldwide marketplace.

In the auto companies' JIT environment, delivery of parts to manufacture an automobile must be frequent and quick. The manufacturer relies heavily on correct and prompt delivery of the parts to minimize disruption to the production process. The supplier must send an ASN of the parts shipped to the manufacturer. The automotive company must rapidly review such documents and respond to the supplier when there are errors or discrepancies. Because EDI is mostly a batch-oriented method of data exchange, lag time is unacceptable; suppliers must communicate directly with the auto manufacturer's computer, and can expect a response within minutes. This approach allows the supplier to correct any errors in shipment before delivery.

Automotive companies have taken this process a step further and eliminated invoicing. When parts arrive and are scanned in, the data is matched with the information previously sent via an ASN. The matched records are routed to the accounts payable system, initiating the payment cycle. This process is referred to as evaluated-receipt settlement (ERS). It eliminates invoices, streamlining business procedures between the manufacturer and its suppliers. With ERS in place, all trading partners have better cash forecasting capabilities and can often negotiate better payment terms.

The automotive industry's next step was toward the concept of pay on production, where the parts are paid for not when they are scanned in as received, but when they are scanned in and used at the production line. Today, large automotive manufacturers are developing and building extranets (using standard Internet tools) to make EDI exchange more real-time and to make it more affordable for their smaller suppliers.

EDI in Retail

EDI is a natural solution for retailers as they attempt to provide better values and a wider variety of goods to the consumer. Some large retailers began using proprietary EDI about 25 years ago, when they faced fierce competition from foreign suppliers. Today, they use public standards such as ASC X12 and its retail subset called Voluntary Inter-industry Communications Standards (VICS) as they move to a QR environment.

Retailers generally carry a large number of Stock Keeping Units (SKUs). For example, in the apparel area, retailers must carry one style of pants in various sizes and colors. Managing large numbers of items in the ordering process requires huge administrative efforts. A typical purchase may contain hundreds of items with hundreds and sometimes thousands of different ship-to locations. In paper-based systems, the high volumes of data entered and re-entered is not only time consuming, but very error-prone. EDI allows for quick turnaround of purchase orders and for accurate exchange of information between retailers and their suppliers.

An EDI document with very widespread use in the retail industry is the invoice. Using EDI, the supplier can send a consolidated invoice to the retail headquarters. The systems there can automatically break down the invoices at store level to facilitate verification, eliminating the need for the supplier to send individual invoices to each store location.

QR and EDI are means to obtain critical data quickly so retailers can quickly replenish the shelves with the right products. These technologies also reduce the need for inventory safety stock.

EDI in Grocery

Grocery stores are similar to other retailers in that they must respond to consumer demand. However, their needs are quite different in that the grocery industry uses fewer vendors, the number of SKUs is much more limited, and the rate of movement per SKU is much faster. But from the success of mass merchants and wholesale clubs in the retail food arena, it is evident that the principles of retail QR are transferable to the food industry.

Efficient consumer response (ECR) is a growing movement in the grocery industry. ECR means giving the consumer better value, product, quality, assortment, availability, and convenience for the lowest price possible. These goals are critical to this industry today, as wholesale clubs and mass merchants threaten to capture a large share of the grocery business. Margins in the grocery industry are very tight, and the industry now has to focus on ways to reduce costs to stay competitive and profitable. UPCs and EDI — and, more important, a close working relationship between the grocery stores and their suppliers — make this goal attainable.

The grocery industry uses ASC X12 and its subset Uniform Communications Standards (USC) standards for exchange of key EDI documents, including purchase orders, invoices, promotion announcements, item maintenance, and remittance advice. Originally, EDI was used in the grocery industry for items that were replenished through the warehouses. Significant amounts of goods are distributed to grocery stores directly from the supplier, in a process referred to as Direct Store Delivery (DSD). As EDI is rolled out to DSD systems, it can have a very positive impact on the bottom line.

EDI in Healthcare and Insurance

It is often said that paperwork is one of the reasons that healthcare systems, particularly in the U.S., are expensive. In addition to the large numbers of documents needed in the healthcare system, each insurance company uses a different type of form, making it a significant administrative task to interpret as well as enter the information on the computer systems. With more than 6,000 hospitals, 600,000 doctors, 45,000 pharmacies, and over 10 million employees, the healthcare industry is a perfect candidate for EDI.

In the late 1980s, major companies in the healthcare industry agreed to abandon their proprietary EDI systems and adopted ASC X12 so that they could communicate with each other more quickly and effectively. In 1991 a nonprofit organization, Healthcare EDI Corporation (HEDIC), was formed to provide EDI education and to assist in the rollout of EDI among hospitals and their suppliers. Today, volunteers from the healthcare industry actively participate in the development of ASC X12 standards to accommodate their specific needs in the areas of procurement, settlement, and patient information. Naturally, care must be taken to ensure patient confidentiality as sensitive data travels through telephone lines and computer systems. Proper control and authorization issues are more important than ever.

In September 1995, a movement known as Efficient Healthcare Consumer Response (EHCR) was begun in an effort to drive unnecessary costs out of the entire medical supply chain, from manufacturer to healthcare provider and patient, by applying EC technologies to a re-engineered supply chain. According to the findings, about half the costs (totaling $11 billion) in the healthcare supply chain is wasteful. EHCR recommends the adoption of best practices and enabling technologies that include use of the Health Industry Number (HIN) (to identify all healthcare entities), use of the Universal Product Number (UPN) (to identify all healthcare products), bar coding, and, not surprisingly, EDI.

A typical healthcare EDI environment is depicted in Figure 1.5.

FIGURE 1.5
Healthcare Claims Processing

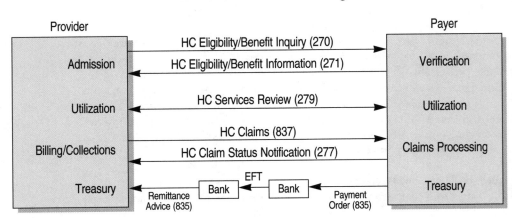

The real objective is to move the healthcare industry beyond its current emphasis in the exchange of claims processing via EDI toward access to clinical data and ultimately real-time access to such information.

EDI in Government

Government work, like healthcare, is very paper intensive. Some U.S. government agencies use thousands of different forms for purchasing, transportation, administration of contracts, and requests for quotes. As the debt of the U.S. government has grown over the past two decades, there has been a concentrated effort to find means of reducing expenses and streamlining business procedures. EDI is the right solution for the government, not only to eliminate paperwork, but to speed up processing of business transactions.

The U.S. government, although not an early EDI user, has been rolling out EDI to many of its agencies. In fact, many government agencies, such as the Department of Defense, use EDI capability as a vendor selection criterion. The Internal Revenue Service uses EDI for tax return filing, and the U.S. Navy uses EDI for purchase orders and bills of lading.

EDI customs documents are gaining popularity as governments around the world search for a means of making trade with their country easier and less costly. And many companies, such as those in waste management or environmental cleanup, have always had to perform compliance reporting to the government. Efforts are underway to standardize such reporting to use EDI to make it easier for such companies to comply with government requirements and to perform reporting within required time frames.

EDI around the World

International trade has always faced physical, cultural, and technical barriers. Each company in each country uses different algorithms and different documents to determine such things as customs duties.

Companies and governments across all continents have perceived the value of EDI and have been actively promoting its use as a means of improving trade opportunities by working closely and efficiently with businesses in other countries. With EDI, everyone can speak the same language.

EDI in Europe

The European Community countries have been working toward the goal of a single European market. To reach this goal, the European Community countries need to remove tariffs and quotas, harmonize product standards (such as units of measure) across borders, and allow open bidding for government construction and telecommunications contracts without regard to the bidder's country of origin.

The European Community has recognized that EDI can assist the free movement of goods, capital, and labor across national borders because it lets business partners exchange information quickly and eliminates misinterpretation due to language or cultural differences. By providing the means for more rapid and effective business communications than mailing or faxing papers, EDI can speed Europe to its target. EDI can result in increased growth and lower costs in Europe due to more sufficient resourcing (through the use of computers and communications rather than people) and more efficient communications and distribution.

Europe 1992, an agreement designed to create a cooperative and coordinated business environment throughout the continent by 1992, included two prevalent EDI initiatives, TRADACOMS and ODETTE (see Chapter 3). These initiatives focused mainly on the automotive industry because this industry pioneered EDI as a way to reduce expenses to remain competitive with Japan.

Following this pioneering effort, many other industries, including electronics companies and freight carriers, produced their own EDI initiatives and are using EDI today. For example, in 1988, many shipping, freight, and export companies from Western Europe began a pilot project to test transmission of international transportation data via EDI. This effort, named COST-306, includes UN/EDIFACT-based messages for invoices, bills of lading, and status reports. (See Chapter 3 for more information about UN/EDIFACT.)

EDI in Asian/Pacific Countries

In Asian/Pacific countries, including South Korea, Japan, Hong Kong, Singapore, Australia, and New Zealand, EDI has reduced the effects of relative geographical isolation and removed technical and information barriers. These barriers include not only different languages but also different character sets, which can require complex coding for computers.

This part of the world has yet to implement EDI widely, but Asian/Pacific countries have been eagerly rolling out EDI. Private interests and, particularly, government agencies have been funding and promoting EDI heavily.

The reason for such interest in EDI is simple: Facilitating the flow of business information between trading partners can bring the Asian/Pacific nations more securely into the international marketplace. Although Asian/Pacific countries are important players in the international market today, the world is changing. For example, many companies in these countries sell to the U.S., where domestic companies are desperately seeking ways to reduce costs. EDI seems to be an answer, so the U.S. companies want everyone, including trading partners in Asian/Pacific countries, to do business with them via EDI. So, if a company in Singapore does not use EDI, the U.S. will turn to a competitor in Hong Kong who does, and Singapore will lose its marketshare.

If your company conducts business with companies or governments in these countries, keep in mind that EDI is relatively new to them. Many U.S. companies that buy goods and services from Asian/Pacific countries deal with very small companies that lack not only an understanding of EDI's importance but also funding for such technology. You may consider assisting these suppliers with EDI education, as well as implementation. The benefits to you are that you will have EDI-capable trading partners outside the U.S.

EDI in Other Parts of the World

Not surprisingly, EDI has captured the attention of Russia. In 1990, transportation companies in Russia formed the Association of Electronic Data Interchange Users to begin EDI awareness and education. Today membership includes customs agencies as well.

In Eastern European countries, SITPRO (the Simplification of International Trade Procedures Board) has been providing EDI education and encouragement to countries such as Poland and the Czech Republic since the early 1990s. SITPRO is an organization that works with trade and payment procedures, develops and promotes translation software, and provides consulting services.

In 1991, the Advance Cargo Information Service was established in Africa to establish an electronic network for exchange of data between ocean carriers and ports. CIS uses a combination of proprietary and UN/EDIFACT standards.

EDI efforts are underway in all industries and within all functional areas. In some industries it has reached critical mass and in others it is being rolled out so quickly that it has become a matter of survival. Around the world, EDI is emphasized in private and public sectors, and standards are being developed to make EDI possible. Many governments fund EDI education opportunities to encourage the use of EDI in the private sector.

EDI CHALLENGES

As we face EDI implementation, we often overlook the obstacles we'll confront on the way to a successful, long-term EDI program. But it's important to remember that EDI offers many challenges — challenges that can impact the cost of your EDI implementation. An awareness of potential obstacles will help you to better plan for the resources and budgets required to overcome them. Let's look at the most significant challenges you'll face.

Management Commitment

Gaining management commitment is perhaps the biggest challenge in implementing EDI. Why is it so difficult to get the budget and resources you need for EDI implementation when, according to the experts, EDI saves money? The answer is that in most instances, EDI is a middle-management initiative and needs to be sold to upper management as either a customer-service necessity or a cost-saving tool.

If EDI is required to keep a customer, you generally get approval for a quick, inexpensive EDI system to satisfy that customer's requirement. Unfortunately, this approach does not usually provide for a sound long-term implementation plan or promote good business planning.

If you present EDI to upper management as a strategic, cost-saving tool, corporate executives may require a cost/benefit analysis, which can be a problem. Although it is possible to estimate EDI's *costs*, it is initially difficult to measure EDI's *benefits* in dollars and cents. Most EDI advocates claim that the greatest benefits of EDI are in improving customer service, gaining a competitive edge, and streamlining business procedures — benefits that are relatively intangible and difficult to measure in bottom-line terms. So when an executive asks how many dollars you can save with improved customer service, you can respond only with the revenues that a particular customer generates, explaining that if you do not become EDI-capable, you may lose those revenues.

Nevertheless, there are some strategies for cost justifying EDI. For example, you can present case studies of companies that have successfully implemented EDI. An effective example would be a direct competitor who has excelled with EDI. A much more convincing approach is to perform a cost justification at your company.

Procedural/Cultural Changes

EDI requires a whole new way of thinking about and doing business. Technical managers tend to focus on the computer side of an EDI implementation, preparing mainly for the technical changes to come. However, EDI also profoundly affects the way business is conducted, and this is a challenge you must meet head on.

In today's world, documents define our jobs. We create paper purchase orders and send them to our suppliers, who must sort and file them after entering the data into their computer. In turn, the suppliers generate loads of paper to define the internal tasks necessary to fill the order. We send paper with the order shipment and then more paper asking for payment. In an ideal world, customers oblige and promptly send us a paper check.

One advantage of EDI is that it eliminates the need for such paper documents. The much greater advantage of EDI is that it can modify and eliminate business procedures as it removes paper from the process. The challenge is in the fact that as a result of an EDI relationship, companies rely on one another much more than ever before to manufacture the goods "just in time" and replenish the shelves on time. Because each company's business procedures are different, it can be difficult to align your objectives and procedures with your business partners'.

Procedural change often brings cultural change with it. One consideration should be to employ the assistance of experts in organizational change management (OCM). OCM experts can help your company's employees, from clerical to executive personnel, be better prepared for the changes to come. With timely knowledge of change, people are better able to adapt and embrace changes, from shifts in daily routines to entirely new job responsibilities.

Learning Curve

Changes in process are not only a challenge in themselves, but they trail further challenges in their wake. Everyone involved in EDI must adapt to the new paperless environment, and adapting to anything is a challenge. But before users can adapt to EDI changes in procedure, they must learn how to use the new systems and learn what the resulting procedural differences will be.

EDI introduces technical challenges for the implementers. It also changes what many employees do and how they do it. And adjustments are necessary because EDI requires partnerships. People within a company must work together more closely than before EDI and must share important information. In addition, everyone must now rely on and trust the information exchanged with customers and suppliers.

With EDI, not only do you need to understand your internal business procedures, but you must be familiar with your trading partners' procedures in order to align them with yours and make them work together more efficiently. This level of collaboration is critical. Success means partners must depend on one another, and survival requires ongoing meetings with customers and suppliers to ensure an understanding of their needs, particularly as those needs evolve.

For an EDI implementation to be successful, you have to overcome reluctance to accept change and help coworkers master the application of EDI.

Resources

Today, with IT resources more valuable than ever before and market demand for qualified IT staff at an all-time high, it has become increasingly difficult to hire and keep EDI resources. EDI personnel must possess a combination of unique skills, including not only strong technical and managerial skills, but strong communication and people skills. Depending on the size of your organization and the volume of your EDI activity, you may need several people to achieve the wide range of skills an EDI environment demands.

Your EDI staff must have strong interpersonal skills. Strong communication skills are crucial because often your EDI staff is the first line of contact for your EDI customers. You certainly do not want to upset a customer who cannot clearly communicate with your staff. Your technical EDI resources must also have the ability to respond quickly and to prioritize customer issues daily.

Dealing with Standards

We are a long way from the ideal world in which all EDI users adhere to one set of standards. As Chapter 3 explains, EDI's history is based on standards that evolved from corporate-proprietary to industry-specific to generic-public standards. But because each industry has unique business requirements, the need to accommodate differences in standard EDI documents will always exist. You may need to use industry-specific standards if you do business in multiple industries. You may also need to use different standards if you do business internationally. You may have to adapt to the standards of your trading partners. You will probably find that because ever-changing business requirements define standards, ongoing updates are necessary to EDI standards.

Perhaps the biggest concern EDI users have about EDI standards is how they are used. Often because it is easier for a trading partner to extend the use of a standard rule, they override, shift, or bypass the syntax or content of a transaction set. This is a form of *standards abuse.* Trading partners sometimes make up their own rules (some based on their interpretation, others based on easier mapping opportunities). Standards abuse causes headaches for IT people, who often have to create and maintain a separate map for that trading partner and may have to modify the interface and applications software to handle the differences between how trading partners send or expect to receive data. Because so many standards are in use, knowing upfront what standards or subsets you must work with will better prepare you for implementation.

Consider participating in the standards development process. Your participation will help ensure that your business requirements are considered. Otherwise, you will be forced to use what others define as a standard. To become involved in the standards development process, you need to become a member of ANSI ASC X12, the responsible organization. The ASC X12 membership meets three times a year and, during week-long meetings, defines and refines the standards.

Dual Systems

The move to EDI is further complicated by the fact that you'll likely need to maintain two systems: one for EDI-capable trading partners and one for non-EDI-capable customers and suppliers. Even EDI-capable customers are not likely to be prepared to exchange all business documents electronically, so you have to maintain dual systems to accommodate this.

Another need for dual systems arises when you deal with small businesses that cannot afford EDI implementation. You must assume that there will always be exceptions to the "all EDI or nothing" ideal and be prepared to deal with this challenge from a technical standpoint.

Hardware Configuration

One challenge that may not be immediately obvious is the need to select the hardware platform(s) on which you'll run your EDI applications. The choice of hardware is a very important one, because it affects issues such as cost of EDI implementation, processing speed, upgradeability, and ease of integration with application data.

The three hardware approaches available are host-based, front-end server, and standalone server. Key factors to consider in determining the right hardware configuration for your environment include cost, disk capacity, processing speed, security, and application integration. Chapter 5 explains these issues in detail.

Communications Support

Because EDI requires transmission of data over telephone lines, you have to consider how to set up communications with your EDI partners. The choices you make here will affect the cost of your EDI implementation, the time it takes for the transmission to get to the recipient, as well as the technical expertise you'll need in house and your security considerations. The communications alternatives include direct communications, VANs, and the Internet. (For details about EDI communications issues, see Chapter 6.)

The Internet has been the long-awaited alternative for EDI document exchange. The Internet is a viable option for EDI processing, but careful consideration should be given to issues such as security, reliability, and other value-added features we have grown accustomed to with the VANs.

Operational Evaluation

Before you implement EDI, you need to face the challenge of identifying the processes and applications that are suitable for conversion to EDI. Knowledge of internal and external information flow will help you to identify which applications to consider and how to prioritize them. You must understand the following operations procedures in your company: the use of paper, telephone, facsimile, e-mail, or face-to-face interactions to convey information. The following list presents the questions to ask to determine information flow within your company.

- What information is exchanged within and among departments or divisions?
- How is the information conveyed (paper, e-mail, fax, telephone, personal visit)?
- How many copies are produced?
- How are copies routed?
- Who uses each copy?
- Is the information in a particular document available through other existing sources?
- Are copies stored?
- How long are copies stored?
- Where are copies stored?
- How often are stored copies retrieved?

You must also evaluate information flow with trading partners. State how the information is being exchanged, such as e-mail, fax, telephone, or paper documents. This analysis allows you to develop a process diagram of your external (inter-organizational) information flow.

Once you have identified the internal and external information flow, you can determine what changes are necessary for EDI implementation. You can develop an EDI model showing where EDI replaces current exchanges of information, such as replacement of paper purchase orders with EDI purchase orders. In addition, the EDI model must show how EDI can eliminate specific procedures or documents due to the data being available from other sources (or unnecessary).

Potential Applications

Once you have completed the operational evaluation, you are ready for the challenge of deciding where to implement EDI. To ascertain which business procedures are most suitable, find out which areas in the company are most paper- and labor-intensive. You can perform an operational evaluation, an internal study of procedures in your company, and build a data model to decide where EDI can reduce manual intervention, paper, postage, and labor. Also, survey your trading partners to find out their EDI application areas. The information you gather will help you prioritize potential EDI applications.

Be aware that the challenge of selecting appropriate EDI applications will continue throughout the EDI implementation effort as your need for additional transaction sets arises. Because the need to implement EDI in new areas will be ever-growing, it is important to compile and prioritize a list of all potential EDI applications and documents, such as purchase orders and invoices. This list will help you prepare for and justify each successive step of the implementation.

Audit and Security

A move to EDI usually requires you to think very differently about auditing and security. When you switch to EDI, auditors can no longer rely on traditional methods of using paper documents as audit trails and must develop and use new methods of substantiating transactions (see Chapter 10 for a detailed discussion of audit considerations). It is crucial to educate auditors about EDI and to let them participate in the EDI project.

A paperless environment means you must incorporate additional auditing controls into information processing and other business procedures. These controls can be application-specific or general. There are many application-specific controls, some mandated by standards and others that users must add to ensure completeness, accuracy, and authorization of EDI information exchange. In addition, there are non-application-specific controls that address restart and recovery procedures, program and file backups, and disaster recovery. (Examples of these controls are discussed in Chapter 10.) Also, VANs offer a variety of detailed control reporting.

Security in a paperless environment is more crucial than ever before. Internal security systems must limit access to EDI systems or the VAN and Internet by means of passwords or other proven methods. After all, you don't want hackers to gain access to your data, and you don't want employees to have the system automatically write checks to themselves. External security systems may include encryption (coding and decoding of data to prevent hacking), authentication (using electronic codes to identify sender and receiver), and use of key management. See Chapter 11 for more about security.

Legal

The legal aspects of a paperless environment have called the legal community into action. The challenges here include such questions as what constitutes a contract when no paper documents exist, what can be considered equivalent to a signature as a commitment, and what kind of document is necessary to formalize a trading partnership. (Chapter 13 provides a thorough discussion of legal issues.)

Many companies overlook the importance of a trading partner agreement in their EDI relationships. But before the start of an EDI relationship, it is imperative for you and your trading partners to review and define the legal issues in a paperless environment in order to avoid future disputes.

Trading Partner Policing

EDI requires active participation from two parties. Although you have some level of control over your internal processes, budgets, and timing, you will find that you have very little control over your trading partners. A common challenge is coordinating the activities and timeframes of EDI implementation. Despite your relentless efforts to keep your trading partners in line, you'll often find at the eleventh hour that they are not as ready as they promised to be. Policing the activities of your trading partner is impossible unless you can be onsite working the EDI resources of your customer or supplier. Even then, you have limited control over their decision-making processes. However, you can make adjustments to your implementation efforts as needed if you are informed about their true commitments and capabilities.

Trading Partner Rollout

The legal challenges and all the other challenges multiply when it comes time to expand your EDI program to include as many trading partners as possible. Implementing EDI purchase orders and invoices with 10 or 20 customers may increase the cost of doing business. However, as you roll out EDI to more customers and suppliers, the return on investment increases because establishing an EDI transaction link with a customer will lay out the proper foundation, making it easier and faster to establish the same link with others.

Trading partner rollout is an economic imperative that will affect your hardware and software setups, audit and security controls, trading partner agreements, and just about every other area of EDI implementation. This is a challenge you must be prepared to handle. Many companies offer free education in the form of white papers or seminars to educate and entice their trading partners to do EDI with them. In fact, in many instances, larger suppliers fund their customers' EDI implementation efforts because it saves them a lot of time and administrative efforts, thereby reducing their cost of doing business.

Chapter 2

Leveraging EDI in the Electronic Commerce Era

Electronic commerce (EC) is the use of integrated technologies to streamline external business procedures to facilitate trade. As EDI and other tools and technologies are implemented, issues arise from changing procedures. You may need to conduct a business re-engineering analysis for changing the way you do business using new technologies. It is sometimes as a result of a re-engineering project that companies look to technologies such as EDI to improve their business procedures, streamline relations with trading partners, and reduce costs. This drive toward the use of technology takes businesses into the world of EC. With EDI as its cornerstone, EC assumes use of other technologies, including bar coding, e-mail, and the Internet. Often, many of these technologies are used together in an effort to enhance data gathering, storage, and use to create a faster, more productive work environment.

CRITICAL SUCCESS FACTORS

Today's EC is only a subset of what it will be in the future. The move to EC must be carefully weighed and must be a strategic decision. In many companies, use of technology is often left to the discretion and management of IT departments. While IT departments play an important role, the decision to adopt EC must be a joint effort between IT and upper management, with participation and input from various functional areas. Before selecting EC components, it is important for upper management to define the objectives of a move to EC. One way to outline these objectives is to define your company's critical success factors and determine how EC tools might help you achieve them. Among the top critical success factors most companies have are customer satisfaction, price competitiveness, and quality assurance. Although EC does not guarantee the achievement of any of these objectives, it can make their realization more certain.

Customer Satisfaction

EC technologies can provide quicker access to the information necessary to respond to customers, thus providing better service. And because electronic data is more reliable than paper-based data, you should experience increased customer satisfaction by providing customers with exactly the goods, services, and information desired, often in a more timely manner.

Price Competitiveness

The cost of computers and communications is generally less than that of paper-based systems. EC allows companies to reduce warehousing costs, increase inventory turns, and reduce labor and administrative time. By reducing expenses, you can maintain lower prices and remain competitive.

Quality Assurance

You achieve quality assurance by making good products that meet or exceed your standards as well as those of your customers. EC can help ensure that you realize this goal. For example, with EC, a retailer can capture daily sales and return information and send it directly to the retailer's headquarters as well as to the supplier to analyze trends and identify possible quality issues. Or using bar coding, the retailer can capture and analyze data about a product throughout its manufacturing life cycle, isolating any problem areas.

EC Technologies

EC is a business initiative that improves the automation of intracompany and intercompany movement of data and fosters efficient and widespread access to information. Selection and prioritization of EC components varies for each company and each industry. It is therefore important to understand these technologies before you can determine whether and how they can be applied to your environment. In this chapter, we look at several of these technologies: e-fax, electronic document management, automated data capture, swipe cards and smart cards, computer telephony integration, workflow automation, e-mail, and extranets.

E-fax

EC-eager companies must occasionally compromise to accommodate trading partners that are not technologically sophisticated. Such a compromise can be achieved simply with a fax machine, which remains more common in today's business environment than Internet access.

EDI-to-fax and fax-to-EDI conversions have been in use for some time. These conversions are handled by service bureaus, which generally charge a setup fee and monthly charges for storing letterhead graphics. For EDI-to-fax conversion, a service bureau receives an EDI document, translates it, formats the data into a custom form, and faxes it to the intended recipient.

Fax-to-EDI conversion is much more complex and relatively expensive, and requires scanning tools such as Intelligent Character Recognition (ICR) and Optical Character Recognition (OCR) to translate paper documents into their electronic equivalents (see "Electronic Document Management (Imaging)" below). The quality of the fax documents has a significant impact on the reliability of the scanned information, rendering ICR and OCR output data only 95 percent accurate. Some faxed documents are rejected and suspended to await manual review and correction, a process that is costly and time consuming. Another disadvantage of using a fax for exchange of EDI information is the absence of a reliable audit trail. The functional acknowledgment available with most EDI processes is not possible with the fax machine, which can provide only a printed log.

The primary advantage of using fax technology for EDI transactions is that it lets companies conduct business electronically with less sophisticated partners, consolidating processes as interaction via disparate methods (the telephone, the Internet, the postal service, etc.) are replaced by communication between an EDI system and a fax machine.

Electronic Document Management (Imaging)

Electronic document management (EDM) is an image-processing technology that replaces paper-based systems. Image processing involves the creation, storage, and retrieval of electronic versions of paper documents. With up to 15 percent of a company's paper documentation lost or misplaced, resulting in the average worker spending up to 30 percent of the day looking for paper documents, EDM is a technology whose time has come. These days, many companies are storing official records of business transactions electronically, usually on unalterable media such as write once, read many (WORM) optical disks. Images of internal documents are stored using computer output to laser disc (COLD) technology.

An EDM system includes several components: personal computers or file servers, scanning devices, storage devices and media, communications devices and lines, document management software, and printers. An EDM system can range from a multimillion dollar client/server-based solution to a simpler setup that can cost less than $100,000, making it an affordable choice for most businesses today.

EDM lets you capture information from paper documents (including handwritten notes), faxes, and photographs, and the captured information is easily stored. The electronic information can later be retrieved easily and quickly to be revised, forwarded, printed, or refiled. EDM brings reduced cycle times, cost savings, and improved customer service. But the greatest benefit of EDM is that it allows companies to integrate imaged information with other EC technologies (workflow, e-mail, the Internet), which streamlines business processes internally and externally.

Today, EDM is used most effectively and beneficially by companies with paper-intensive processes — companies such as financial institutions, insurance companies, and transportation companies, among others. Let's look at some of the EDM tools these companies are using.

OCR, ICR, and Other EDM Tools

With EDM, data is captured and routed automatically using technologies such as OCR, ICR, MICR (Magnetic Ink Character Recognition), and imaging.

OCR matches patterns of letter images with a dictionary of character templates. When a close match is made, the scanner creates the ASCII equivalent of the character and stores it. ICR also recognizes letters and words by extracting key features of a character and comparing them with a dictionary of features that are enhanced with rules of grammar and language. OCR is usually used to scan typed or printed material, while ICR is used to recognize handwriting. The accuracy of the captured data depends heavily on the quality of the original document and the sophistication of the scanner hardware and software. OCR and ICR are said to be 95 percent accurate, making imaged data fairly reliable, but a degree of manual cleanup is sometimes required.

With imaging, you generally have two options. One is to scan the original and display the electronic version for an operator, who extracts the relevant data for entry into a database. This does speed up the process, but the manual entry into the database introduces the risk of data-entry errors. Another option is to have OCR or ICR automatically convert key data and map directly to the database. Both of these options are better alternatives than traditional methods.

EDM can play an important role in an EC environment as part of a total EC solution. Let's take a look at how a typical company can benefit from EDM.

A manufacturing and distribution company receives orders from its customers around the country. Some orders are sent via fax and mail, some are taken over the phone, while others are sent using EDI. All EDI orders, once translated, are edited in the interface software area and are posted to order entry. All faxed, mailed, and phoned orders can be scanned in using OCR and ICR, cleaned up, and funneled through the same interface programs. This streamlining ensures consistency and increases accuracy. Finally, another point of streamlining is in the storage of the order data. Generally, imaged data is sent through a COLD system for backup and archival. It's good to route EDI orders through the COLD system as well. Streamlining the capture, integration, and archival of data reduces confusion and loss and increases data integrity and reliability.

The new era of EDM, called compound document management, packages text, voice, images, photographs, e-mail, fax, and multimedia to consolidate the document-management system. Imaging offers multiple users instantaneous and simultaneous access to the same information, in text or image form. Imaging products today are off-the-shelf and run on many hardware environments, making them affordable for everyone.

Automated Data Capture

Automated data capture technologies are used to capture and use information automatically to improve the timeliness and quality of data and to let users manage and track transactions. Simply put, automated data capture is keyless data entry.

For automated data capture, you need a bar code printer, scanner, or radio frequency equipment. These devices do not add as much value by them-selves as they do when the data they gather is appended with EDI and inte-grated with applications. Interfacing the captured data with application systems is the key to taking full advantage of automated data capture.

Bar coding is commonly used with EDI and an advance ship notice (ASN). In a traditional system, information is gathered and sent in for data entry when products are picked in a warehouse. This is an inefficient process because the inventory level information is obsolete as soon as the data is entered. With bar code technology the process is moved out of the warehouse so that as soon as the products are picked, invoices are confirmed, cartons and pallets are packed, weighed, labeled, and ready to go. All relevant data is captured and inventory levels and accounts-receivable systems are updated. Customers can scan package bar code labels, matching the goods received with the ASN information to identify any discrepancies. After this information is reconciled, the customer can generate an accounts-payable record and initiate the payment process.

The ability to have accurate, up-to-the-minute inventory information is one of the greatest assets an organization can have. Manufacturers and distributors often lose sales because they can't respond quickly to customer demands. This type of technology can enable the sales force to respond more quickly and accurately to customer requests. Tying the warehouse to the sales force is therefore critical. Because many companies use third-party warehouses, inte-gration of inventory information is also an important factor in accuracy.

Bar codes have been widely used for more than 25 years. Today, bar codes are used for everything from identifying conference attendees to insurance forms. Using automated data capture tools means fewer errors and faster turnaround times.

Swipe Cards and Smart Cards

Swipe cards are widely used today and are familiar to most of us. Swipe cards include credit/debit cards and access key cards, and work by storing small units of data that can be accessed by card readers.

Smart cards differ in that each contains a microprocessor chip. Thousands of bits of data can be stored on a smart card. A more significant difference is that smart cards can perform computations — in addition to a microprocessor, smart cards contain an operating system, files, and algorithms. They can be used for payment, authorization, identification, and much more.

Smart cards interface with card readers in two ways. Contact smart cards must be inserted into a reader; contactless smart cards exchange information with a reader using a radio frequency device.

Although both types of cards can be very useful to the everyday con-sumer, the contact cards are much more prevalent. The contactless card can play a significant role in business because there is no action required by the cardholder other than being within inches of the card reader to exchange signals.

Smart cards are intelligent devices that effectively combine several technologies. They can be used for tracking product or product status. In addition, they can be used to exchange data (certainly in a standard format) and to help manage workflow. In most environments today, applications that work with bar codes could be implemented with smart cards. The difference is that bar codes can only be read, while smart cards can perform logical computations and have data written back to them, making the data more accurate and meaningful.

For example, in a manufacturing and distribution company, the contactless smart card can be used to better track products. Containers, pallets, and boxes can interact with the card reader as they travel via a conveyer during a manufacturing or distribution process. Data can be read and written back onto the card as they move. In the transportation industry, train cars can check in and out at key contact points, allowing users to check on the exact status of a shipment.

In the health care field, each insured patient could be issued a smart card containing personal information (Social Security number, date of birth, etc.) as well as insurance information (policy number, group number, deductible, and copayment). The patient could use the card to check in with the primary physician. At the conclusion of the visit, the primary physician could request lab work or prescribe medicine, and could simply upload that information to the smart card. The card could then be used at the pharmacy for medications (with the smart card containing personal drug interactions or allergies), or could be used at the laboratory to download exact specifications, the doctor's office notes, and other relevant information.

Coupled with complimentary technologies such as EDI, smart cards offer a compelling advantage to those who use it as a business strategy. Imagine that in a distribution company, as the smart card identifies the items traveling to the shipping department, the ASN can be created on the fly. In the health care example, the lab request can be uploaded to the card as a standard EDI transaction; in the financial industry, payments can be processed as standard EDI transactions. Smart card technology is not yet standardized. But organizations such as the International Standards Organization (ISO) and the American National Standards Institute (ANSI) are working together to develop industry standards.

Computer Telephony Integration

Computer telephony integration (CTI) is a technology that merges voice and data services — specifically, telephone systems and computer systems. This is EC at work: technologies working together to facilitate trade.

Call centers have been used for years for telemarketing and help-desk assistance. Banks and credit card companies are examples of companies that use CTI systems. When you call a credit card company, you usually have to enter account information using your telephone keypad. When you eventually talk to an operator, that person knows your name, address, and purchasing and credit history. With this information, the operator can handle the call more efficiently and in a way that makes it seem more personal to the customer.

CTI is used in catalog-sales call centers with image processing and EDI, two other EC technologies. When a customer calls, an operator accesses customer records and scanned images of hundreds of catalogs stored on laser disc. The operator eventually takes the customer's order and enters it into the system. This creates an EDI transaction set that is routed to the appropriate vendor for drop shipment, saving time and labor for everyone involved. The catalog-sales company's applications are updated with the new order information when the EDI transaction set is sent, streamlining the process and ensuring the accuracy of the data.

Call centers have used CTI successfully for retail-to-consumer trade, so companies are starting to take advantage of call centers (and related EC technologies) to facilitate business-to-business transactions.

Workflow Automation

Workflow automation, as its name implies, is the automation of information processing. With workflow, internal and external processes and transactions are electronified. Transactions enter businesses through such gateways as direct connections, private networks, VANs, and the Internet, and are exchanged in the form of EDI, FTP, proprietary formatted files, fax, telephony, e-forms, images, e-mail, and traditionally entered data on legacy systems. The objective of workflow automation is to allow for the efficient manipulation of electronic data: the data can be consolidated at the workstation level, routed to appropriate users based on specified criteria, queried for further action, or integrated with application systems. Without workflow automation, processes could be held indefinitely, transactions could be dropped and not noticed, and we would have to rely on manual procedures to ensure that information gets to the right people on time.

Workflow automation tools use the latest technology available today to make them user friendly. They employ graphical objects to develop diagram flows, and the workflow definition can be designed using a mouse and point and click. Within the process definition, logic processing allows for the information or transaction to be routed to different users based on specific criteria. Consider, for example, vendor invoices coming in from a variety of sources. Some invoices must always be reviewed by accounting personnel. Some invoices, depending on dollar value, may be routed directly to the accounts-payable system, while others must be reviewed, have general ledger numbers assigned by one person in accounting, and be forwarded to another person for final review and approval before integration with accounts payable. Other invoices may need to be queued for a rendezvous process because additional data or transactions are needed for further processing. Workflow holds the invoice until the specified data arrives, integrates everything, and releases the document for the next decision step. Should there be a need for a change in the process, changes to the workflow process are an easy point and click away.

The key to using workflow automation successfully is to view it not as a process automation tool. It is best when used to provide companies with the ability to quickly identify and respond to changes. Workflow has traditionally provided the opportunity for internal connectivity; now it can be used for inter-organizational connectivity as well. While EDI, e-mail, document management, workgroup, and other similar technologies allow us to automate and expedite information access, workflow allows for the automation of the processing of this information. It is the process that defines the capturing, scheduling, routing, decision-making, archiving, integrating, and finally automating the information exchange. The power of workflow automation lies in its use with other EC technologies.

E-mail

In an electronic commerce environment, there are two approaches to exchanging information such as drawings, photographs, and graphics. You can attach the information to an EDI transaction set, or you can incorporate it within an X12 transaction set.

X.435 is the protocol that lets you attach graphics to an EDI document. X.435 evolved from X.400, which, as the protocol for e-mail exchange, could only accommodate ASCII and binary format, text-only messages. X.400 was renamed X.435 in 1990 after standards had been updated to handle all types of digital data and enhanced to address EDI-related issues.

X.435 features include

- data encryption
- proof of delivery
- verification that message contents were not altered
- proof of sender/receiver IDs
- proof of receipt
- verification that contents were sent by the sender

To incorporate graphics within an X12 transaction, you must convert them to a .jpg file and incorporate the binary data in the BIN segment of the transaction set. The detail area of the transaction within an appropriate transaction set can contain a wide variety of data types, including text, graphics, images, and audio. The transaction set can be transported via the Internet when encased in an X.435 envelope.

Extranets

An extranet, a term derived from "extended intranet," uses Internet technology to allow parties — business partners, customers, and employees — to share information and conduct business electronically.

The success of extranets and electronic commerce depends heavily on the use of standards. Internet and communications standards govern access to extranets, and EDI standards define the purpose and layout of transaction sets.

By the year 2000, more than half of hub companies will employ such standards as they grant their spokes access to their extranets. Through an extranet, a spoke company can exchange information with hub-company databases and internal applications.

The difference between EDI access to databases and EC access to extranets is that EDI gives access only to data, while extranets allow sharing of data and knowledge, which together give EC users a competitive advantage.

EDI AND COLLABORATION

The terms *electronic commerce* and *collaboration* are becoming more and more closely related. EC is about two companies conducting business electronically, but it requires a high level of collaboration. Vendor managed inventory (VMI) is one example of how companies are collaborating.

VMI streamlines the inventory ordering process by eliminating the purchase order transaction. With VMI, the customer sends sales data directly to the supplier's applications, which determine reorder numbers and delivery dates. VMI tightens things up, improving turnaround time, increasing customer satisfaction, and saving money by reducing inventory levels

For collaboration to be a part of an EC strategy, both parties must benefit. A major retailer decided not to deploy VMI because the company felt its forecasting system was sophisticated and accurate enough. Unless the suppliers offered added value, this retailer was not interested. The suppliers can add value by improving their service levels. They can offer the retailer solutions that will help increase inventory turns (which will help both parties).

EC collaboration should be limited to stable customer-supplier relationships. It may need to be limited to moving specific products or automating some processes. No matter what, EC collaboration should be used where it is most cost effective: with high-volume, high profit-margin products or processes.

Another factor that plays a role in making EC and collaboration a success is openness in sharing information. The customer should openly give the supplier access to relevant information for better decision-making. This may include forecasts, promotions, and store-specific trends. Armed with this information, the vendor can better plan its activities and be proactive rather than reactive.

EC and collaboration with one or two suppliers does not offer tremendous advantages. It may, in fact, increase your costs. Organizations planning to work collaboratively with their EC partners should plan for trading partner rollout to maximize the benefits. Additionally, having the right technologies in place is key to the success of this type of initiative.

CONCLUSION

Although EDI has been the key EC tool for more than two decades, it is only a part of the solution today. You must consider other technologies that can be incorporated with your EDI system in an effort to further leverage your investment. Remember that electronic commerce is a business solution that embraces multiple technologies.

Chapter 3

EDI Standards

What sets EDI data exchange apart from other methods of electronic information transmission is that EDI data is defined and exchanged in a standard format. The evolution of EDI began with standards, and you can't begin thinking about EDI without understanding what EDI standards are, what their function is, and how they work.

Standards define the way an electronic business document (such as a purchase order) looks to a computer. Defining standards for an EDI purchase order is similar to defining the field layouts of a file that contains purchase order information. Standards determine such a document's format, content, and data integrity by defining exact locations for data and exact valid codes so that a trading partner's computer will know how to interpret and validate information it receives via EDI. For example, standards help trading partners determine where one electronic document begins and ends, what type of document it is (a purchase order versus an invoice), and where to find certain fields of information.

Today, several sets of standards are in use. Once you understand what EDI standards are and how they function, you can make informed choices and decisions about standards in your own EDI setup. (For more information about the evolution of standards and how standards development works, see Appendix A.)

WHAT ARE EDI STANDARDS?

The goal of EDI standards is to make an electronic business document the same regardless of origin, industry, or country. Although a purchase order to a leasing company contains different details (fields) from the details in a purchase order to a retail distributor, all purchase orders have the same purpose and convey similar information. EDI standards ensure that similar parts always follow the same patterns and rules, even though documents for different industries may choose to use different fields of data.

EDI standards are built on the concepts of data elements, segments, codes, transaction sets, and functional groups. The rules that hold these EDI pieces together are called syntax. Let's look at what these terms mean.

An EDI *data element* is one character or more that represents a numeric or alphanumeric field of data and is the smallest unit of information in a standard. For example, on a purchase order, the item number and item price are two elements. Data elements are defined in the Data Element Dictionary. Each data element is identified by a reference number. For each data element, the dictionary lists all code values and their definitions or indicates in an appendix where the valid code list can be obtained.

A *composite data element* is formed when two closely related data elements are communicated in the same element, using a delimiter for separation. For example, a composite element may consist of the sender ID and ID type.

A *segment* consists of logically related data elements in a defined sequence: a predetermined segment identifier (which is not a data element), one or more data elements (each preceded by a data element separator), and a segment terminator. An example of a segment is a line on a purchase order: the item number and quantity ordered elements make up a line item segment. Data segments are defined in a Segment Directory, which gives the segment identifier, name, purpose, and the data elements it contains in their specified order. Unused contiguous optional data elements appearing at the end of a segment are omitted; transmission of the segment terminator signifies this omission. The omission of data elements other than those at the end of a segment is specified by successive data element separators.

The standards mandate certain segments (GE, GS, ST, SE, ISA, etc.) to be used to identify the sender and receiver of the documents and the times and dates of the transaction, for example. Other segments are available for optional use.

Codes are numeric or alphanumeric representations of text for exchanging commonly used information. Codes are like building blocks that create transaction sets or messages. Some elements in a transaction set require the use of valid codes (to identify sender and receiver IDs and DUNS (Dun and Bradstreet) number, federal tax ID number, and telephone number).

A *transaction set* is the EDI term for a business document. For example, a purchase order is a transaction set. In the creation of EDI transaction sets, rules are followed to standardize the document. For example, a rule might state that the purchase order number appears before the purchase order date. *Syntax* is the collection of these data formation rules.

Each transaction set ID has a three-digit numerical representation that identifies it. Table 3.1 shows examples of transaction sets and their IDs.

TABLE 3.1
X12 Transaction Set IDs

Transaction Set	Transaction Set ID
Purchase order	850
Invoice	810
Remittance advice	820
Advance ship notice	856

To build a transaction set, you refer to a table of available segments (you find tables of segments in standards reference material or in translation software packages) for that transaction set and select the segments you need. For example, Table 3.2 is an excerpt from a purchase order transaction set. This table lists segments (such as N1, DTM, and ITD) you can use to create a purchase order transaction set. The table explains the purpose of each segment.

TABLE 3.2

Segment Table Excerpt from a Purchase-Order Transaction Set

Segment Name	Purpose
N1	To transmit name information
DTM	To transmit date information
ITD	To transmit terms and conditions information

The X12 record format in Figure 3.1 shows an example of an N1 segment. In this example, you can see how the segment is broken down by elements. The elements are separated by a special character (in this case, the asterisk). Each element appears in a predetermined sequence, and each has special qualifications. For example, the first element of the N1 segment, N101, is a mandatory field. It is exactly two bytes, and you can obtain further information about it by looking up its cross reference number 98 in the X12 data dictionary.

The function of each transaction set is defined in a purpose and scope statement. Each transaction set is composed of one or more tables that list the segments in a predefined position. Tables display a transaction set header segment as the first segment, then one or more data segments in a specified order, and finally a transaction set trailer segment.

Many transaction sets are divided into three tables, which generally relate to the format of a printed document. Table 1 is the heading area, in which information common to the entire transaction is placed. Table 2 is the detail area, which is usually one large loop. Table 3 is the summary area. When the same segment appears in more than one table, the following semantic rule applies: a segment appearing in Table 1 applies to the entire transaction set, but this may be overridden for the duration of a specific occurrence of a loop in Table 2 when the same segment with a changed value is present in that occurrence of the loop.

Other specifications are also listed in tables. The requirement designator defines a segment's need to appear in the data stream of a transmission. The maximum use designator affirms the number of times the segment is permitted to be used in that position in the transaction set.

Groups of segments may be repeated as loops, designated by a bracket; within each bracket a loop identifier and the maximum occurrence are given. Loops themselves are optional or mandatory. There is a specified sequence of

FIGURE 3.1
X12 Record Format

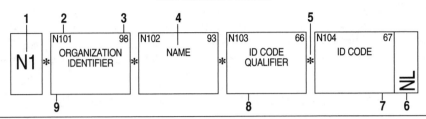

No.	Data	Description
1	N1	Segment identifier for name
2	N101	Reverence designator (segment plus sequence number)
3	98	Element cross-reference number in data dictionary
4	NAME	Element name
5	*	Segment delimiter
6	NL	New line character
7	2-17	Minimum-Maximum length of element
8	ID	Type of record
		AN Alpha-numeric
		DT Date
		TM Time
		N# Implied decimal (# is the number of places to the right of the decimal
		R Decimal with required decimal point
		ID Identification
9	M	Indicates whether the information is required
		C Conditional
		F Floating
		M Mandatory
		O Optional

segments in the loop, and the first segment in the loop may appear only once in each iteration. A segment may be mandatory within a loop, and loops may be nested within other loops. For nested loops, the same segment in an inner loop will override the data in an outer loop. Notes and comments may be provided with the tables, to provide additional information to users.

A *functional group* is a group of similar transaction sets (e.g., three purchase orders). A functional group, when transmitted, is bound by a functional group header segment and a functional group trailer segment. Each transaction set is assigned a functional identifier code, which is the first data element of the header segment. Only those transaction sets with the same code are considered members of one functional group. The functional identifier code is often used by the receiver to route the transmission to the proper internal application.

X12 SAMPLE TRANSLATION MAP

A translation map provides the information you need to translate a typical business document, such as an invoice, into a standard X12 transaction set.

The transaction map includes an explanation of what is being translated, gives the X12 format for that information, and shows an example of what that might contain. In this example, we follow the N1 segment, which is used in the standard EDI document to identify the name of the company. The first element of the N1 segment is specified as BT, the standard code for Bill To. Therefore, we know the name that follows the BT element is that of the party to be billed, namely the Acme Distributing Company. Notice that the N1-N3-N4 loop is repeated two other times with different standard codes to convey name and address information belonging to the Ship To and Remit To parties.

When you have built your EDI transaction set (such as a purchase order), you are ready to send it to your trading partner(s). If the purchase order were on paper, you would put it into an envelope and address the envelope to the proper person. But what if you had both invoices and purchase orders to send to different departments of the same company? You might put all the invoices for the accounting department into one addressed envelope and all the purchase orders for the fulfillment department into another addressed envelope. Then, because both envelopes are going to the same company, you might package them both in a larger manila envelope. When you have electronic purchase orders and invoices, EDI provides a way to put these documents into electronic "envelopes."

ELECTRONIC ENVELOPE STRUCTURE

An *electronic envelope* consists of codes that mark the boundaries of electronic documents. The electronic envelope "contains" the document. To transmit EDI transaction sets to trading partners, you must enclose the transaction sets in electronic envelopes.

An electronic envelope can have three layers. The first layer contains a document. The second contains groups of like documents (e.g., all purchase orders). Finally, the outermost envelope contains all documents for a specific trading partner. Figure 3.2 illustrates the three layers of electronic envelopes.

As depicted in Figure 3.2, the first layer uses the ST (transaction set header) and SE (transaction set trailer) segments to mark the beginning and end of each transaction set; the second layer uses the GS (functional group header) and GE (functional group trailer) segments to mark the beginning and end of groups of similar transaction sets; the third layer uses the ISA (interchange control header) and IEA (interchange control trailer) segments to enclose the first two and identifies the sender and receiver information.

Your translation software places an ST segment preceding a purchase order transaction set and an SE segment following it to identify the beginning and end of a transaction set. Often, in the same transmission, you send a variety of transaction sets, such as invoices and ASNs, to one customer. To separate groups of like transaction sets, you use another layer of enveloping, identified by the GS and GE segments. You do the same for all the ASNs, grouping them separately and surrounding them with a GS and a GE segment.

FIGURE 3.2
Interchange Envelope Structure

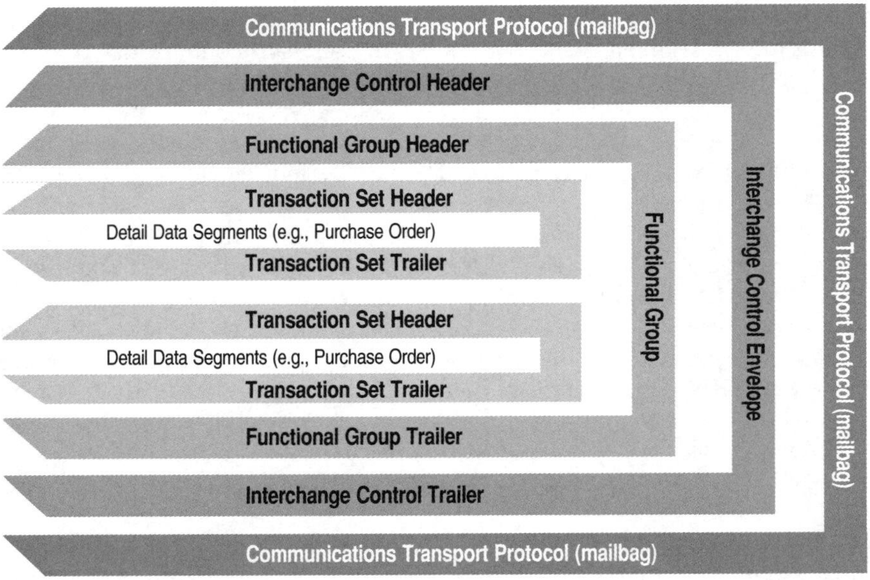

Communications Transport Protocol (mailbag)

Interchange Control Header

Functional Group Header

Transaction Set Header

Detail Data Segments (e.g., Purchase Order)

Transaction Set Trailer

Transaction Set Header

Detail Data Segments (e.g., Purchase Order)

Transaction Set Trailer

Functional Group Trailer

Interchange Control Trailer

Communications Transport Protocol (mailbag)

Functional Group

Interchange Control Envelope

Communications Transport Protocol (mailbag)

In the outermost envelope, the interchange control layer, you place all documents you want to send to each trading partner before you add communications protocols and transmit the data. The ISA identifies the sender and receiver of the documents, as well as date, time, and control number information. The IEA indicates the end of the envelope.

It is quite common to send EDI documents to multiple trading partners in the same communications session. You compile all envelopes (ISA/IEA layers), place them in a mailbag, and send them to the VAN or ISP for delivery to the recipients. The communications software simply piles them together in a mailbag and sends them out. ("Mailbag" is an EDI term meaning an electronic manila envelope that contains batches of EDI mail.) This provides a more efficient means of transmitting EDI documents over telephone lines than sending each trading partner's mail separately.

The whole point of EDI standards is to let your computer know what to expect when you receive an electronic document. The computer needs to know where one electronic document begins and ends, determine whether a document is a purchase order or an invoice, be able to tell which is the ship-to name and which is the bill-to name, and so on. Imagine how confusing it must have been when companies first started using EDI without public standards! That mental picture gives you an idea of how companies reached the conclusion that without standards, electronic exchange of business documents would be an administrative burden.

In Figures 3.3a, 3.3b, and 3.3c, you can see how the data from a paper invoice has been formatted according to X12 and UN/EDIFACT standards. Please note that all of the data may not be included in each example.

FIGURE 3.3A

SMITH CORPORATION   **INVOICE No.** 1001
900 Easy Street
Big City, NJ 15155
(618) 555-6765

INVOICE DATE: 7/13/98   **SALES PERSON:** NTO

CHARGE TO: Acme Distributing Co.   **SHIP TO:** The Corner Store
                  P.O. Box 33327   601 First Street
                  Anytown, NJ 44509   Crossroads, MI 48106

YOUR ORDER NO.	CUST. REF. NO.	ORDER DATE	TERMS
P989320	66043	6/25/95	2% 10 Days

QUAN.	UNIT	NO.	DESCRIPTION	UNIT PRICE	TOTAL PRICE
3	Cs	6900	Cellulose Sponges	12.75	38.25
12	Ea	P450	Plastic Pails	.475	5.70
4	Ea	1640Y	Yellow Dish Drainer	.94	3.76
1	Dz	1507	6" Plastic Flower Pots	3.40	3.40
			PLEASE PAY THIS AMOUNT:		$51.11

PLEASE DIRECT CORRESPONDENCE TO:
C.P. Jones (618) 555-8230

DATE SHIPPED: 7/13/98   **SHIPPED VIA:** Consolidated Truck

FIGURE 3.3B

ASC X12 Format	Sample Invoice Content	
GS*IN*012345678*087654321*960713*2219* 000000001*X*003040! ST*810*0001!	Invoice	
BIG*950713*1001*950625*P89320!	DATE ORDER DATE INVOICE # CUSTOMER ORDER #	7/13/95 6/25/95 1001 P989320
N1*BT*ACME DISTRIBUTING COMPANY! N3*P.O. BOX 33327! N4*ANYTOWN*NJ*44509!	CHARGE TO	Acme Dist. Company P.O. Box 33327 Anytown, NJ 44509
N1*ST*THE CORNER STORE! N3*601 FIRST STREET! N4*CROSSROADS*MI*48106!	SHIP TO	The Corner Store 601 First Street Crossroads, MI 48106
N1*RI*SMITH CORPORATION! N3*900 EASY STREET! N4*BIG CITY*NJ*15455!	REMIT TO	Smith Corporation 900 Easy Street Big City, NJ 15455
PER*AD*C.P.JONES*TE*6185558230!	CORRESPONDENCE TO	Accounting Dept. C.P. Jones (618) 555-8230
ITD*01*3*2**10!	TERMS OF SALE	2% 10 days from invoice date

	Quantity	Unit	Supplier Brand Code	Description	Unit Price
IT1**3*CA*12.75**VC*6900!	3	Cse	6900	Cellulose Sponges	12.75
IT1**12*EA*.475**VC*P450!	12	Ea	P450	Plastic Pails	.475
IT1**4*EA*.94**VC*1640Y!	4	Ea	1640Y	Yellow Dish Drainer	.94
IT1**1*DZ*3.4**VC*1507!	1	Dz	1507	6" Plastic Flower Pots	3.40

TDS*5111*!	Invoice Total
CAD*M****CONSOLIDATED TRUCK!	Via Consolidated Truck
CTT*4*20!	(4 Line items, Hash Total 20)
SE*21*0001!	
GE*1*000000001!	

FIGURE 3.3c

UN/EDIFACT Format	Sample Invoice Content				
UNH+1+INVOIC:D:95B:UN'					
BGM++1001'	INVOICE #	1001			
DTM+3:950713:101' DTM+4:950625:101' DTM+11:950713:101' RFF+ON:P989320'	DATE ORDER DATE SHIP DATE CUSTOMER ORDER #	7/13/95 6/25/95 7/13/95 P989320			
NAD+BT+++ACME DIST. COMPANY' P.O. BOX 33327+ANYTOWN+NJ+44509'	CHARGE TO	Acme Dist. Company P.O. Box 33327 Anytown, NJ 44509			
NAD+ST+++THE CORNER STORE' 601 FIRST STREET+CROSSROADS+MI+48106'	SHIP TO	The Corner Store 601 First Street Crossroads, MI 48106			
NAD+RE+++SMITH CORPORATION' 900 EASY STREET+BIG CITY+NJ+15455'	REMIT TO	Smith Corporation 900 Easy Street Big City, NJ 15455			
CTA+AR+:C.P.JONES' COM+6185558230:TE'	CORRESPONDENCE TO	Accounting Dept. C.P. Jones (618) 555-8230			
PAT+22+ZZZ:::2% 10, Net 30+9:1:D:10' PCD+12:2'	TERMS OF SALE	2% 10 days from invoice date			
TDT+1+++31+:::CONSOLIDATED TRUCK'	Via Consolidated Truck				

	Quantity	Supplier Brand Code	Description	Unit Price
LIN+001++6900:BP' IMD+F++:::CELLULOSE SPONGES' QTY+47:3:CS' MOA+38:12.75'	3	6900	Cellulose Sponges	12.75
LIN+002++P450:BP' IMD+F++:::PLASTIC PAILS' QTY+47:12:EA' MOA+38:.475'	12	P450	Plastic Pails	.475
LIN+003++16404:BP' IMD+F++:::YELLOW DISH CONTAINER' QTY+47:4:EA' MOA+38:0.94'	4	1640Y	Yellow Dish Drainer	.94
LIN+004++1507:BP' IMD+F++:::6" PLASTIC FLOWER POTS' QTY+47:1:DPC' MOA+38:3.40'	1	1507	6" Plastic Flower Pots	3.40

UN/EDIFACT Format	Sample Invoice Content
UNS+S' CNT+2:4'	(4 Line Items)
MOA+39:51.11'	Invoice Total
UNT+34+1'	

CONCLUSION

EDI standards are the basis for all EDI transactions. With an understanding of what these standards are and what they do, you can begin looking at how to implement EDI.

Chapter 4

EDI Software

Software in an EDI environment is multilayered. Application software lies at the top of the software pyramid, depicted in Figure 4.1, which is where data ultimately needs to be. To get there, incoming data must travel through the EDI communications software at the pyramid's base, through the EDI translation software, and through the interface software. Outgoing EDI data must travel back down through the pyramid before it can be sent to EDI trading partners.

FIGURE 4.1
The EDI Software Pyramid

Application

Interface

Translation

Communications

Incoming EDI Data

Outgoing EDI Data

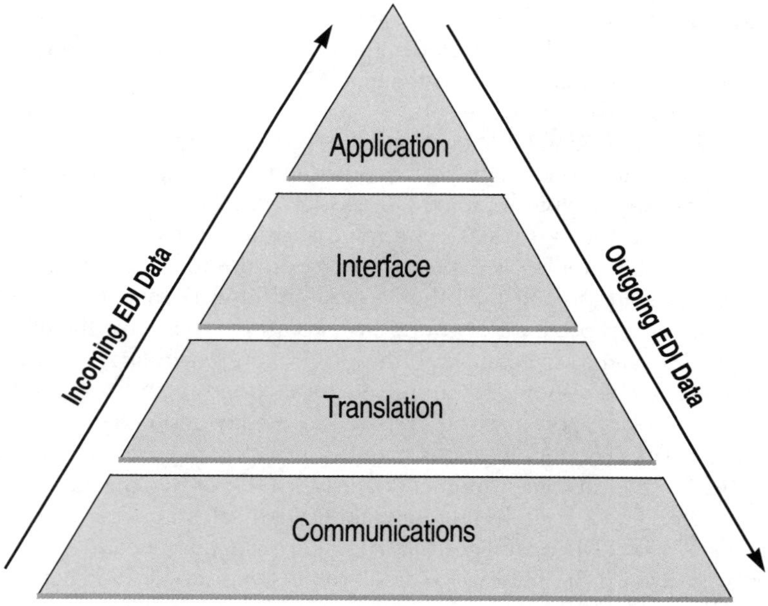

When you implement EDI, you need to evaluate your application software for its ability to work with EDI data. You also need to investigate developing, leasing, or buying the communications, translation, and interface software layers that form the EDI software pyramid. Each of these software layers requires you to consider several factors, but the issues involved with translation software are especially numerous and complex. Let's tour the software pyramid, starting at the top. We first examine the EDI considerations for your application software. Next, we move down one layer and examine the interface layer. We then skip down to look at the communications layer at the pyramid's base, saving the complexities of translation software for last.

APPLICATION SOFTWARE

EDI brings about changes in business procedures, and application software must be able to accommodate such changes. For example, today, many retailers send one EDI purchase order with many ship to points. For a large retailer, this can mean one purchase order is allocated to as many as 2,500 ship to points. To properly fill and ship the retailer's orders, the suppliers must modify their order-entry programs to split multi-ship orders into multiple orders.

In other cases, companies send data in an EDI purchase order that must be returned to them via another EDI document, such as the advance ship notice (ASN). In some instances, the application software cannot accommodate this data. Therefore, supplemental files are built to cross-reference and return the data when the outbound document is transmitted to the trading partner. Other examples of supplemental data includes the customer's purchase order number and associated line numbers, the customer's PO release number, department number, or dock door number.

While EDI is changing traditional business processes, quick response (QR) and JIT manufacturing concepts, which incorporate EDI, are also causing changes that affect application software. Some QR and JIT companies, especially original equipment manufacturers (OEMs), send forecast data to their suppliers via an EDI document. The supplier is expected to process the forecast data in lieu of a purchase order. In this situation, the application software must have the flexibility to create and process orders from the forecast data, or have the ability to create necessary data to integrate with the production scheduling application.

As these examples show, if you implement EDI with your application software already in place, you must be prepared to modify and enhance it for handling EDI data. The modifications may begin with a minor addition of an EDI flag field to the customer and vendor master files, or the changes may be comprehensive. If you are selecting new application software, you should carefully evaluate it for EDI capabilities that suit your particular needs.

You can save on the number of modifications your application software will require by letting the other software layers perform some of the processing that prepares and checks your EDI data. Let's next look at the layer just below your application software, the interface layer, which serves as a buffer between electronically transmitted data and your application.

INTERFACE SOFTWARE

Incoming EDI data usually requires some work before you can confidently add it to your application database. You want the data to be in the proper format, and you want to be sure it's correct. Your application software may be able to perform any editing and formatting, but such capability could require extensive modification to the application. Thus, most companies opt to add a layer of software, called interface or bridging software, between the incoming EDI data and the application database.

Interface software edits, formats, and audits data before you integrate it with your application. For example, EDI standards require date information to be in YYMMDD format. If the same data in your application file is in a different format, such as MMDDYY, interface software can reformat it. If your translation software does not allow for logic processing, you can use your interface software to perform data conversion to convert cases to units of each, for example, or to check for item number validity. Data audits in the interface software can perform checks and balances to ensure the validity of transactions and proper values or value ranges.

In addition, you can use interface software to process turnaround documents. Turnaround documents are used to communicate specific information and data back to the trading partner following receipt of a transaction set. For example, after receiving a purchase order, a supplier may send a purchase order acknowledgment back to the customer to confirm and verify specific details of the order. Although some translators are able to automatically create and send turnaround documents, others cannot. This could mean you have to develop interface software to do so.

You can develop your own interface software to be sure you get all the functionality you need, or you can try to purchase this software. The EDI interface software packages that are available through major application software vendors provide minimum functionality. While these off-the-shelf packages are much less expensive than custom development, you will still have to reckon with making your own modifications and enhancements. Whether you purchase or develop interface software, it is important to ensure proper design: The software must be flexible and generic enough to accommodate most of your trading partners' specific data requirements.

There are application software packages that come with built-in EDI interfaces. However, they do not include everything you need. Most come with interfaces with the most commonly used EDI documents. And what comes with the applications software is not always comprehensive enough to meet your specific needs. For example, the application vendor may have selected key elements and segments in a specific transaction set, but the specific data you need to trade may not have been included. Although not comprehensive, what vendor application software packages provide is a great help and saves some development time and effort.

COMMUNICATIONS SOFTWARE

You need communications software to add appropriate protocols to the EDI document in preparation for transmission over telephone lines. This level of software, the least complex, is inexpensive. You can buy it from your translation software vendor.

In fact, most translation software packages offer the necessary communications scripts required to connect to major VANs. Often these packages include the necessary software to communicate with proprietary links to major auto manufacturers and retailers.

The advantage of the communications software you get from translation package vendors is that it requires little or no communications expertise to use. The communications setups are menu driven. However, if you occasionally have to establish a direct link with a trading partner, you may need some knowledge about communications.

TRANSLATION SOFTWARE

After the communications software has established a link to let you retrieve the EDI data and before the interface software can audit and format it, the translation software receives a standard EDI document, such as an X12 purchase order. The translator takes this document from the form in which it was communicated and translates it into a format your company's computer can recognize. The translation process is illustrated in Figure 4.2.

FIGURE 4.2
Translation Process

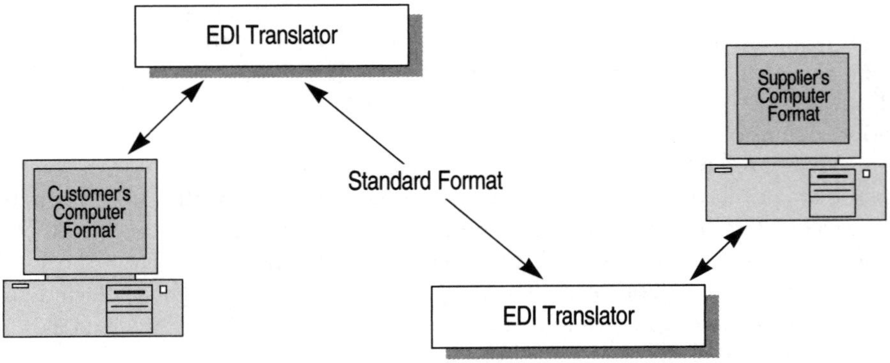

Because the layout of every corporation's database files is different, EDI requires that we map the files' data fields into a standard file format. Mapping is the process of defining the road map used to move data fields from a specific location in one file to a specific location in another file. Figure 4.3 depicts mapping.

FIGURE 4.3
Mapping Data Fields

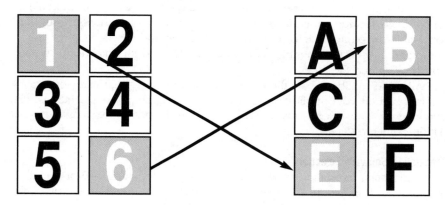

Translators are usually menu-driven tools that let you select the standard transaction map, the segments, the elements, and codes and map them to the trading partner's file specifications. There are two approaches to mapping a transaction set: trading partner-specific and generic. Trading partner-specific mapping occurs when you map the trading partner's exact segment and element requirements, with the idea that the map is used only for that one trading partner. Generic mapping means you try to fit multiple trading partners' requirements for a transaction set into one. The initial effort in mapping a trading partner-specific transaction is relatively quick because the map specifications are already available. Generic mapping requires a study of multiple maps before you can design a single generic transaction set, so initial development will take longer. However, because multiple trading partners will be using the same map, it lowers long-term testing and maintenance efforts. Although generic mapping is preferred by many due to its long-term administrative and maintenance simplifications, it is not always possible to have all trading partners use the same transaction map. For example, if the trading partner's business or data requirements are unique or significantly different than most others, it is a good idea to create a map specifically for that partner, rather than modify the generic map to the point that it begins to lose some efficiencies.

Today, many EDI users are looking to their translation software to minimize modifications to their application software. These users have the translation layer perform sophisticated tasks that the application software previously had to handle. The usual functions of the translation software are to support all public standards, revised versions of standards (so translation software should be easy to update), and options that individual trading partners require (such as verification of transaction and group IDs, acceptance of a trading partner's standards version, acceptance of production/test modes, allowance for various envelope choices and contents, acceptance of various network IDs, and establishment and maintenance of control numbering).

To unburden the application software, the translator can perform additional tasks. These include audit and security functions, control numbering, support for a table-driven approach, adjustment to the size and functionality of your computer, usage reporting, transition modes, VAN and ISP interfaces, and support for required file types.

All these capabilities — the usual ones and the ones that take some processing load off your application software — are important considerations when you evaluate translation software. The following discussion explains these evaluation points in detail.

Translation Software Selection

You can obtain translation software in three ways: You can lease or purchase the software from a supplier, have a third party (a VAN or a service bureau) perform your translation, or develop the translation software yourself. In general, the most cost- and time-effective alternative is to purchase or lease the translation software. If you develop your own, in addition to the cost of the initial development efforts, you have to consider the cost of ongoing maintenance, incorporating new releases of EDI standards, adding new transaction sets (that is, the record formats for the data sent/received in a business transaction), and performing required audit and control reporting. Translation software vendors offer a maintenance agreement that addresses all these requirements. Using a third party to perform the translation may be a good option for small companies who do not have the in-house expertise or resources to perform and monitor the necessary tasks. Some firms believe that low transaction volumes do not warrant the initial expenses of EDI software purchase and setup, making the third party option a very viable one.

Because translation software must include so many important features, the evaluation and selection of the translation software package is key to implementing EDI, but also to minimizing investment in your application software. Below, we discuss the most important criteria to consider when selecting translation software.

Standards Support

Standards are the key to EDI's success. Consider the following before committing to any translation software package.

Public standards. Translation software should support all public standards, including X12 and UN/EDIFACT, because you may need to use either standard with your trading partners. Some packages let users define proprietary standards as well. However, this feature is one you may not need because proprietary standards are no longer recommended in EDI, and use of such standards is strongly discouraged.

Subsets of public standards. Most packages support subsets of public standards. For example, subsets of X12 include CIDX (for the chemical industry), PIDX (for petroleum), and VICS (for retail). If these are missing and you do business in those industries, you may have a problem because basic X12 alone may not be enough.

Compliance. The software should check for errors with compliance to the standards you've selected for the specific document and trading partner (for example the sequence of data fields may be different from what the standards dictate). Compliance checking should reject any document in error, issue a translate error, and then allow valid documents to continue processing. Compliance monitoring is a must, and in its absence, you may experience delays in processing what turns out to be non-standard information.

To get additional information regarding X12 and UN/EDIFACT standards, you can contact DISA, the X12 secretariat. You can obtain industry-specific standards information directly from the industry group that develops them (see Appendix C for a listing of EC industries and organizations).

Version Support

Version support in translation software is important because EDI standards are always evolving. We discuss the version support issues you need to consider below.

Current version. Translation software should always support the most current published standards. Standards are revised and published several times a year. If you are involved in the standards development process, you will know which standards are current. Otherwise, you must rely on vendors or your trading partners for this information.

Previous versions. Because your trading partners are not always on the most current version and release of the standards, the translator should support all previous versions as well. The minimum support you should expect is at least four earlier versions of the standards.

Draft versions. Throughout each year, standards are updated to add fields to or remove them from existing documents or to create new transaction sets. Before ANSI approval, these changes and additions are called drafts. Because users often request changes, documents are in draft for years before ANSI approval, providing time to "perfect" them. During this period, draft versions of standards are published for trial use, and many translators support them. Support of draft versions of standards is an important feature of translation software because the draft version of a document may more closely fit your requirements than an existing version.

Trading Partner Options

The translation software should support the trading partner-specific options discussed below.

Transaction ID. The translation software should let you define the specific transaction set for each trading partner. For example, you can define a purchase order as the only valid transaction set you can send to company XYX. This option is necessary to verify the establishment of a specific EDI document with the trading partner. The translation software should reject for review any transaction sets that are not properly set up — they should not be integrated with the applications but should be placed in a reject pile for you to review and determine why you received them.

Group IDs. Some translators let you set up a group of transaction sets to be sent to and received from specific trading partners. You tell the translator that you can receive only POs and remittance data from company XYZ and that you can send only PO acknowledgments and invoices to them. This option lets you capture invalid document groups, which can save you from an embarrassing situation (such as sending your class A customer price list to a class B customer).

Trading partners' standards versions. The translation software should let you set up (map) any document and identify its standards version. This capability allows version control. Should a trading partner send a new version of a document that was previously established with you, the translation software will reject the document for review because it won't match your map setup. For example, the new map may include a new data field, and your system won't know what to do with it.

Production/test modes. You should set up each transaction set for each trading partner in test mode and promote it to production later, so it does not interface directly with your applications. It is important that the translation software allow this option because this may be the indicator you will use to place the EDI document in a test or production mailbox at the VAN or ISP. To illustrate why this is important, imagine that you are in test mode and receive a purchase order. Your software automatically integrates the purchase order with your applications, and your people pick and ship the goods only to find out you were just testing. Test and production documents should always be treated separately.

Electronic envelope choices/contents. An electronic envelope contains the electronic document itself and so is usually specific to each individual trading partner. The translation software should let you establish EDI documents for each trading partner. For example, some like to use BG instead of ISA because BG has another password tier. The software should allow the option of setting up trading partners so that they can use their own envelope type for each document. For instance, you might use BG for payment orders because of the added password tier, but use ISA for other documents.

Network IDs. Each of your EDI trading partners can choose a different communications vehicle. For example, your trading partners may use various VANs or ISPs, which means you are required to use a different network ID for each. The translation software must recognize various network IDs.

Control numbering. To keep track of your transactions, you need to establish and maintain sequential control numbers for each trading partner. The control numbers in EDI are of key audit importance so you can match receipt records to control numbers. This matching lets you make sure you are not missing any documents if there is a skip in the number. The translation software should give you this ability. Having a control number for each document for each trading partner is the best, but some translators assign the control number to trading partners regardless of the document.

Further Trading Partner Options

As you evaluate translation software, keep in mind your own specific needs as well as the general requirements of EDI. In addition to the considerations we've discussed, you'll need to review the following trading partner options to see which ones apply to your environment.

Multiple GS03s for each ISA. If your ISA envelope specifies that a transmission is from ABC company to XYZ company, you can use the GS03s to specify further that it is from Division A of ABC Company and that you're sending it to Division C of XYZ Company. In other words, within an ISA envelope, you can further break down the details of the sender and receiver IDs, using the GS segment to specify multiple envelopes. This is extremely important because it lets your customer place one order with you, and you can automatically break it down and distribute the order to the right division within your company. This is customer service!

Distribution based on GS03. Translation software should have the ability to automatically separate and disburse EDI documents to the intended recipients based on IDs provided in the GS segments, as illustrated in the previous example.

Internal number for partner. In the translation software, you should be able to use an internal number for each trading partner you establish. The internal number is the common identifying key between the application, interface, translator, and VAN or ISP. If you use a different ID number for VAN or ISP communications, the translator should automatically retrieve and use that before it dials out to send the electronic mail to the communications supplier.

Proprietary headers. Proprietary headers are envelope labels that are not defined by public standards but are specific to a company. Although proprietary headers are not in wide use, it is possible for a trading partner to use them. For example, the trading partner might have been using them for a long time, they are embedded in the system, and changes would be too expensive. The software should let you maintain the option of proprietary headers at the partner level.

Element/composite element delimiter. An EDI element is one or more characters that represent a numeric or alphanumeric field of data. A related group of elements makes up a segment. Composite elements are used extensively in EDIFACT, and have been adopted by X12. In a composite element, rather than use two elements to define sender ID and ID type, you use one element and break it down into two subelements of sender ID and ID type. Delimiters are characters that separate elements/subelements from each other. Each trading partner may use a different character as a delimiter to separate EDI elements and subelements. The translation software should let you specify which delimiter to use for each document and each trading partner.

Segment terminator. Each company may use a different character called a segment terminator to indicate the end of a segment. An EDI segment is a unit of information (analogous to a record) composed of elements in a transaction set. You can use a segment in multiple transaction sets or multiple times in the same transaction set. The translation software should let you specify and maintain the segment terminator for each document and trading partner.

Last control number sent/received in ISA. The translation software should automatically generate and track a sequential control number for each document from each trading partner. Although the ability to maintain the control number is not recommended from an audit perspective (you lose your trackability if you mess around with control numbers), the translator may let you maintain them. This function is useful in testing to help you avoid duplicate errors. Also, a trading partner may require a specific control number every time, so you need the ability to conform to such requirements. Changing control numbers is absolutely not recommended, but sometimes you have to.

Audit and Security Functions

In translation software, audit and security functions are important because they provide information necessary to ensure the sending and receiving of electronic documents. When you're evaluating the audit and security capabilities of translation software, consider the following criteria.

Reconciliation of functional acknowledgments. The software should reconcile functional acknowledgments (which report the results of transmission of electronic documents) with their associated documents and notify you if acknowledgment is not received for successfully transmitted documents. For example, if you send a purchase order and you don't receive a functional acknowledgment, you should not rely on the ordered products arriving when you need them.

Other audit reports. Translation software can provide a wide variety of audit reports to indicate document arrival and departure, transmission batch numbers, and whether the electronic mail is sent/received successfully. Make sure the package has as much detail as you need to feel comfortable that your business procedures won't halt.

Multiple levels of security. Translation software also provides various security options to ensure authorized access to specific menus and to limit access to specific functions by user ID. This is important, for example, to ensure that an unauthorized user does not set up and send confidential data in a transaction set to a competitor. At a minimum, the translation software should have a two-tiered password structure, secured menus, and secured menu options.

Backup and recovery. Timely backup of your data and recovery of lost data is of utmost importance to ensure that business procedures are never held up. Translation software should include backup and data retrieval routines. The minimum requirement is backup of EDI files before and after translation, automatic archiving, support for the user to define the timetable, and criteria to use to automatically clear EDI files. Here, you may wish to use different criteria to clear files that contain sensitive payment data versus less sensitive inventory level information.

Capture of rejected transactions. At a minimum, the translation software should capture and report any transaction sets that are in error for standards noncompliance, invalid ID numbers, invalid standards version, and incorrect document type because you want clean, concise, standard data to integrate with your applications.

Continuation of error-free documents when documents in error are detected. The translation software should continue processing valid and error-free EDI documents despite the existence of any erroneous transactions in the same transmission batch. Be sure that if a transaction is in error, the entire transmission will not be left hanging.

Control Numbering

Control numbering is important because it is the way the system tracks documents sent and acknowledged as received. When you evaluate a translation software package's control numbering capabilities, the features it should have are discussed below.

Automatic assignment. Generally, translation software automatically generates and maintains control numbers, each control number corresponding to the trading partner or the trading partner and document type. The numbers should be in sequential order by trading partner (i.e., in the order in which trading partners are set up).

Reporting of duplicate numbers. The translation software should capture and report any envelopes containing a duplicate control number. A duplicate number could indicate a duplicate transaction, and you don't want to fill a purchase order twice!

It is necessary to turn off this capability for any trading partner that chooses to send the same control number with every transmission. Turning off this capability for a particular trading partner allows duplicate control numbers for that partner without disrupting the processing, while other trading partners' duplicates continue to be rejected as erroneous.

Reporting of missing numbers. As with the duplicate number processing, the translation software should capture and report any missing control numbers. You need to know whether you are missing a document. If your customer sends you an order and is waiting for the shipment, you know you are missing something if there is a skip in the control numbers for purchase orders from that trading partner. Again, it may be necessary to turn off this capability for a certain trading partners or documents.

Table-Driven Setup of Transaction Sets

EDI translation software should be menu driven and the setup of the transaction sets should be completely table driven to minimize your efforts. With this method, you have a table of values to select from, which is easier than having to type everything in. Look for the features discussed below.

Listing of transaction sets. The transaction software should provide a complete list of all available transaction sets for each standard and standard subset, along with the corresponding document IDs. If not, you have to thumb through huge manuals to find the number that corresponds with a transaction set in a given standard.

Listing of segments/elements in transaction sets. When a transaction set is selected, the translation software should list all available segments/elements and corresponding IDs in the sequence that the standards mandate. At the same time, the software should display requirements for use and related loop information, minimum/maximum length requirements, data dictionary reference numbers, and other related information. It is a lot easier to select from a list on your screen than to thumb through manuals.

Enforcement of mandatory segments/elements. The translator should enforce the setup of mandatory segments and elements but give you the option of overriding the requirements. Although it is highly discouraged, you may need to override the standards requirements on occasion.

Code lookup capability. As elements are mapped in the translation software to your corporate files, the standards require special codes to define the type of data being mapped. The translation software should do code lookups online, using tables in the translation software to avoid manual lookup.

GUI. Having the option of a graphical user interface makes the translation software much more user friendly. GUI capabilities may be important to you if your resources are not necessarily application developers (programmers).

Split screen mapping. Some users find it easier to look at a split screen while they set up transaction maps. One window shows the standard EDI transaction, while the other displays the map being currently set up.

Size and Functionality

Look for the following features:

Disk usage. If you are concerned with disk capacity, it is important to determine the amount of disk space the translation software requires. This consideration may affect your choice of translation software, or you may need to acquire additional disk capacity.

Version comparison reports. As trading partners update their transaction sets to new versions of the standards, a version comparison report helps you identify the differences between the previous documents and the new document. This is very useful, especially if you can copy the old version map and simply modify it according the changes you find in the version comparison report.

Version conversion. Some translators can detect a new version of a document and reformat it to the version setup on your computer. This can be a time-saving feature, particularly if you have numerous trading partners and documents that require updating.

Concatenation/decatenation. The ability to concatenate and decatenate data elements within the translation software can also save a lot of time and effort. For example, if your internal order number consists of data that is being sent to you in two different elements (for example, a purchase order number may consist of the first letter of the customer's name and their order number, which is how you may choose to make the number unique on your computer), concatenating the two fields in the translator means that you don't have to do the concatenation in the interface software to create the correct order number for the application files.

Simple logic processing. Another way to minimize the interface software efforts is to have the translation software perform some simple logic processing. For example, the software might call a program to perform a function if a specific data element is null or blank.

Document forwarding. The translation software can minimize your manual efforts. Suppose you wish to forward a customer order as is to your supplier. Document forwarding lets you establish this link automatically. When the EDI purchase order is received, the translation software revises the envelope to reflect the new sender/receiver IDs and to add new control and date and time stamp information. The translation software then automatically forwards the document to your supplier through the communications link.

Document turnaround. The translator can be set up to generate specific turnaround documents. A turnaround document is one that is sent to confirm or acknowledge the detail that the trading partner may have sent. For instance, you may want to send back a PO acknowledgment to your customer to confirm the details of a purchase order. The translator can be set up to automatically create the PO acknowledgment upon receipt of the order, prepare the new electronic envelope information, and place the document in the communications outbox.

Multiple record writes from one EDI segment. It is often necessary to write data to multiple records in a file from one EDI segment. This practice is now very common with the use of SDQ segments to place one order with multiple shipping points. In this instance, one order record must be written to multiple records in the interface file because each location's order quantity may need to be treated as a separate order.

Read forward/backward. It is sometimes necessary to perform certain activities based on conditional data. The conditional data may reside in the header, detail, or summary areas of a transaction set. It is important for the translator to have the ability to read forward and backward throughout these transaction set areas to perform the specific action.

Paper-clipping. Some companies need to send nonstandard data, such as a CAD/CAM drawing or spreadsheets, with a standard transaction set. The translation software can let you paper-clip the two together and send them in one electronic envelope.

Cross-reference table. Many translation software packages include use of cross-reference tables, which let the translator cross-reference a field of data, such as matching a Universal Product Code (UPC) number to your internal part number. The software can automatically place your part number in the files to interface with your applications. This can greatly minimize efforts in the interface software. If the translation software does not do cross-referencing, you have to write the logic in the interface programs to do it.

Map copying. To save a lot of time, the translation software can let you simply copy existing maps for new trading partners and modify the copied maps to fit any new requirements. This is much more efficient than creating each new map from scratch.

Automatic map generation. One of the newer features offered by some translators is the ability to automatically create transaction sets based on incoming EDI data. The translator can read the data and generate the associated segments and elements. Although user review is important, this can significantly reduce the amount of time required to set up maps.

Multiple computer use. Many companies use multiple computers for development and for production. The capability to copy document maps and trading partner setups automatically from the development computer to the production computer can save manual backup and retrieval efforts.

Usage Reporting

Translation software packages provide a variety of reports to assist in the audit, control, and review of EDI documents. These reports, discussed below, are necessary if you are trying to track a lost order, look up the time it was sent to you, etc.

Transaction type. This type of report shows specific transaction sets received from or sent to trading partners. You can select reports for a given period or for documents sent via a selected VAN or ISP.

Trading partner. This report type lists all documents received from or sent to a specific trading partner for a given period or via a selected VAN or ISP.

Time period. You can also get reporting of all or selected EDI activity for a given time period.

Communications session. Reporting of all or selected EDI activity in a given communications session is also available.

Acknowledgment errors. Perhaps the most important error report is the acknowledgment not received or received in error because it is crucial for you to know whether your supplier received your order, and if so, whether errors were noted. Some translation software packages let you specify a window of time beyond which nonreceipt of an acknowledgment is flagged and the user is automatically notified. Other translation software requires the user to request a report of late acknowledgments. Each vendor does it differently

User-defined errors. User-defined error reports list user-defined errors and let you query any needed information. For example, if you want to see the same data that is provided in the above reports, but need to have it sorted differently, this is a very useful option.

In addition, the translation software should offer a variety of other error reports (such as reports of translation errors, invalid documents from receiver, transmission problems), providing all information necessary to correct or resolve problems.

Transition Modes

Translation software packages include various modes of operation. The four transition modes you need to look at in translation software are discussed below.

Tutorial mode. The translation software should provide a tutorial for first-time users and have the ability to simulate a communications session. The user can then learn the operation of the system just as it would take place in production. This is an important feature as new or additional people in your company need to learn to work with the software.

Test mode. A test mode lets new users try the system using real data but without updating live production files. To allow testing, the software should be able to access live files while dialing out to the VAN, ISP, or trading partner to test the communications setup.

Production mode. A full production mode is, of course, necessary for all live EDI processing. Production mode uses real data and real trading partners. You should segregate the production environment from all testing and tutorials.

Unattended operation mode. Some translation software includes a 24-hour job scheduler, allowing users to set up EDI processing (such as translation, document sending, or mail retrieval) to take place automatically throughout the day and night. The unattended operation mode means you do not have to rely on manual actions for EDI activity to take place. You can set up activity, such as mail pickup and sending and translation, to take place at predetermined times, without having to rely on a person to take action.

Communication Interfaces

Translation software must have the interface capabilities discussed below.

Interface with major VANs. Translation software packages generally provide all necessary communications software to interface with major VANs. Be aware that some vendors charge an additional fee for each VAN interface.

Interface support to proprietary organizations. If you require an interface to proprietary (nonpublic) organizations, such as RAILINC, the translation software should be able to accommodate the interface. This service is sometimes provided for an additional fee.

Internet scripts. In addition to the ability to connect to major VANs and proprietary organizations, it is critical for the translator to provide the scripting necessary to connect to the Internet or to major ISPs.

Files

Files are an important consideration with translation packages because we rely a great deal on the files' data content. Look for the options discussed below.

Predefined flat files. Flat files are built to temporarily hold EDI data before translation and transmission to a trading partner, and following receipt and translation. EDI data is sometimes edited while in the flat files. Many translation software packages, in particular those for the PC, format the data by predefining the flat files to which EDI data is mapped. Many PC EDI users receive EDI data and print it, so they don't care about the file layouts. On midrange or mainframe systems, you do care about the layout of the files. You want them to look like or be similar to your application files so it is easy to integrate data with them once the editing is completed, so the ability to define the file is important.

Although small companies that do not have inhouse technical expertise sometimes want the package to format the data by predefining the flat files, this is a limiting practice in establishing EDI data requirements in an integrated solution setup. It is much more practical to set up the flat files to closely resemble the application files to which the data will be integrated.

Self-cleaning files. The translation software should let you define the period after which it will automatically clear EDI files. Otherwise, the files will grow too large, and you really don't need the data to sit around too long because it is already somewhere else (at the VAN, in your archives, etc.). Specifying each file and the corresponding time to clear it is very important because you may want different file types cleared at different intervals. For example, you may wish to clear all purchase order flat files within 48 hours, but you may want to keep invoicing files longer.

Archiving. Translation software should provide the option of archiving all EDI and related files based on creation date, trading partner, and document type. It should also allow easy retrieval of archived data.

Documentation

A variety of documentation, including a user guide, initial installation guide, release upgrade guide, and online help text, should be available and provided to EDI users. Documentation requirements are discussed below.

User guide. This document is for the IT user who will set up the EDI software. The guide should provide step-by-step instructions for setting up trading partners, transaction sets, communications with third parties, and so on. In addition, it should include sample reports, flow charts of the way the software operates, and a list of file names used.

Initial installation guide. This document is for the IT manager or the IT person who will set up the EDI software. An initial step-by-step installation guide will greatly assist in setting up the software the first time.

Release upgrades. As the software is updated, the vendor should provide ongoing, up-to-date documentation of release upgrades, the bugs that are corrected, and the enhancements made. The documentation should describe how these changes affect existing setups.

Online help. The software should also include online user documentation for the technical staff. It is very important for the software to provide field- and screen-sensitive help. It is much more convenient to look for quick answers online than it is to read through a few pages of help, even online, to get an answer to a field-specific question. You may also find it useful to be able to customize the online help text.

Technical Support

Technical support is an important factor in your decision about a translation software package because your day-to-day ability to use the product depends on whether you can get the support you need when you need it. Technical support covers a variety of vendor services; the important ones are discussed below.

Electronic customer support (ECS). ECS is a very efficient process that lets the translation software vendor sign onto your computer and check your EDI setup to determine and correct a problem online. Many manufacturers of hardware (such as IBM), as well as software package vendors, use electronic customer support today. This is not an essential consideration, but it is good feature. ECS lets software vendors see and correct problems from wherever they are.

Installation support. Some vendors provide installation support, while others provide instructions for you to install the software. If your in-house technical expertise is limited, installation should be an available service.

Ongoing support. One of the most important keys to selecting EDI translation software is choosing the right vendor and getting superior customer service after the initial installation and setup. You often need ongoing help as you set up new trading partners and new documents. Ongoing support, whether electronic or via the telephone, is vital.

Support hours. Software vendors have a wide range of support hours. Most do not provide round-the-clock support, so their hours may be important to you, especially considering such factors as time zone differences. Those who offer 24-hour support may charge users an additional fee.

Support staff. The number of support staff and their expertise will give you an indication of the kind of support you will get when you need help. Some vendors who claim offer 24-hour telephone support simply have a non-technical staff member take a telephone message for someone to call you back with an answer at a later time. If this type of support is not what you have in mind, keep looking.

Response time. You should inquire about the expected or guaranteed response time once your call for help is placed. Some vendors respond to you immediately, while others work on a call-back basis.

Price

A variety of costs are associated with translation software packages. Below we cover costs and note which are broken down in the price of some translation software packages and are included but not listed separately in others.

License fee. The fee for the software package license is usually a charge per CPU.

Communications software. Sometimes third-party (VAN/ISP) communications software is included with the translator, and sometimes there is a charge. The charges can vary for the type of protocol software.

Standards included. Some vendors include all public standards, while others charge an additional fee for each standard set.

Transaction sets included. Some vendors include all publicly approved transaction sets, while others charge for each transaction set individually.

Installation. Vendors may charge a fee to install the software on your computer. However, in many cases, they will usually provide free telephone assistance if you install it yourself.

Training. The vendors provide training for their software. Most training is offsite, but some will provide onsite training as well. Although some vendors include some training with the cost of the software, additional or special training costs extra. A key consideration may be to negotiate for follow-up training beyond the initial sessions offered or included. The follow-up training gives you the opportunity to learn more about the advanced features once you have become comfortable with the basics.

Multi-site discount. Vendors are usually open to discounting the cost of software when you purchase multiple licenses. Most vendors will not charge you for an extra copy of the software operating on your development computer.

Trial period. Most vendors provide a free 30-day trial period for you to evaluate their software. This period is an excellent opportunity to work with the software as well as experience the vendor's customer service support.

Consulting fees. Many vendors provide consulting services above and beyond what they deem necessary for the installation and support of their software. You may wish to inquire about their hourly or daily rates and compare those rates with other consultants with the same or similar experience.

Maintenance charges. There is generally a 10 to 15 percent annual maintenance charge for EDI translation software. Even if it is optional, the maintenance agreement is highly recommended. This service provides you with all new releases of the software that are affected by standards upgrades, program fixes, and enhanced capabilities.

User-group membership. There is usually no charge for membership in the vendor's user group. However, there may be fees to attend the user-group meetings.

Other

Several other considerations will affect your choice of a translator; we cover the important ones below.

User-group sponsorship. Some vendors sponsor user groups with periodic meetings across the country. This service provides a platform for users to collectively voice concerns to the vendor, to share issues and solutions with other users, and to learn of the software's new features.

Hardware platforms. Some vendors market translation software for a variety of hardware platforms. This can be a plus if you use multiple platforms in your corporate environment, if you might perform EDI processing on more than one, and if you would like to the same vendor for the software solution. On the other hand, if you use only one platform you might want to select a vendor who focuses on and invests in just that one hardware platform.

Source code. Most vendors do not provide the source code with translation software. If source code is a requirement for you, you will want to know the programming language in which the product is written so you can assess the feasibility of modifications and enhancements you may wish to make. The vendor should be willing to put the source code in escrow, so that it is available to you if the vendor ceases to support it or goes out of business.

CONCLUSION

When you're evaluating EDI software, the number of considerations you have to keep in mind can seem endless.

In addition to making sure the software has all the functionality you want, to do a really good evaluation of a vendor, you need to talk to each vendor's customers. Their comments and level of satisfaction will give you a realistic picture. You can use the form at the end of this chapter to simplify the task of getting vendor references and to help you keep track of responses.

Translation Software Vendor Reference Worksheet

Company name	
Contact	
Telephone number	
Date of installation	
Hardware platform and model	
Number of trading partners in production	
Transaction sets in use	
Level of in-house EDI expertise	
Standards used	
Proprietary formats used	
Enveloping used	
Is EDI distributed using GS segment?	
Compliance checking performed?	
Check for duplicate/missing control numbers?	
Is built-in file archiving available? Used?	
Is Standards version control functional?	
How many transactions are processed?	
How long does the translation take?	

Are cross-reference tables used? How?	
Are logical expressions used in mapping?	
Reporting used	
Unacknowledged transactions	
Number of transactions sent/received	
Mapping error reporting	
Communications error reporting	
Compliance error reporting	
Running in unattended operation mode	
Quality issues	
Quality of software	
Learning curve	
Quality of training	
Quality of documentation	
Quality of hotline support	

Off-hours support	
Call-back timeliness	
Problem-fix timeliness	
Standards-release update timeliness	
User group involvement/quality	
Software strengths	
Software weaknesses	
Recommendation (Yes/No)	
Other comments	

Chapter 5

Hardware

You can implement EDI on just about any hardware platform or any combination of platforms. In fact, in many cases, many computers are used to process EDI data in a distributed environment. The three most common hardware choices for EDI processing are host-based, a server as a front-end processor to the host, or a standalone server.

Which platform or combination of platforms you choose will depend on your software needs in conjunction with cost, disk capacity, processing speed, security, application integration, and your business strategy. Let's look at each alternative with these considerations in mind.

HOST-BASED

The host computer is defined as the hardware platform containing the applications with which EDI must integrate. Host does not imply the main computer or a larger hardware platform. If your accounting systems reside on a PC-based system and your order-management software is on a midrange computer, then the host for financial EDI data is the PC, while the host for order processing is the midrange computer. When you use EDI in a host-based environment, your company's host computer performs all EDI activity, including receipt of the transaction set, mapping, translation, and population of interface files. In addition, the data is edited through interface programs on the same host before integration with the applications software. The host system can be a PC, midrange, or mainframe. Both partners' host systems do not have to be — and often are not — the same platform. Trading partners can choose whichever hardware platform and whichever hardware configuration they like.

Figure 5.1 illustrates the host-based EDI approach. Note that the customer's host computer sends data to the supplier's computer. (You can also use a VAN or ISP.) The trading partner may or may not use the same hardware approach as you.

FIGURE 5.1
Host-based Approach

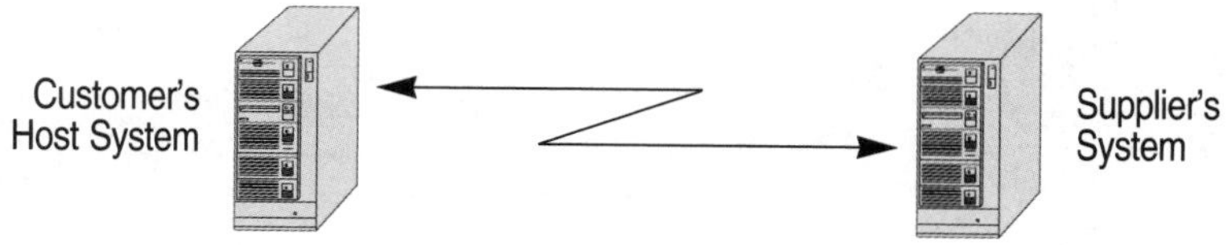

Customer's
Host System

Supplier's
System

Advantages

- **Application integration**. With EDI data received, translated, mapped, and integrated on the same computer, you minimize steps and possible points of failure. You also minimize the need for monitoring and manual intervention in case of communications failure in uploading/downloading the data to another platform.

- **Cost**. Of the three hardware choices, the host-based approach usually requires the largest initial investment. However, in the long term, this approach may also be the most effective solution because you minimize the risk of data loss and can automatically integrate all EDI data with your application database without manual rekeying.

- **Auditability**. The host-based approach provides a more controllable communication environment by eliminating the need to monitor multi-hardware communications issues.

- **Resource needs**. You can leverage your existing resources — you do not need to provide additional training for a new platform or to hire additional personnel with expertise on a different system.

Disadvantages

- **Cost**. Because most host computers are midrange or mainframe computers, the host-based approach means higher hardware costs. In many cases additional DASD and communications ports are needed, and annual maintenance costs are higher as computers are upgraded. In addition, EDI translation software is more expensive for midrange and mainframe computers than for the PC, as is generally the case with any software.

FRONT-END SERVER

You can use another server to front-end EDI processing into your host system. Most companies use a PC for front-end processing; others use midrange computers. The front-end server sends, receives, and processes EDI data, and the data is then integrated with (uploaded to and downloaded from) the host system(s), as Figure 5.2 illustrates.

FIGURE 5.2
Front-End Server Approach

Customer's Host System

File Extract

Customer's Front-End Server

Supplier's System

Advantages

- **Cost**. This approach can be less expensive to set up because the cost of front-end hardware is often lower than the cost of additional memory or disk space for the host. Those who choose the front-end server approach for cost savings generally use a PC. PC translators are less expensive than translators for midrange or mainframe computers.

- **Ease of setup**. Smaller companies with limited resources opt for a PC front-end to minimize the reliance on technical resources. PC translators are usually more user friendly than those for larger platforms. Also, many vendors of PC translators provide the most commonly-used transaction set maps, which are not usually provided for the midrange and mainframe platforms.

- **Security**. For security reasons, many companies do not like to give trading partners a direct link to applications on their host computer. A front-end server prevents such access and isolates the EDI data that resides on the host.

- **Performance**. EDI processing can diminish the performance of your host system by overloading it. The front-end server offloads the processing of EDI data to another platform, freeing your host system for normal processing.

- **Application integration**. Using the front-end server approach, EDI data can be uploaded and downloaded for integration with the applications on the host, eliminating the need for manual data entry or intervention.

Disadvantages

- **Capacity and performance**. Because most computers used in a front-end approach are PCs or smaller midrange computers, you may experience capacity and performance issues — especially as EDI volumes increase. The PC or midrange can take the load off the host processor but cannot provide the mainframe or midrange computer's capacity and processing power.

- **Communications link**. By using another server for interim EDI processing, you add another link to a series of communications that must take place between you and trading partners as the EDI data travels between you. With the addition of another potential failure point, you must add and closely monitor the communications link between the front-end and host computers.

- **Realtime processing**. Adding another hardware layer in EDI processing will add processing time. Realtime EDI processing becomes less dependable.

STANDALONE SERVER

Many companies, often in reaction to customer demand and with a fast-approaching deadline, use a standalone server for EDI processing, creating a "make-believe" EDI system. You make the trading partner believe you are doing EDI, but you really are not. This approach is like using a fax machine. With the other hardware alternatives, EDI data is not manually re-entered on your computer; it is integrated with your applications exactly as the senders entered it on their computer. But when you use a standalone server for EDI (see Figure 5.3), data received on the server is printed on paper and processed as if it had been received as a paper document. If the host is not the EDI server, you must manually re-enter the printed data on the host computer. For outbound data, the traditional paper document is printed as usual, and the data is re-entered on the EDI server to be translated and sent out.

FIGURE 5.3
Standalone Server

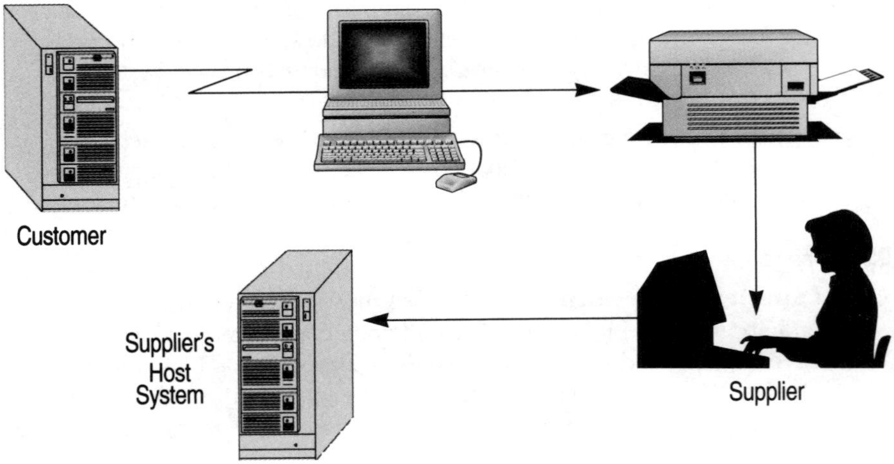

Customer

Supplier's
Host
System

Supplier

Advantages

- **Customer retention**. Using this approach, your company appears to be EDI-capable. When a customer sends an EDI transaction set, you are able to receive and process it. Your customers do not have to know that you are manually rekeying the data on your host system.
- **Cost**. You'll need to invest in a small server (such as a PC) and translation software. Translators for smaller servers are fairly inexpensive and easy to use, and because the EDI data is manually rekeyed, there is no cost in the development of interface software.

- **Implementation speed**. You can set up the standalone server approach relatively quickly. Translation software vendors can generally provide the document maps, so all you have to do is plug and go.
- **Resource requirements**. Because small servers (usually PCs) are pretty user friendly, and most people are used to working with them, there is a level of comfort in using them.

Disadvantages

- **Processing speed**. Small servers usually do not have the processing speed of larger computers, which may not be a disadvantage if you are working with only a few transaction sets and several trading partners. But as the volumes of data increase, performance degradation may occur.
- **Manual intervention**. Once received and printed, EDI data must be rekeyed, which is time consuming and error-prone.
- **Functionality**. Generally, translators for small servers have diminished capabilities for translation and mapping. Although simpler to use than their midrange or mainframe equivalents, they lack sophistication and functionality (the more the translator can do, the less you have to do in programming and interfacing of the EDI data).

Sometimes companies combine all of the alternatives we've just discussed, using a variety of hardware platforms for internal information processing. For example, you might use PCs for financials and a midrange for manufacturing applications. Many companies with multiple platforms integrate EDI with all of them because the applications that require EDI reside on various platforms, which means you must install an EDI translator on each hardware platform and integrate it with the residing application software.

HARDWARE PLATFORM SELECTION

You can use one hardware alternative for EDI or combine them all, but you need to be aware of all the considerations involved in using a particular platform for EDI. Selecting the right hardware platform is an important step toward saving a lot of time and money. For example, many companies jump to the inexpensive, easy-to-install PC solution, only to face problems with performance or inadequate functionality in the future. They end up throwing away their initial investment because EDI maps and trading partner setups are not portable from one hardware and translation software package to another. They have invested twice. If they choose the right platform the first time around, they spend less money and effort in the long run.

Before you decide on an EDI platform, you need to examine the hardware alternatives for your environment. We look at the important factors below.

Determine Your EDI Commitment

Your reasons for implementing EDI play an important role in planning a long-term EDI strategy. If you are implementing EDI because your only alternative is to lose an important customer, your choice of hardware will probably center on a solution that is inexpensive, quick, and easy to install. You won't be terribly concerned with flexibility, expandability, or integration with your applications. On the other hand, if you have a long-range goal of making EDI an integral part of your electronic commerce (EC) strategy, you'll be interested in getting a solution that is expandable and viable in the future. You'll want to examine the hardware alternatives in detail, based on your interest in EDI.

Are You Reactive?

For many companies, EDI implementation is customer-driven. One or several key customers force a supplier to use EDI for sending purchase orders and receiving invoices. The coerced parties may not think of EDI as a cost-saving tool. Rather EDI becomes a necessity to keep customers and is viewed as an additional expense or cost of doing business. A return on investment (ROI) is not a factor.

In many instances, these companies choose a standalone server approach to minimize expenses and become EDI-capable quickly. This is particularly true if the company is a small supplier and does not have in-house technical expertise for implementing a large-system EDI solution. Standalone-server (generally PC) solutions are fairly user friendly and are thus implemented more easily than other hardware solutions. Another reason, of course, is that these companies must react quickly to customer demand, and the standalone server solution is a quick-fix method of doing EDI.

Unfortunately, today's quick fixes usually turn out to be tomorrow's throwaways. Some of these companies eventually realize that if EDI had been integrated with their applications, it would have saved them time and money. These companies must reinvest in a turnkey EDI solution. This is a costly way of implementing EDI because EDI transaction set maps that are set up on the PC are not transferable to another translator on a different computer. Moving to a new platform means starting all over again. A major disadvantage of this type of migration effort is that you must retest all transaction sets with your trading partners again. Many trading partners find this disruptive to their business and incur additional expenses when they have to go through this process with you again.

Are You Proactive?

Proactive EDI implementers fall into two distinct categories: those who are forward-looking and internally driven to implement EDI, and those who view EDI as mission critical.

The first group consists of companies that haven't been forced into EDI but recognize its benefits. These companies implement EDI to become more competitive or to improve customer service.

These internally driven EDI users take the time to develop a long-term plan for EDI implementation. They are usually medium-sized companies with internal IT departments. They may use multiple hardware platforms, but their applications usually reside on a midrange computer or a client/server platform. Such companies usually opt for the front-end or the host-based approach to EDI. Those who select the front-end approach are comforted by its added sense of security (isolation of EDI data), are somewhat concerned about costs, and may have limited technical expertise for ongoing addition of documents and trading partners.

The second group of companies, which view EDI as mission-critical, consider EDI, bar coding, document management, the Internet, and other advanced technologies to be critical tools that they must use to remain competitive and offer their customers added value. These are usually large corporations that operate in JIT environments.

Examples of this second group include automobile manufacturers and large retailers. To order and receive parts directly at the assembly line when they need it, the big automotive companies use EDI in very tightly controlled plans. In these plans, if the timing is slightly off, the manufacturing process can fail. In fact, these companies do not assume ownership of the supplier parts until the parts reach the assembly line, where they are scanned and mounted on vehicles. In the retail industry, retailers expect suppliers to replenish merchandise sold today within two or three days. These businesses plan receipt of the merchandise very carefully, using EDI documents such as the advance ship notice (ASN). Mass merchants, for instance, use ASN information to schedule their receiving processes and assess substantial penalties if the supplier fails to send the ASN, or even if it contains incorrect information that changes the dock scheduling.

Organizations in this mission-critical category generally use the host-based EDI approach. Because the EDI data must reach applications as quickly and effortlessly as possible, the data is sometimes integrated directly into the applications without any interface programs.

If you've examined your company's commitment to EDI, you've probably already narrowed down the hardware platforms you will consider. Your next step is to see how this preliminary choice fits with your business requirements.

Review and Evaluate Business Requirements

To select the right hardware for EDI, you need to evaluate both your internal and external business requirements. You must determine the number of transaction sets you'll be exchanging (purchase orders, invoices, bills of lading, etc.). You should review your internal operations to identify areas that are labor and paper intensive; the processes you identify are good candidates for EDI application. Then ask your customers and suppliers which transaction sets they are transmitting via EDI, and compare the two to develop a priority list. You must

assess what your EDI platform must accommodate: how many trading partners, how many document maps, what volumes of transactions. You should
also consider future growth requirements.

In reviewing your internal business issues, consider whether your present
IT department can support your hardware choice for EDI. The amount and
level of existing technical expertise is an important factor when you're
selecting EDI hardware. Large companies can have either a decentralized EDI
system with its own hardware platform and perhaps a separate technical support staff, or a centralized system. If decentralized, EDI processing can be
done on each center's hardware. If centralized, EDI processing is naturally
done on the main computer(s).

Evaluate Hardware Approaches

When you think you've found the right platform, be sure you consider the
availability and strength of the translation software packages for that platform.
(See Chapter 4 for information about translation software selection.) As a
matter of practice, the software sometimes has more influence on the hardware
decision than other factors. For example, if you choose the standalone or
front-end approach using a PC as an interim solution, do so knowing your
long-term costs will be much higher because the EDI setups are not transferable to another hardware platform later.

If the relatively high initial cost of translation and interface software will be
offset by long-term cost effectiveness, and your host processor's capacity
(which high EDI volume can negatively affect) is not an issue, and the lack of
an insulation layer (such as a front-end server) does not pose a security threat
in your company, the host-based approach will be most beneficial because
you'll be able to directly integrate EDI data with your application data. If those
are crucial issues, you must measure the costs versus the benefits of each alternative to select the right hardware approach.

Conclusion

Whether you are a proactive EDI user or are forced into it, EDI can be a costly
tool or a cost-saving tool. The right choice is different for every company. The
most important role of EDI in today's business is to eliminate manual intervention. Following that dictum, you'll find that the hardware approach that requires
the least manual processing is ultimately the best choice for every situation.

Hardware Selection Procedure

✔	**Determine your EDI commitment**
	Are you reactive?
	Are you proactive?
✔	**Review and evaluate business requirements**
	Determine the number of transaction sets you'll be exchanging
	Identify application areas that are labor and paper intensive
	Ask your customers and suppliers what transaction sets they are doing via EDI, and compare the two to develop a priority list
✔	**Assess what your EDI platform must accommodate**
	How many trading partners?
	How many transaction maps?
	What volumes of transactions ?
	Consider future growth requirements
✔	**Review your internal business issues**
	Can your present IT department support your hardware choice for EDI?
	Evaluate the amount and level of existing technical expertise
✔	**Evaluate hardware approaches**
	Consider the availability and strength of the translation software packages for your chosen platform
	Select the hardware approach that requires the least manual processing

Chapter 6

EDI Communications Options

Several communications vehicles can be used to exchange EDI transaction sets. These include direct link, private or proprietary networks, third-party VANs, and the Internet. The choice you make will depend on the number of trading partners and transactions you have; your in-house technical expertise, security needs, budget; and several other factors. Let's look at each alternative and discuss the relevant factors in the decision as well as the advantages and disadvantages of each alternative.

In a typical scenario, all of the available communications vehicles can be used for EDI exchange (see Figure 6.1). Each trading relationship may justify a different option, therefore there is no "best" option today.

FIGURE 6.1
Communications Scenario — Direct, Private, VANs, and the Internet

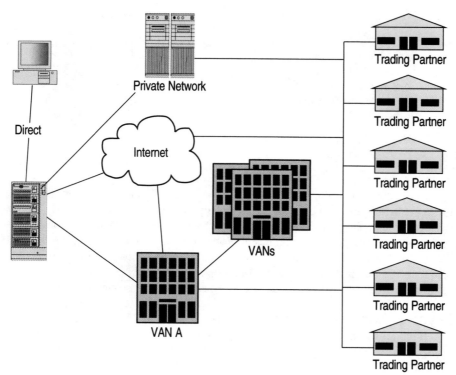

DIRECT LINK

To establish direct communications, you use modems and telephone lines to connect two computers. Each computer has communications protocols that define its "language" of communication. (Commonly used EDI communications protocols are asynchronous and bisynchronous.) If two computers using different protocols must communicate directly, protocol conversion is necessary to let them to speak the same language. You can use direct-dial access for beginners and low volumes, but as volumes increase, a leased line is more cost effective.

You can use direct communications for an EDI link-up with trading partners. Figure 6.2 shows a supplier's computer linking directly to a customer's computer via modem. Using a direct communications link, you must be prepared for such inconveniences as busy signals, time-zone differences, and your trading partner's system downtime. Additionally, you are responsible for implementing proper audit and control procedures to ensure that EDI documents are sent to and received from the right party, are timely, and are complete. (See Chapter 10 for more information about audit and control procedures.)

FIGURE 6.2
Direct Communications

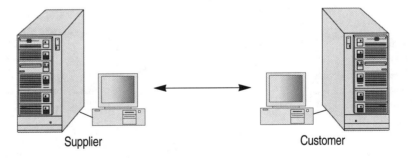

Supplier　　　　　　　　　　　　　　　　Customer

Direct communications is usually the method large companies prefer because the cost savings are greater for high volumes than with the other methods. Companies that use direct links must be prepared for its challenges such as protocol conversion, having sufficient communications ports, modems, and data lines. Furthermore, skilled resources are required to manage this type of an environment. With direct links, remember that you must put in place security, archiving, and restore/recovery procedures to ensure the integrity of the communications link.

PRIVATE OR PROPRIETARY NETWORKS

To eliminate the need for a third-party network provider, many major corporations create a closed, proprietary network. The network is only available to the hub (host) organization and its trading partners. This arrangement amounts to establishing private network services for their EDI business partners. The spokes (trading partners) establish communications using a dial-up to the host private network. In this scenario, you pay only the cost of the telephone call because most host trading partners do not charge for their network service. You usually do not have to be concerned with communications protocols because the hub can accept most protocols and will perform the necessary conversion. The hub usually provides limited data restore and restransmission opportunities in the event of communications failure. And the audits and controls, although limited, are sufficient. Even if the host company archives the data files, you must have your own archiving. In addition to the speed of access to stored data, your own archival of data provides you with the necessary evidence in case of dispute with the hub. Because proprietary networks are only open to authorized trading partners with set limitations, security features are fairly reliable.

VALUE-ADDED NETWORKS (VANs)

Today, most companies use VANs to exchange EDI documents. VANs electronically perform the basic functions of a post office or delivery service. For example, Figure 6.3 shows how one trading partner exchanges documents with many trading partners through a VAN. You place your EDI documents in electronic envelopes (see Chapter 3 for a definition of electronic envelopes), identifying sender and receiver information. Then you mail the electronic document to the VAN in a transmission via telephone lines. The VAN places the EDI mail in the recipient's mailbox, from which it can be retrieved at any time (VANs are available 24 hours a day, seven days a week). Most VANs will also deliver mail to a recipient by dialing out to the recipient's computer and placing the electronic document directly on their system, usually for an added fee.

VANs offer many value-added services, including translation of data to EDI documents (and vice versa), archiving, EDI-to-fax, and e-mail. The VAN's main function is to act as the delivery agent of EDI mail. Because each computer can use a different protocol, the VAN must convert various communications speeds and protocols. If you use a VAN for EDI exchange, you don't have to perform such communications protocol conversions. In addition, VANs act as a security buffer by not allowing your trading partners direct access to your computer.

Both trading partners can use the same VAN to perform these functions. Figure 6.3 illustrates both a supplier and customer conducting EDI business through one VAN.

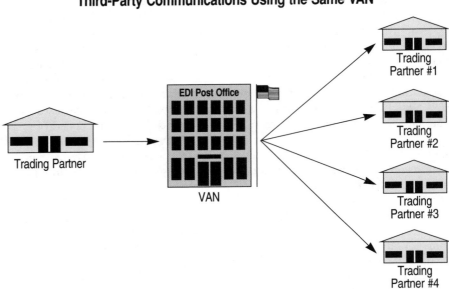

FIGURE 6.3
Third-Party Communications Using the Same VAN

The VAN of your choice is often different from your trading partner's choice. However, this is not a problem because most VANs have the ability to communicate with each other. This capability, known as a gateway or interconnection, lets you send your EDI mail to your VAN of choice. As Figure 6.4 shows, your VAN will sort the mail and, if any mail is addressed to trading partners on another VAN, forward that mail through to the appropriate VAN. The trading partner's VAN will then place the EDI documents in the appropriate mailboxes. This option of EDI exchange adds float time, but the float is sometimes minor (a few extra minutes). Another disadvantage is that you have no way of knowing that the addressee's VAN received your transmission and put it into the addressee's mailbox. You can be certain only that your VAN received your transmission and sent it on to the correct trading partner VAN.

Using VAN interconnects is quite common today. However, some companies prefer to maintain multiple mailboxes, one on each VAN where their trading partners' mailboxes reside. The disadvantages of multiple mailboxes on various VANs include the cost of the mailboxes and of maintaining communications with multiple VANs. The advantages include minimizing float time and eliminating failure points where data can get lost or misplaced. Also, some trading partners will not accept an interconnection; they require that you maintain a mailbox on their VAN.

Figure 6.4
Third-Party Communications Using a Network Gateway

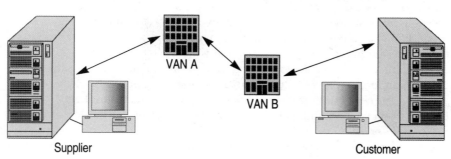

VANs have reliably delivered EDI for many years in a secure environment, notifying senders and receivers of perceived or real problems. They have trained professionals monitoring EDI traffic 24 hours a day, seven days a week. They identify and track problems, unauthorized access attempts, invalid trading partner IDs, unauthorized transactions, and much more.

Finally, a key piece of information you should have is that VANs are not liable for damages in case of message delivery failure or delay. The only liability of the VAN to its EDI customers, should a transmission not be delivered, delivered improperly, or delivered late, is the cost of communication transmission. This means you must conduct reasonable audits and checks to monitor inbound and outbound transactions.

THE INTERNET

The Internet has quickly gained the attention of the EDI community and the world. Although the Internet has been touted as a cheap, easy-to-use communications vehicle, most companies are still hesitant to use it for exchanging EDI transaction sets. There are a lot of reasons for this apprehension, despite the high costs of using VANs.

The Internet is a network of networks linked around the world, using TCP/IP communications protocols. In a way, it is in line with EDI because the concept behind both is standardization: EDI defines the standards for exchanging business data in a transaction set, and the Internet requires use of a standard communications protocol, standard Web browsers, and other standard Web technologies. The Internet makes good sense for transporting electronic messages, but how reliable is it for EDI?

For EDI transactions to travel via the Internet as messages, they must be wrapped inside a Multipurpose Internet Mail Extension (MIME) envelope. The MIME protocol is a standard method of sending and receiving attachments, including an EDI document.

Today, fewer than 10 percent of companies using EDI exchange transaction sets over the Internet. This number has been growing slowly and cautiously over the past few years. The biggest draw to using the Internet for EDI seems to be cost savings. If we look strictly at the cost of transmitting messages, EDI exchange via VANs can cost anywhere from two to 10 times more than using the Internet, depending on the volumes.

The Internet also offers the opportunity for immediate transmission to trading partners, while VANs use a store-and-forward approach. Using VANs, an EDI document can take several hours to reach the recipient. Using the Internet, a transaction and its response can be completed within minutes.

Careful selection of an Internet Service Provider (ISP) can ensure the likelihood that your EDI transactions are traveling safely to your trading partners. To provide a one-stop shop for their customers, most major VANs offer Internet access. This lets a trading partner send all its EDI transaction sets to its VAN, with the VAN managing and forwarding the messages through the appropriate channels to a resident mailbox, to another VAN, or via the Internet to a trading partner. Besides the cost, the major difference between using VANs and the Internet for EDI exchange is that VANs do a lot more than just data exchange.

The biggest concern most companies have about using the Internet for EDI is security. But security is no more or less of a concern than when using traditional approaches to conducting business. We do not hesitate to provide credit card information to a telephone sales representative or to a waitress (who can and sometimes does abuse the information), but we do hesitate to send the same information across the Internet. You can take some steps to make your EDI via the Internet environment more secure by using encryption and electronic signatures. There are numerous software packages available on the market that provide this level of security. (For more information about security, see Chapter 11.)

Web-based EDI

Web-based EDI, a new offering in the world of electronic commerce, lets companies with access to the World Wide Web conduct EDI in a seemingly inexpensive and uncomplicated manner. With Web-based EDI, spoke companies rely on software developed by third-party vendors. The software lets a trading partner enter information on an e-form using a standard Web browser. The information is then translated into an EDI transaction and sent on to the hub company.

Hub companies have invested in Web-based EDI because they believe its simplicity, user-friendliness, and low cost will entice second-tier companies to use EDI. Web-based EDI can, indeed, be easier and cheaper for second-tier companies, but there are disadvantages. It is often limited in that only very common transactions such as purchase orders and invoices can be sent. Also, the third-party vendors often allow only in-network traffic, so VAN-to-VAN transactions are out of the question. And with Web-based EDI, second-tier trading partners must manually key information into the e-forms, inviting delays and errors. Finally, standardization — one of the initial goals of EDI — is compromised as hubs roll out their own unique Web-based systems.

Communications Standards

Each type of computer uses a different protocol to communicate with another computer. There are many standards for exchanging EDI documents among trading partners, including asynchronous, bisynchronous, SNA, LU6.2, and X.400. The most notable for our purposes is X.400, because it is the one favored for use with EDI.

X.400 is an international standard developed in 1984 to accommodate store-and-forward messaging for what has become millions of e-mail users worldwide. By making the exchange of e-mail messages consistent, timely, and secure, early versions of X.400 facilitated the widespread use of e-mail. In 1984, X.400 could handle only ASCII and binary format, text-only messages. By 1988, the X.400 standards had been enhanced to carry all types of digital information in a more organized and secure fashion, by providing additional security features, remote user agents (for sending and retrieving e-mail through an agent, such as CC:Mail), message storage, and directory services. In 1990, the X.400 standard was enhanced to address EDI-related issues. For example, X.400 now provides strong notification and security features that are very desirable in an EDI environment. At this point, the standard was renamed X.435.

Like X12, X.400 uses electronic envelopes. An X.400 envelope consists of an outer P1 envelope and the contents of the envelope, whereas X12 envelopes use the outer ISA envelope. The equivalent of X12 transaction sets, or functional groups, is termed "body parts" in X.400. (See Chapter 3 for more information about the X12 standard.)

Today, many VANs offer X.400 products to ensure consistency and timeliness of delivery and to deal with security issues, such as easy use of encryption and authentication in the exchange of EDI documents. X.400 standards let you easily move authenticated and encrypted data. The X.400 standards also provide proof of delivery, verify that the contents of a message were not modified, and make the data unreadable except to the intended recipient. Additional features of X.435 provide proof of sender/receiver IDs and of the source of the EDI document, and proof that the contents were received, that the contents of a document were sent by the sender, and that data received is exactly what was sent. These capabilities are important for security and auditing purposes. (See Chapter 9 for more about audit requirements.)

In addition to these superior security capabilities, X.400 lets the same message carry and deliver e-mail as well as standard EDI transaction sets. This capability means that a standard EDI document and binary data (such as a CAD/CAM drawing) can be channeled through the same message.

Batch, Event-Driven, and Interactive Sessions

Communications sessions in an EDI environment can take three approaches. EDI is traditionally a batch-driven system, with transaction sets batched and saved to be sent at one time. Batches of transactions are forwarded to the VAN or ISP on a predetermined scheduled job.

Another option is an event-driven approach. Based on predetermined criteria, an event is triggered, similar to using a workflow automation tool. For example, the EDI system can be set up to translate and send transaction sets to a mailbox based on specific transaction sets being created, a total quantity of transaction volume being reached, or when a trading partner specific activity takes place. In other words, a specific event drives a specific process.

As the need for more real time data is achieved, interactive communications environments are becoming a necessity in many companies. Here, an interactive communication session can be initiated based on a transaction set being generated or any time a transaction is ready for a specific trading partner.

It is important to assess your needs for these options as you select your communications environment. Your requirements for batch, event-driven, or interactive may affect the hardware as well as software needs.

Chapter 7

Choosing a Service Provider

If you've decided that you want to conduct EDI using a third-party communications provider (and not a direct-link or a private or proprietary service), you still have two important decisions to make:

- do you use a VAN or an ISP
- which VAN or ISP do you use

We examine these decisions in this chapter, looking in detail at the many issues you need to consider.

VAN or ISP — Which One Do You Use?

Today, VANs and ISPs offer different opportunities for EDI users. VANs are traditionally good at storing and forwarding EDI transactions. ISPs are traditionally good at transporting electronic mail. So EDI users are wise to assume that the roles of the ISP and VAN have been quite different. In the near future, we can expect the roles to come together and offer the EDI community a powerful, less expensive solution for exchanging EDI transactions over the Internet. Let's review some of the services and differences between a VAN and an ISP.

Cost. To most, the most attractive feature of using an ISP for EDI is cost savings. Strictly looking at costs of transmitting messages, EDI exchange via a VAN can cost anywhere from 2 to 10 times more than using an ISP, depending on transaction volumes. Many companies use VANs during off-peak hours and negotiate volume discounts to minimize their expenses, but these savings are insignificant when VAN bills are in the six figures. ISPs generally offer a flat monthly rate, regardless of time of access and transaction volumes.

Over the next couple of years, we can expect to see a pricing equilibrium between VANs and ISPs as VANs reduce their prices to remain competitive.

Data throughput. Using VANs, many companies postpone mail pickup until off hours when fees are lower. The Internet can be used for immediate transmission using high bandwidths, allowing increased data throughput to trading partners. However, with the increased use of bandwidth-intensive multimedia Web applications, performance issues will increase with the current Internet infrastructure. As Internet bandwidths increase and the infrastructure improves, these issues will dissipate.

Communications protocols. VANs support multiple communications protocols to support the disparate needs of all trading partners. The protocols supported include asynchronous, bisynchronous, LU6.2, and X.400. The ISPs generally support TCP/IP, the standard communications protocol used by all who access the Internet.

Time sensitivity. The Internet also offers the opportunity for immediate transmission to trading partners. Many companies using VANs delay mail pickup until the off-peak hours of late evening to early morning because of the cost savings. That means that a trading partner's transaction sent first thing in the morning may possibly be picked up the following business day. Using the Internet, a trading partner can receive transactions almost immediately.

Query and reporting. Most VANs offer numerous queries and reports to provide tracking and audit information to trading partners. Reports range from errors to a summary of activities. ISPs do not provide similar services yet.

Encrypted/authenticated data transportation. VANs have been unable to effectively carry encrypted and authenticated data (unless the encryption is embedded within the EDI transaction set), while most ISPs are capable of transporting data that is encrypted or authenticated at the outer envelope layer, much like certified mail.

Control tools. VANs offer unique batch and interchange numbers for each transmission, making it easy to track EDI activity. They include consistent date and time zones when stamping messages (most use Greenwich Mean Time). Many ISPs do not offer unique identifying numbers or date- and time-zone consistency.

Other tools. The Internet offers other benefits, such as GUI interfaces and electronic forms (e-forms). Some use FTP to download EDI data via the Internet. The options are numerous and fairly easy to use.

Popularity and resistance. Many small companies continue to put off EDI implementation because they have difficulty justifying its expenses. So larger corporations are using the Internet as an option to minimize not only their own expenses but also those of their trading partners. Some provide an e-form on the Web to allow entry of order information. Once the trading partner enters the data, automated procedures create EDI documents and route the transactions to the host's computer, streamlining the processing of order data. Because Internet and Web access is inexpensive, most companies embrace it with little or no resistance.

Interactivity. EDI documents can be traded interactively via the Internet. Using VANs, a store-and-forward approach is used, sometimes taking several hours for a document to reach its destination. Using the Internet, a transaction and its response can be completed within minutes.

Using a VAN to interconnect with the Internet may yield different results. Because VAN-to-Internet traffic will probably be modest for the next several years, VANs may be inclined to initiate Internet transmission sessions on an as-needed basis, or when there is sufficient traffic to justify a session, thereby defeating the assumption of immediate delivery. If you plan on using the Internet as an option for EDI mail delivery, you may be wise to consider low-priority documents until the ISPs and VANs are able to improve their joint performance.

Security. Security seems to be the biggest concern for those considering the Internet for EDI. But the same users consider VANs safe for EDI. The common misconception is that VANs assume responsibility of EDI messages. The fact is that the only liability of a VAN in the event of delivery failure is the cost of transmission.

System maintenance. The fundamental difference between EDI VANs and ISPs is that those who use ISPs for EDI will need to install and maintain any additional capabilities (besides simple message delivery) on their own systems, rather than relying on standard services that are provided by most VANs today. There is no ownership of the Internet — no one monitors it, no one guarantees delivery of messages, and no one ensures that our messages or transactions will not be hacked. Some of the limitations of ISPs can be attributed to SMTP/MIME. With the support of other e-mail messaging protocols, such as X.435 (specifically designed for EDI messaging), ISPs may be able to provide the additional security support EDI users require.

Reliability of service. Some VANs offer Internet access today in an effort to provide one-stop shopping for their EDI customers. Most companies are quite happy with their VANs and see no need to switch to an ISP. VANs have been transporting EDI messages for many years and have worked out most of the "bugs." They have proven themselves reliable in delivering transactions, notifying senders and receivers of potential or current problems, and for offering a fairly closed, secure environment.

Value-added services. VANs monitor and track EDI activity 24 hours a day, seven days a week. They identify and track problems, notify their customers of problems, check for unauthorized attempts to access private mailboxes, unauthorized transactions, and much more. The ISPs, on the other hand, do not understand the technical and business procedures associated with EDI and simply offer transport.

VANs offer invaluable features such as archival and retrieval of EDI transactions, disaster recovery, compliance monitoring, audit reporting, carbon copying, distribution list processing, and EDI-to-fax or EDI-to-mail.

Multi-threading. VANs have the ability to receive EDI transmissions for multiple trading partners in the same communications session, a task that has proven difficult for Internet-based systems.

International applications. The Internet is available to the public in the U.S. and is relatively inexpensive to use. But some countries limit public access to the Internet. In other countries, Internet charges are equivalent to VAN charges. Because the VANs offer a lot more features and functions than ISPs for EDI messaging, if the cost is about equal, the natural choice is to use the VAN.

Although we can expect the Internet to play a strong role in transporting EDI messages in the future, it is still not the ideal solution. Cost savings should not be the reason to do EDI via the Internet. Rather, companies should use the Internet as a means to extend their reach to other Internet-connected trading partners around the globe.

VAN AND ISP SELECTION CRITERIA

The selection of a VAN or an ISP is a critical decision. There are many vendors and many services to choose from. Required services vary for each company, so evaluate your options carefully. The wrong provider can mean loss of data integrity, unavailability of data when needed, and lack of future support capabilities. Careful selection of a provider means a secure, long-lasting relationship. The factors to inquire about when selecting a VAN or an ISP are discussed in the following sections.

Transaction Processing Requirements

A major reason for implementing EDI is that it is much more efficient to use than traditional paper-based methods. If a communication link provider's services do not facilitate speed and easy access for your EDI environment, you should keep looking. Here are the most important criteria to evaluate.

Available hours. The network should be up 24 hours a day, seven days a week. Deadlines know no workweek. Make sure you are aware of any downtimes that are used for backup or maintenance purposes.

Transaction processing interval time. The network should process transactions immediately upon receipt. Some providers may queue incoming transactions because of heavy traffic during peak times. If you require immediate turnaround, even slight delays can cause problems. Ask potential providers what their average turnaround time is during peak times.

Peak/off-peak processing. Is there a peak and off-peak time of day when fees are higher or lower? Often VANs offer a significant discount for off-peak processing. You should ask what those times are to determine whether you can take advantage of discounts and whether savings are worth the wait. ISPs generally do not use time of day discrimination.

Priority processing. If you select a provider that performs queuing because of internal capacity, bandwidth or other reasons, it is important that they offer priority transaction processing as an added service. Priority processing puts your transactions in the front of the queue. This generally costs you extra.

Immediate dial-out (continuous send). If you are using a VAN, you may need the capability to dial out immediately for mail delivery when you send certain documents to selected trading partners. Messages are usually routed to the recipient immediately when you use the Internet and an ISP. Whether you use a VAN or ISP, this means that the recipient must have a server that is up 24 hours a day.

Scheduled dial-out. If you are using a VAN, in addition to immediate dial-out capabilities, you may require that the provider support dial-out capabilities on a predetermined schedule. For dial-out services, the VAN should specify the number of attempts to call and to deliver to a recipient and specify the action taken if there's a failure to connect. A reasonable number of attempts is once every 15 minutes until delivery is secured. If delivery does not take place after two to four hours, the VAN should immediately notify the sender.

Bandwidth capacity. Because processing speed is a key attribute of an EC environment, you should inquire about the bandwidth capacity of your provider. VANs have been transporting EDI documents for many years and have made the necessary adjustments to their bandwidth capacity for peak activity times. But ISPs are often overloaded as the demand for their services exceeds their ability to support throughput. ISPs often appear to be playing catch-up with their customers' demands, so bandwidth should be a strong factor in determining your choice of an ISP. And because ISPs are new at the EDI game, they are somewhat unfamiliar with its trends throughout the day.

Support Issues

Superior customer service and technical support from the network provider are of key importance because you depend on EDI transactions to conduct your daily business. Make sure your provider will be available any time you need support.

Customer support. Customer support can be provided in a variety of ways. Is there an 800 number to call? Is vendor response immediate or on a callback basis? Can you use e-mail for inquiries? Does the vendor have the ability to provide online interactive support? How many support staff are available for how many customers? To find out about customer support, talk to the provider's existing customers.

Technical support. The provider should offer technical support 24 hours a day. In some cases, support during regular hours (generally 8 am to 6 pm) is included as a part of your maintenance agreement. Off-hour support may be on a pager basis, and on occasion additional fees apply. Some providers may assign specific technical personnel to a group of customers, making the relationship more personal.

Average problem resolution time. The provider should give you documented evidence of the average time it takes to resolve a problem. Problems are often categorized in order of severity or urgency. You should find out what criteria the provider uses to determine the urgency of your problems.

Reporting and Inquiry Capabilities

Audit requirements are among the most important considerations in EDI environments because auditors no longer have paper documents to rely on (see Chapter 9 for more information about audit requirements). Because this area will be a major part of your implementation, pay close attention to a provider's ability to produce reports and provide inquiry services. Look for the following capabilities.

Audit reports. Ensure that the information a service provider has on its audit reports satisfies your auditors' control and audit requirements. VANs generally offer detailed audit logs of EDI activity; ISPs do not.

Traffic reports. Reporting capabilities of a transaction's status, date, and time of delivery or pickup, in chronological order, can expedite problem resolution. These capabilities are important when you need to look for a trading partner's missing transaction set, for example. Ask the provider how long this information will be available. VANs generally provide this information for 7 to 14 days.

Error-reject report. The provider should be able to provide reports showing errors detected in transmissions (e.g., an error with the trading partner ID, a standard version that was not valid for a given trading partner relationship, errors that prevented a trading partner from receiving a transmission). It is important to know how long this information is available, and how far back it can be traced.

Charge-detail report. Charge detail by transaction and trading partner is not always a standard service. You need this detail to charge transaction expenses to specific business units. For example, you might want to charge the accounting department for all expenses associated with invoices and the purchasing department for purchase order expenses.

Custom or query reports. If you have specific reporting requirements that the provider does not offer as a standard, the provider may give you the query capabilities to design your own queries. This is a nice feature and generally does not cost extra. But it requires that the provider give you access to their tracking data.

Communications Access

You might need to communicate with multiple VANs or ISPs to do business with all your trading partners. Not only must you have this access, but you also need to know it will occur in a timely fashion. Make certain your provider offers the basic services discussed below.

Third-party interconnection. VANs must be able to interconnect with other VANs so you and your trading partners can use your VAN of choice. In addition, check to make sure the VAN can connect to an ISP or that the ISP is able to route your transactions to a VAN mailbox.

Interconnect intervals. Some VANs transmit a document to other VANs immediately upon receipt. Many, however, dial out to other VANs on a predetermined schedule. Ask the VAN for a gateway-transmission schedule to the VANs your trading partners use. In addition, ask your VAN to provide details about how and how often your transactions are routed to an ISP. ISPs are all connected via the Internet on an interactive basis.

Interconnect acknowledgment. An interconnect acknowledgment is electronic acknowledgment of submission and receipt of EDI documents from VAN to VAN. Find out whether your provider can provide you with interconnection information, such as date and time of submission, receipt, and errors. If you are going VAN-to-ISP or ISP-to-VAN, this may not be possible.

Connection to proprietary networks. If you need access to proprietary networks, check whether your provider has this interconnection capability in place. Additional charges may be associated with this service. Most VANs are able to connect to the major proprietary networks today, but ISPs are likely unable to do the same, unless the proprietary network is accessible via the Internet.

Supported protocols. The provider should be capable of supporting a wide variety of communications protocols. As we noted earlier, VANs generally support asynchronous, bisynchronous, LU6.2, SNA, and X.400; ISPs generally support TCP/IP.

International access. If you exchange or plan to exchange EDI documents with trading partners outside the U.S., check whether the service provider can provide the connections to VANs or ISPs in the required countries. If your provider uses a third-party vendor for international access, it should be transparent to the users. Many providers use the PTT (Post Telephone Telegraph) agencies in other countries for EDI mail delivery. This is cause for concern because PTTs don't address EDI security and audit issues.

Internet connection. If you are using a VAN, you should inquire about connections to the Internet. Even if you don't have plans of trading EDI transactions via the Internet today, you may soon be faced with it. So it is better to ensure that your VAN can provide you with Internet access when you need it.

Mailbox and Access Services

To save time and communications costs, the provider should offer services that allow multiple activities to occur at once. Find out whether the provider offers the following services.

Distribution list/carbon copy. A distribution list or carbon copy capability is a cost-effective way of transmitting one document to many receivers. For example, you can send one catalog update to the provider to distribute to all customers. Many VANs can only distribute to those trading partners on their own network, leaving trading partners on other VANs to be handled individually. Carbon copying can save a lot of time and money because it requires that you send only one copy of a transaction for multiple trading partners. This is usually not an issue for ISPs to handle.

Multiple mailbox retrieval. The provider should let you retrieve transactions from multiple mailboxes during the same communications session. This helps reduce the expenses in communications costs, such as telephone and connect-time charges.

Mail slot routing by partner/document type. You need the ability to perform a variety of tasks, including exchanging test and production data with trading partners, by placing such data in separate mail slots. You can send or receive different transactions in different mail slots, which lets you process documents based on their urgency. The provider should give you the capability to define the mailboxes or mail slots this way.

EDI and other messages in same mailbox. For the convenience of access and retrieval, it is important that EDI and other messages, such as images or e-mail, be contained in the same mailbox. Providers often require a different set up for different mail types and require a separation of these transactions or messages.

Standards Support Issues

Because standards are continually changing, you must give some thought to the standards support of the provider you choose. Also, if you use or anticipate using proprietary formats, be sure the provider can transport them without additional administrative efforts. Because ISPs do not review or discriminate against message content, the issues discussed below are most applicable to VANs.

Standards supported. The EDI standards the VAN supports should include those that you and any trading partners use or may use in the future, including X12, UN/EDIFACT, TRADACOMS, ODETTE, and various banking standards.

Versions supported. The VAN should support the current published standards, as well as previous versions and releases. Some of your trading partners may be using older versions of the standards, so it is important that your VAN be able to deliver their documents. If possible, select a VAN that supports approved but unpublished enhancements to existing documents and new documents.

Proprietary formats. EDI's benefits lie in the use of public standards. Because these standards let everyone speak the same language, they reduce effort and expenses in interpreting information. However, some companies still use proprietary formats. In such cases, the VAN you select must be able to support transmission of these formats. Often VANs support proprietary transaction sets as long as standard header and trailer segments surround them.

Security Issues

One of the most important reasons for using a VAN or an ISP for transporting EDI transactions is the security measures they offer. Of course, security is essential any time you deal with communications between computer systems. The importance of security increases greatly when you're sending and receiving vital business information and perhaps even allowing outside access to your applications. Providers should minimally offer the security measures discussed below.

Password. VANs and ISPs can provide many levels of password security. Most offer one or two levels. Some have three-tiered password security, which is ideal. The provider should allow you to change your password at any time should you require it for any reason. They may require routine periodic changes as well.

Encryption. Encryption is a technique that scrambles data before it is sent. The receiver must use the same technique to decrypt the data. Providers should be able to support and deliver encrypted data. There are many different encryption software packages and standards available on the market. You should check to see that the provider can carry all encrypted data regardless of the standard applied. Many VANs are unable to transport encrypted data unless the encryption is embedded within the transaction set, while most ISPs are well equipped to handle it.

Authentication. Authentication is a technique that uses a standard algorithm to compare codes (for example, check digits) created to ensure that data has not been corrupted. If the codes the sender creates match the codes the receiver computes, it is fairly safe to assume the data has not been tampered with. VANs and ISPs should be able to support and deliver authenticated data.

Control Mechanism Issues

You must be able to track documents as they move through your EDI system. The provider should offer the following control mechanisms to let you trace documents easily. (See Chapter 10 for details about audit and control requirements.)

Tracking by control number. Does the provider offer document tracking by interchange, group, or document control number? If there is a problem, can the provider find the correct document by control number and recover by control number if necessary?

Transmission log number. The provider should generate a log number and make it available to users to indicate the chronological order of transmission of documents to each trading partner. Examples of various log numbers used are inbound batch number, outbound batch number, and packet number for sender/receiver for each interchange.

Data tracking (undelivered data). The provider should have a tracking mechanism in place for undelivered data. Often EDI transactions are undeliverable due to unreadable identification information. The provider's tracking system should capture this information over a period to try to find the sender or recipient and notify them as soon as possible. This type of tracking adds a level of security because it can potentially identify attempted unauthorized activities that are repeated over a period.

Date/time stamping. As EDI documents travel through computer networks, it is essential that arrival and departure times are accurately logged. The provider should indicate precise date and time information regarding the sending and receiving of documents and the retrieval date and time by the recipient.

Time-zone consistency. For the date and time stamping to be meaningful, the provider should use Universal Standard Time (Greenwich Mean Time). Providers sometimes use the time zone where their main facility is. As a result, your provider may use Eastern Standard Time, while your customer may use Central Standard Time. If you need to look for an EDI document at a later date, it will be a lot easier to have consistent times and dates stamped on the documents. This is useful in case of dispute regarding timeliness or receipt of a sensitive document. Also, time-zone consistency is important if your various trading partners are in different time zones, especially overseas.

Backup and Recovery

Just as you plan for backup and recovery of your computer systems and data in-house, you need to be prepared for disasters during transmission of EDI data. The provider must adequately protect your documents and data. Make sure your provider has all the necessary protection.

Data restore/retransmission. The provider should have the ability to restore and retransmit a specific transaction set or group of transaction sets. For instance, if you retrieve and then accidentally delete a transaction set, you do not want to make an embarrassing and potentially aggravating call to your customer to resend it. The provider should be able to bring the transaction back online within minutes so you can re-retrieve.

Online data retention. Once data has been retrieved from your mailbox, it is marked as read. But it is sometimes necessary to retrieve documents that you've already retrieved. There may have been a problem with previous tries, or user testing may have caused problems in the transmission. For such cases, you need to know how long the provider keeps retrieved documents. Online data retention should generally be about seven days. Some providers have longer online retention available; two weeks is recommended.

It is important to distinguish data retention of retrieved versus unretrieved data. Data that has not been retrieved should be retained online indefinitely. The provider does not have the authority to throw away mail that is sitting there unread because the mail belongs to the recipient. Only the intended recipient should be allowed to discard it.

Off-line data retention. You should ask your provider about the length of time they keep your data off-line before it is archived. Access to off-line data is much faster and less expensive than accessing archived data.

Archiving. Your auditors may determine your minimum archiving requirements. Data archiving is available for a wide range of periods, depending on the provider. If you go by the IRS rule, everything should be archived for anywhere between three and ten years, depending on state regulations. In addition, the provider should state whether archives are kept on the premises or offsite. Offsite storage is absolutely recommended!

Downtime. From time to time, computers experience downtime due to problems such as disk crash, for regularly scheduled maintenance, and during occasional upgrades. Ask the provider for maintenance schedules so that you don't attempt to access your mailbox at an inappropriate time. You should also ask them whether they notify you about system downtime for problems and what their general experiences have been in this area.

Disaster-recovery plan. The provider must have a written disaster recovery plan to ensure ongoing processing of transactions without interruption. Because interruptions in transactions can cost you and your trading partners time and money, the provider's recovery plan is an important business requirement. Many providers contract disaster recovery services to a third party. Your provider should tell you whether their plan includes a cold or hot site, and if they use a third party, who that is.

Backup facility. The provider must have backup facility arrangements within its own company or must use another vendor for this function.

Data mirroring. To measure your risks of data loss in case of a disaster, a key factor in access to EDI data is whether the provider mirrors the EDI data on its main computer or on a backup machine. If data is mirrored on a separate disk on the same machine, failure of the main disk could minimize interruption to your daily processing because the provider can quickly switch to the backup disk. If backup data is on a different computer, you may experience longer delays as the provider switches to the backup computer. It is also important to know how real-time the mirrored data is. If the data is real-time, you won't lose any. If "real-time" means 15 minutes to your provider, you risk losing the data sent in the last 15 minutes. You need to get a clear definition of what the provider means by real-time.

Audit of activities. The service provider should be periodically audited — either internally or externally — for security, recoverability, etc. The auditor's reports should be available to you upon request.

Problem Handling

It goes without saying that problems will arise with transmissions. What's important is the way your provider handles them when they do occur. Not only can problems be irksome, but they can also be highly embarrassing: Imagine sensitive information going to the wrong trading partner! Protect yourself by knowing exactly what your service provider is responsible for doing and how quickly it acts in case of problems. Consider the issues discussed below.

Problem notification. In the event of transmission or operational problems, the provider should notify the sender. The method of problem notification can be important to your daily procedures. Some providers notify the customer electronically, some send a fax, and others notify via telephone. Some providers use all these notification methods but select the one that is appropriate based on the error severity. It is important to discuss your specific needs with your provider and document your agreement, rather than leave such decisions to their discretion.

The method and timeframe for notification depend on the severity of the problem. For example, if the provider does not receive a batch of documents properly, they should call the sender immediately because the sender may have sent advance ship notices (ASNs) to its customer that must get there before the truckload of products does. Things are supposed to happen quickly with EDI, so when there is a problem, immediate telephone notification is the preferred method. Most providers do not pick up the phone because of the administrative costs. If someone is monitoring your system, e-mail notification can suffice.

Rejection of invalid sender/receiver. The provider should validate the ID of the sender and receiver of EDI documents and notify the sender and/or receiver (if identifiable) of the error. You do not want unauthorized users accessing your system. Many VANs offer this service; however, most ISPs do not hold back mail as long as it is properly addressed to you, leaving this task to you.

Rejection of invalid document. The provider should be able to reject documents that have not been set up for exchange with specific partners. This can save embarrassing or unwanted situations, such as a customer accidentally receiving your purchase order intended for a vendor. While many VANs offer this value-added service, most ISPs do not.

Cost

While you're considering all the offerings from various providers, it is not likely that you will overlook cost considerations. Just keep in mind that providers use a variety of factors to determine their charges, including installation, segment and element, and logon time charges. Inquire about expenses you may incur for using other services, such as archiving, priority message delivery, and translation. VANs and ISPs are quite different in their pricing, so make sure that you evaluate the costs and the services provided (compare apples to apples). Some costs to consider:

- Startup fee
- Mailbox fee
- Transaction cost
- Character count
- Connect time
- Peak/off peak prices
- Unretrieved document storage fee
- Interconnect charges
- Monthly flat charge
- Bandwidth traffic charge

Other

The criteria listed so far are the most important for selecting a VAN or an ISP. However, there are some additional issues that are less important but can make the difference in your selection if all other factors are equal.

Knowledge of EDI. It is very important that your provider has a working knowledge of EDI messages and their delivery. EDI transactions require unique care in processing, and such provider knowledge means better and more targeted service. The provider's involvement in the standards-development process is one factor that helps in their understanding of user needs and their knowledge of current standards requirements. Select a provider that is EDI knowledgeable and is involved in standards development.

Electronic billing. Receipt of electronic invoices from the provider will allow easy integration with your accounts payable system. Although choosing a provider who has electronic invoicing is not an absolute must, it is a convenience that might be the deciding factor.

EDI-to-fax. Some VANs can generate and send a fax of an EDI document to specified trading partners. This is a valuable option for customers or suppliers who are not EDI-capable. This lets you streamline all like transaction sets (e.g., all your invoicing functions) to be funneled to the provider, with some being delivered as EDI transactions while others are converted and sent via fax.

E-mail. Because EDI is for the exchange of standard electronic business documents, e-mail is a distinct requirement for many companies. Companies that currently use e-mail to talk to each other cannot replace this capability with EDI, but need to continue to use it in addition to EDI. Some providers let you combine all e-mail and EDI documents and route them to trading partners in the same mailbox, thereby integrating the two technologies. This capability may be important to companies that streamline the two functions. For example, you might wish to send an updated price catalog to your customers and an accompanying free-form message to direct their attention to a special sale on certain items.

Trading partner rollout support. Many providers offer value-added services to help manage their major customers with trading partner rollout programs. Ask whether this service is available, how many hubs they have assisted, how successful they were (how many trading partners-or spokes they brought up in what amount of time and what the established goals were), and whether there are any fees involved.

Online catalog support. Does the provider support maintaining a catalog of item numbers and associated information in an area accessible to other trading partners? Some VANs offer this as a fee-based service only for those who maintain a mailbox on their network.

VAN AND ISP VENDOR EVALUATION

Selecting the people you do business with is very important, particularly when you rely on them for delivery of important business documents in a paperless environment. Some information about the company's background can help you evaluate vendors. Look into the provider's history, revenues, market share, number of customers, and the other products/services they offer.

Find out the date the business was established; the longevity of the business will tell you how well established the company is. If the company's sole business is being a communications network provider, the age of the company tells you how much experience they may have.

You can also learn a lot by looking at the company's growth history in numbers or percentages. This may be one measure of success of the provider. If the provider has grown a lot and very rapidly, you may need to investigate whether the company has adequate resources, infrastructure, and proper business management to sustain growth.

Another way to evaluate a vendor is to check into the company's annual revenues. This information tells you the company's size. If you can obtain annual revenue figures from previous years, a comparison will tell you about financial growth. If you spot a big jump in revenues one year, you may investigate whether an acquisition or merger occurred and if so, with whom. You may also investigate the company's market share.

Finding out how many customers specifically use EDI mailbox services helps you measure how large the vendor is. You should be aware, however, that many providers include e-mail users or non-EDI network users in these figures. Again, this information is simply a measure of size and not quality.

For long-term strategic use, it helps to know what other services the provider offers. For example, some VANs provide electronic collection services, thereby serving an important function to help in managing your accounts payable and receivable systems.

With this outline for provider evaluation, you have the means for shopping intelligently. However, nothing tells you as much about a vendor as talking to their customers. To help you ask the right questions and document the results of your conversations with vendor references, you can use the reference form on pages 99–101.

CONCLUSION

The size and technical ability of your business and EDI's strategic importance to your company are the major factors that will help you determine which communications solutions — direct communications, proprietary networks, VANs, or ISPs — are best for your EDI implementation. If you decide to use a VAN or an ISP, the number of considerations quickly multiplies. But the number and variety of factors you must consider need not be intimidating. With the information this chapter offers and the vendor evaluation form, your task should be greatly simplified.

VAN and ISP Reference Form

Company name	
Contact	
Telephone number	
Service start date	
Hardware platform and model	
Protocol(s) used	
Number of EDI customers in production	
Standards supported	
Compliance checking performed?	
Speed of transaction turnaround	
Immediate outdial used?	
Connect to other VANs? ISPs? Which?	
Interconnection schedule	
International service used?	
Distribution list used?	
Security used	

VAN and ISP Reference Form

Audit reports used	
Archived data retrieved? How was service?	
Problem notification techniques: telephone/electronic/e-mail	
Invalid sender/receiver noted?	
Invalid document for sender/receiver noted?	
Down time experienced? How often? For how long?	
Receive electronic billing?	
E-mail used?	
EDI-to-fax used?	
User group involvement/quality of meetings	
Quality of overall service	
Quality of training	

Quality of documentation	
Quality of hotline support	
Off-hours support?	
Callback timeliness	
Problem fix timeliness	
Support of other technologies? Which?	
Provider's strengths	
Provider's weaknesses	
Recommendation (Yes/No)	
Other comments	

Chapter 8

Analyzing EDI Costs

EDI cost justification is closely related to the benefits we discussed in Chapter 1. When it's time to present an EDI proposal to upper management, you need more than just a list of benefits. You need bottom-line numbers that demonstrate EDI's business and strategic value. By tying the benefits we've discussed to the actual costs of the EDI components we've been examining, you can do a bottom-line evaluation that will give management the cost justification they need.

Many people fail to plan for EDI implementation beyond the initial investment. The initial setup costs are usually easily identifiable, but they depend on the hardware platform you choose for EDI and whether the EDI data is integrated with your application files. But more important and more elusive are the ongoing maintenance costs, which include all the monthly and yearly fees, processes, and procedures you'll need to reckon with. In this chapter we examine in detail how to figure the initial and the ongoing costs of EDI.

IMPLEMENTATION COSTS

Let's look at the costs associated with an initial EDI implementation effort (the list on page 112 summarizes these costs). The implementation costs that you can fairly readily estimate are those you'd have for just about any IT project. You can get quotes for software you'll need to purchase, or you can use your own estimating methods to figure out what it would cost to develop the necessary software in-house. Similarly, once you've analyzed your needs, it's relatively easy to get quotes for hardware costs and for message transportation (via VANs and/or ISPs). Your experience and company standards will provide reasonable estimates for development, training, and documentation costs.

The cost of implementing EDI will depend on your hardware platform. Generally, costs will be lower if you select a standalone or front-end server approach and higher if you choose a midrange or mainframe host solution (see Chapter 5 for details about hardware implementation choices). This generalization also applies to the three layers of software you'll need for EDI: translation, communications, and interface software (for details about software requirements, see Chapter 4).

Translation Software

Let's begin our look at implementation costs by examining translation software. First, to save costs, you should probably discard the idea of developing translation software in-house. Such development requires solid knowledge of EDI standards, industry applications, editing/auditing requirements, and computer communications. Developing a translator takes months, and translation software requires continual modification and enhancement to keep up with new standards and releases, new transaction sets, and audit and reporting requirements.

The better solution is to purchase translation software for your hardware platform and let the package vendor do all the updating and enhancements. Remember to evaluate the software for your needs and select the solution that best fits all your requirements.

PC translation software packages start at around $600. Some vendors charge several hundred dollars for each document and for each standard you want to include in the translator. Others include all transactions for about $3,000 to $5,000, but may charge more for mapping software. Midrange platform translation software ranges from $7,000 to $50,000 and is tier priced, based on CPU size. Translation software for mainframe computers varies in price depending on CPU size also, but can be anywhere from $55,000 upwards.

Transaction Set Mapping

Once the translation software is in place, you must map the transaction sets you plan to trade. There are two approaches to mapping: trading partner-specific and generic (see Chapter 3 for a further definition). The initial cost of developing a trading partner-specific map is lower because the map specifications are provided; generic mapping requires transaction design before implementation. Costs of transaction set mapping can therefore vary depending on the approach you take, but can generally range between $500 and $1000. In addition, the complexity of the transaction set determines the amount of time required to develop its map.

Communications Software

Translation software vendors for midrange and mainframe platforms often offer the necessary communications software for EDI exchange with major VANs and for Internet connections. Some PC translation software vendors charge separately for communications software. For midrange computers, the additional cost for communications software is about $1,000 to $2,000. On the mainframe platform, communications management software can cost as much as $75,000 to $90,000. Mainframe communications software sometimes offers more than simple store and forwarding of EDI messages. Some packages can, in fact, act as a "mini" VAN operation and perform more complicated messaging and mailboxing functions. In addition, many translators include the necessary proprietary communications software for EDI dealings with major corporations, such as the big three auto manufacturers and major retailers or mass merchants.

Interface Software

The software that will cost you most is probably the interface software. It is estimated that interface software development is nearly 30 percent of the cost of implementing EDI. You should plan to develop interface software in-house. Some package software vendors offer interface software for EDI integration, but this software will generally satisfy only part of your total integration needs. For instance, vendors will include file layouts and interfaces for commonly used transactions (such as purchase orders and invoices), but may not have the same capabilities built in for advance ship notices (ASNs) or inventory inquiry transactions. Furthermore, the vendors must assume certain business needs for the transaction set. So vendors don't tend to allow for all segments and elements available in a given transaction set; rather they select the common ones, leaving you to make additions and changes for the rest. And, whether you buy or develop interface software, because each EDI trading partner has different requirements, you'll have to make adjustments to suit particular trading partner needs. Also, each EDI document you add will require additional interface software. So, all things considered, some in-house development is nearly inescapable for interface software.

The cost of interface software development depends on the specific transaction set and how many applications it integrates with, as well as how sophisticated you need it to be — and you'll probably want it to be pretty sophisticated. It's a good idea to delegate some processing to the interface software instead of troubling your application software with formatting and editing data and performing data validity and authorization checking. The interface software layer can (and probably should) also act as a security buffer between EDI data and your application database. You should also note that the interface software is where many auditors like to perform substantiation and authorization checking of data, count of data, and other check points. You'll probably want to accommodate auditors by having these checks available where the auditors expect to find them.

Typical costs of interface software development vary for each document. Development cost for a purchase order document range from $15,000 to $30,000. Similar interface program development for an ASN document can cost $15,000 to $50,000, depending on whether the ASN is integrated with a bar coding system.

Message Transportation

In addition to software costs, your EDI implementation costs will also include the cost of transmitting data over telephone lines, either directly or through a VAN or ISP. Small companies often do not have the technical expertise to establish and maintain direct communications. However, if you can accomplish direct transmissions via dial-up with your trading partners, the only cost is that of the telephone call, unless the trading partners charge for their network service. With increased data volumes, most companies move to dedicated leased lines. These dedicated data lines will have installation fees ranging from $1,500 to $4,000. In addition, you will incur charges of $350 to $2,500 per month, based on physical distance and the line speed. For example, a 56K line is about $350 per month; an ISDN line (128K) is around $100 per month, with possible additional meter charges of about 10 cents per minute; and a T1 line (256K to 1.5 MB) can cost between $600 and $2,500 per month.

For small companies or where EDI volume is low, VANs, ISPs, and service bureaus are a more cost-effective alternative. Each of these vendors uses different cost structures. Some charge for each byte of data you send or receive, causing costs to soar as you add trading partners and documents (which is why large companies prefer direct communications). If a typical purchase order contains "from" and "to" names and addresses, five line items with descriptions and prices, and shipping instructions, the EDI transmission cost can range from $0.80 to $2 using a VAN. The difference depends on the VAN you use, whether you send or receive the data during peak or off-peak hours, the modem baud rate, and whether the data is packed to eliminate spaces.

Additionally, some VANs charge an initial setup fee of a few hundred dollars and a monthly mailbox fee of about $50 (or charges for connect time). Be sure you find out all costs, including charges for added services, such as priority processing and immediate dial-out. Also, ask whether the VAN offers volume discounts.

If you plan to use the Internet for EDI mail exchange, the charges are calculated differently. Through an ISP, there is usually a flat monthly fee that allows unlimited usage. You can use a simple dial-up connection for about $20 per month that enables you to send outbound documents on demand, but such a connection is not so easy to use for inbound receipt. Inbound receipt of transactions would require the system to be up and available 24 hours a day, seven days a week. Typical Internet access charges depend on the type of line speed selected. You will incur about $2,000 in hardware to enable the Internet connection.

Whether you plan to use an ISP or VAN, if you have high EDI data volumes, you should expect data line expenses. Cost will vary depending on the capacity of the line and on whether you require a direct link to the provider.

Hardware

The next implementation cost factor to consider is hardware. If your EDI solution is host-based, you have to think about the cost of disk and memory upgrades and the possibility of adding communications ports and modems. Typical modems used for EDI are usually 9600 Kbps and cost about $1,000.

If your EDI implementation is on a PC, you will probably want to dedicate a PC to EDI processing. In this case, your hardware cost will be that of a PC and a modem.

Security

If you plan to secure your EDI system, you should consider both hardware and software expenses. A firewall is a combination of hardware and software that acts as a security buffer to your computer hardware. If you use a VAN, a firewall may not be necessary; but if you use the Internet, a firewall is an absolute necessity. Two approaches to firewall installation include use of a PC with network cards, which will require additional firewall software (for a total of $15,000 to $30,000), or use of a real-time, embedded firewall system, which can cost about $20,000. Encryption and authentication software varies depending on the hardware platform it is used on, but can start at $300 to $400.

Project Plan Development/Management

An implementation cost associated with any IT project is the cost of developing a solid business plan, stating objectives, resources, and timelines. The cost of developing such a plan for EDI implementation can range from $2,000 to $10,000, depending on the scope of the project and the EDI knowledge necessary to plan it.

Training and Education Expenses

Your EDI implementation costs will also include training and education for you and your staff. Local EDI classes can cost from $400 to $1,200 per person. For out-of-town classes, you'll have to add travel expenses. There are other sources of education that are cost effective, including EDI- related publications and a world of information that is available through a number of Web sites at no charge.

Standards Documentation

Not only will you require general EDI education, but you'll need to learn about EDI standards and buy standards documentation. Involvement in EDI standards development is the best way to gain this knowledge, but it is also very expensive and time-consuming. For participation in standards development, ASC X12 membership costs from $500 to $5,000 annually, depending on the size of your organization. In addition, you'll have to budget travel expenses for attending the development meetings three times a year. It is imperative that you purchase the standards manuals (both printed and CD-ROM versions are available) for proper data mapping of EDI documents. X12 manuals cost between $150 and $600 per version/release. ASC X12 members receive a 50 percent discount.

Trading Partner Survey

Surveying trading partners from time to time is necessary to obtain information relevant to your implementation efforts. Trading partners change direction, obtain new application packages (which affects EDI), and incorporate other technologies that can affect your plans. Survey costs vary depending on how many trading partners are involved, but costs can range between $500 for a dozen or fewer trading partners to $2,000 for about 200 prospects.

Legal Negotiations

Before you can implement EDI, another cost factor you must consider is that you need legal contracts with your trading partners (see Chapter 13 for details about trading partner agreements). Because many corporate attorneys have little or no EDI knowledge, it is imperative for an EDI specialist to review your trading partner agreements. Attorneys specializing in EDI charge a minimum of $200 per hour, and they can compile a contract in a few hours. Be aware that because each trading partner agreement requires negotiation, attorney fees can soar. However, a good trading partner agreement can save you thousands or even millions of dollars in legal fees in the event of a dispute.

Implementation Guide Development

Developing an implementation guide not only serves as a form of documentation for internal use, but can also be disbursed to trading partners to communicate your specific technical EDI requirements. Costs can vary depending on the number of transaction sets included, but you can estimate approximately $1,000 per transaction set.

ONGOING COSTS

Calculating the cost of EDI gets more complicated when you start thinking about the long term. Not only are the ongoing costs more difficult to estimate than the initial costs, but you can be sure that ongoing costs will surpass initial EDI implementation expenses. The list on page 112 presents the most important ongoing costs.

Trading Partner Addition

As your EDI implementation becomes an integral part of your company's business, you'll want to add trading partners and documents. It is difficult to cost-analyze the necessity of bringing up trading partners. You must establish each trading partner in the translation software and flag each as an EDI trading partner in the application software. Trading partners use various communications means, set up their transaction set maps differently, and have limited EDI resources; these factors make the cost of bringing them up on EDI difficult to measure. Figures of $3,000 to $4,000 per added trading partner are not unusual (assuming they can be fitted into an existing transaction map), with the average cost being about $3,000. Being prepared for this reality in terms of budgeting and resources is the best assurance of successful rollout of your EDI program.

Addition of New Maps

Not only will you be adding trading partners, but you'll always be adding new EDI documents. For each new document, you must consider its complexity and the resulting amount of time you'll need for implementation. Outbound invoices, for example, are relatively easy, taking one to two weeks to establish. Documents such as ASNs can be complex, particularly if they are integrated with a bar coding system for container labeling. Establishing such documents can take from three weeks to three months. The cost of adding a new document with an established trading partner can range from $500 to $5,000.

You can, however, bring down the cost of implementing a new document. Your strategy should be to choose several experienced trading partners, review their mapping requirements, and create the most effective blend to map on your system.

Map Updates

You and your trading partners will need to revise EDI maps to carry new pieces of information or to take advantage of new versions and releases of standards. This ongoing cost can vary depending on the tools you have available. If new maps must be created for the new version/release, costs can range from $500 and $2,500. If your translation software offers automated tools such as auto-mapping from inbound EDI data or version conversion routines, your costs will be significantly lower.

Software Modifications/Enhancements

Further complicating an ongoing cost analysis is the fact that with continuing development of your EDI implementation comes the need to continually modify your software to fit your trading partners' needs. For example, your EDI ordering system might be set up to accept purchase orders from several customers. A new customer might require you to accept multi-point shipment orders, which can mean major modifications to your application and interface programs, as well as file structure changes. Similar changes may be necessary to accommodate updates in EDI standards.

Software modification costs are difficult to estimate. If you want to minimize expenses in this area, thorough up front analysis and design of the interface software is essential. For example, if you build the interface software based on one or two trading partners' requirements, every additional trading partner will require additions and modifications to the software. Knowledge of and experience with what most companies require allows a more global view of interface software requirements and helps you estimate the potential costs. Costs can vary between $500 and $5,000, depending on the complexity of the transaction set implemented and how many different applications are affected by the integration.

Message Transportation

These ongoing costs can vary depending on whether you use dial-up access or a dedicated leased line. In addition, expenses to transport the actual messages will vary depending on whether you use a VAN or an ISP. You can easily calculate ongoing expenses by referring to the flat monthly charges listed under initial expenses. In addition, if you use a VAN, you will incur a monthly mailbox fee of about $50 and transaction costs of $1 to $5 will be incurred (transaction cost is dependent on the amount of data).

Standards Documentation
From time to time, you will need to purchase new copies of the standards documents as new releases and versions are published. These costs range from $150 to $600 per set.

Training and Education
You'll also need to integrate standards modifications regularly and keep yourself and your staff up to date on EDI developments. Once everyone has had initial training, your staff can maintain their expertise by attending one seminar a year for approximately $2,000. They can read EDI publications, which are sometimes free (see Appendix D for a list of EDI publications and Web sites), and they can be active in user groups. User groups usually meet monthly and have a membership fee of $20 to $50 per month.

Legal Negotiations
Ongoing negotiations of EDI trading partner agreements is another cost you should plan for. Total costs will vary based on the amount of time spent. You can expect legal fees of about $200 per hour.

Implementation Guide Maintenance
Your EDI implementation guide will require ongoing maintenance for changes made to existing transaction sets as well as to add new transaction sets. Average annual maintenance fees are about $2,000 to $5,000.

Trading Partner Rollout
Once EDI is implemented, you will incur ongoing costs as you try to convince your trading partners to use it with you. You should plan on budgeting funds and resources to the marketing of your EDI program to prospective partners. This cost is variable and depends on the degree of your conviction and the variety of activities you employ (developing marketing material, conducting trading partner seminars, promoting at trade shows, etc.).

Awareness of these ongoing cost considerations lets you plan for and properly manage them. Many EDI implementors don't recognize the importance of ongoing costs and run the risk of budget overrun and having to put the EDI project on hold while they obtain additional funding.

JUSTIFYING EDI COSTS
EDI justification is easy when a major customer requires you to be EDI-capable; otherwise, it must be sold as a cost saving tool. To calculate the cost savings of a typical EDI transaction, follow a few simple steps. First, add up the costs of

postage and paper in the existing system. Determine labor costs for filing, mailing, data entry. Add up how long it takes someone to enter the data for a particular trading partner, how long to file it, etc. Multiply the worker's hourly rate by the resulting number of hours. To that result, add the postage and paper cost.

Then calculate how long it takes to post the transaction if received via EDI. Here, include the labor cost to handle exceptions (estimate a certain percentage of error). Add VAN, ISP or communications charges. The resulting figures provide a good measure of the costs involved.

The above calculations assume EDI is already in place. If it is not, consider the initial investment needed. Initial setup costs are easily identified, but vary depending on the choices you make.

Measuring tangible benefits of EDI becomes easier once it is implemented. It is then that you can measure the reduced inventory turns, the new business you have secured because a competitor is not EDI-capable, or the personnel headcount reduction.

Although cost-justifying EDI is not easy, neither is it impossible. These figures should give you a good start. But you should not limit your attempt to convince management of EDI's value by simply presenting cost-justification figures. In particular, do not overlook one important measure that will help: Identify an EDI champion or sponsor at the executive level. The commitment of this individual can mean the difference in getting the appropriate resource allocation and staff reassignments. This strategy will also help with the cultural battles resulting from the changes EDI can bring to a company.

WHEN WILL EDI PAY OFF?

Although EDI is said to have saved millions of dollars for many companies, others feel it has cost them more to do business using EDI — testimony that can make it difficult to justify EDI implementation and rollout. Let's look more closely at EDI cost savings throughout three distinct phases: communication, integration, and optimization.

Communication (Phase I)

During the communication phase, EDI implementers replace a paper-based document with an equivalent electronic format. They translate a paper transaction into its electronic equivalent field by field. For example, if a company currently prints a customer name and address on a purchase order, they will map the same data into its EDI equivalent. Companies that implement EDI in this fashion are usually reacting to customer pressure and feel they must do EDI. This approach does not save a lot of money, if any. Although there are a lot of benefits — including customer satisfaction, reduction in data error, and faster turnaround — simply put, Phase I implementers are duplicating a paper transaction electronically.

EDI Costs

Implementation Costs

- Translation software
- Transaction set mapping
- Communications software
- Interface software development
- Message transportation
- Hardware acquisition or upgrades, including modems
- Security hardware/software
- Project plan development/management
- Training and education
- Standards documentation
- Survey of trading partners
- Legal
- Development of implementation guide

Ongoing Costs

- Trading partner addition
- Addition of new maps
- Map updates
- Interface and application software modifications
- Message transportation
- Acquisition of new standards documentation
- Maintaining EDI expertise
- Legal negotiations
- Implementation guide maintenance
- Trading partner rollout

Integration (Phase II)

Although most companies begin with Phase I, they quickly realize that there are additional benefits to be gained by eliminating the redundant and unnecessary exchange of data. For example, by sending and receiving customer name and address information, you are paying for the transmission costs to and from a VAN or ISP as well as storage costs. But it isn't really necessary to convey this information to our trading partners if their computers also contain name and address information based on a unique key or ID, like the customer number. So Phase II implementers attempt to replace a paper transaction with an electronic "version," not a duplicate. The electronic version usually contains only the necessary information, with the rest being looked up via cross-referencing. Here, you can even eliminate the exchange of redundant information. For instance, you can choose to receive a purchase order without the item prices. If you have already agreed to a price in the purchase order quote transaction set, the purchase order should simply confirm the quantity ordered; you could look up the price. Similarly, you could receive an invoice without specific item pricing, because the quote or perhaps the purchase order transaction sets have already communicated the agreed to prices. This eliminates the need for the exchange of redundant and possibly contradictory data. If you receive the same information twice (via a quote and invoice), which one holds up? Phase II can certainly save a few bucks, but it still does not seem worthwhile to many.

Optimization (Phase III)

During this phase, companies realize that the biggest EDI cost savings come with the elimination of not just redundant data exchange but of redundant business processes. Here, organizations question whether a purchase order or invoice transaction set are necessary at all. After all, if the supplier receives the point of sale or usage information from its customer, (s)he knows how much needs to be replenished and when. The purchase order serves no real purpose. Also, the customer can pay its supplier for what has been received, and not wait for the invoice. This can certainly speed up the payment process. Naturally, in this paper and process elimination, discrepancies and disagreements can and will occur. But if you focus your time and efforts on resolving the discrepancies and allowing for authorized and acceptable transactions to go through, you can save a lot of time and money. These major cost savings are experienced mostly by Phase III implementers.

CONCLUSION

EDI can be a cost saving tool or a cost burden. It all depends on how well the technology is implemented, whether it is seamlessly integrated with the applications, and how many trading partners are on board. Once an EDI transaction set is implemented, the cost savings increase as it is rolled out to additional trading partners.

Once you've done your cost analysis and have your EDI solution lined up, two other areas require attention before you can begin your implementation: audit and legal considerations. No company can escape auditors and their need to be able to track and verify transactions. Because EDI changes business procedures, it also changes the traditional methods auditors use to perform their jobs. The requirements for auditing will influence your EDI implementation in many areas, but will be a particularly important factor in your software considerations and VAN or ISP selection criteria. Legal protection for you and your trading partners is especially important in an EDI environment because paper contracts and signatures no longer exist as proof of an agreement.

Chapter 9

Preparing an Auditable EDI Environment

Whether you conduct business using traditional paper documents or implement EDI, you need internal controls to ensure and verify the validity and timeliness of business transactions. These controls are essential to the auditors responsible for the checks and balances in a company's books to ensure proper reporting of funds and to prove the absence of misappropriation.

Traditionally, internal controls have used paper documents as evidence. For example, a purchase order is used to ensure and verify that an order was placed. To an auditor, paper documents such as purchase orders serve as the major form of a transaction's existence.

In an EDI environment, your dependence on computer and communications systems increases. With these new dependencies comes a decrease in dependence on paper documents, which will be obviated. When you adopt EDI, you lose paper evidence important to an auditor. But EDI can provide the same evidence electronically and, in fact, give more detail than is practical on paper. EDI electronic evidential matter, such as an electronic copy of the EDI document, can make the audit process more efficient and effective than with traditional paper documents. After all, retrieving information on a computer is faster than going to and searching through a file cabinet, and on a computer, you can save more information more accurately for longer periods.

When conducting business using EDI and a public medium (the Internet or a VAN), we must be able to provide evidence of the existence, timing, and privacy of a transaction. *Content authenticity* means you must be able to prove that the contents of the EDI document are complete and that the sender and receiver of the document are in fact authorized users. *Transmission authenticity* means you must prove the creation and transmission of the document from point of origin through arrival at the recipient's computer. Finally, *privacy protection* means you must have sufficient and reasonable systems and procedures in place to ensure untampered flow of the EDI data through the communications network.

SUBSTANTIATING THE AUTHENTICITY OF EDI DOCUMENTS

Auditors collect evidence to verify an account by using *substantive procedures*. For example, in a paper world, auditors can substantiate evidential matter by confirming that invoices or purchase orders are printed on paper with a company's name and logo and by verifying the signature on the printed form.

In an electronic environment, substantiating the authenticity of EDI invoices and purchase orders is not as straightforward as authenticating paper documents: Electronic documents can be generated on any computer and sent at any time, and they therefore lack the tangible, external quality that helps to substantiate their authenticity.

However, substantive procedures for collecting evidential matter in an EDI environment have been developed. These procedures include historical electronic confirmation, dynamic configuration, electronic signatures, and a combined approach. To help you include the proper audit controls in your EDI implementation, let's look at each of these procedures in detail.

Historical Electronic Confirmation

The auditor can request verification of transactions from your trading partners and check that information against your internal data. This method has some inherent problems. First, the trading partner may not be willing to supply the archived data because of the inconvenience involved in finding it. Second, trading partners may use different standards that can vary over time, making it difficult to interpret old data. Third, the trading partner's backup of data may contain duplicates. For instance, a backup might pick up two transmissions of the same document. Finally, trading partners might not separate EDI data from their application files, in which case they may be unwilling to give you the necessary data because it can include proprietary data that the trading partners cannot easily separate from your transaction.

Dynamic Confirmation

This procedure lets the auditor match your internal data with data retrieved from the VAN or ISP. The match can be performed with a sample of transactions for a given period.

Electronic Signatures

Electronic signatures are a form of authentication that let you identify and validate a transaction by means of an authorization code. For example, as Figure 9.1 shows, the sender of a transaction would include an authentication code, an 8-byte code with a check digit.

The auditor can verify the authenticity of transactions by verifying the electronic signatures. The two main problems inherent with this method are that the trading partners can make comparison difficult by using different electronic signature standards over time, and implementation of electronic signatures can be cost-prohibitive for many companies because trading partners may use different algorithms. Management of multiple electronic signature algorithms is another deterrent.

FIGURE 9.1
System Security

Authentication/Electronic Signature
Sender: $5942.68 to Supplier Smith Manufacturing
Receiver: Must know and verify the authentication code | 2A93-19DBZ

Combined Approach

The combined approach involves creating log files in your database to capture data, such as sender and receiver IDs, passwords, and associated transaction sets. The auditor can retrieve this logged data and sort it in any way necessary to verify transactions. This solution is valid as long as the logged EDI data is not purged and is available for auditor review. Be aware that this approach requires you to keep the EDI data archived.

Regardless of which of these substantive methods you select, you need to be sure the necessary internal controls are in place for your auditor. Auditors in an electronic environment rely on two types of internal controls to ensure the authenticity and validity of EDI business transactions: application controls and general controls.

APPLICATION CONTROLS

EDI changes business transactions and their flow through an application. In a paper environment, a customer may send its supplier purchase orders when inventory levels reach a low point; with EDI, customers send forecast information and expect the supplier to manufacture and ship the goods automatically when the forecast indicates they will be needed. To support EDI processing and the new procedures that accompany it, you must add layers of communications, translation, and interface software to deal with EDI data before it reaches your application software. When an audit is performed, the auditor must ensure the validity and correctness of electronic transactions in each significant accounting application, including purchases, cash disbursements, and accounts payable. Application controls must address completeness, accuracy and authorization of EDI transaction sets. To accomplish these audit requirements, the computer application must monitor nine control points when the transaction is initiated and as it is processed. These audit functions, called application controls, ensure that all transactions are

- real/authorized
- recorded
- recorded in a timely fashion

- valued properly
- posted
- summarized correctly
- classified correctly
- complete
- accurate

To identify these control points (and to assess what could go wrong and how controls are designed to prevent or detect errors), you need a detailed understanding of the flow of transactions. Until application software vendors design their EDI interface software to include and integrate the additional controls needed in a paperless environment, you will need some form of control database or series of files to control transactions throughout this new flow.

Let's look at each of these nine application controls to see what an auditor looks for and to learn what your software system needs to do and where best to do it to support the auditor's needs.

Transactions Are Real/Authorized

Auditors must ensure that transactions are real — that your company was meant to receive and act on them. To meet this need, you must set up controls to limit access to your application systems, to check authorization, and to ensure trading partner ID validity.

The audit controls that limit access to your application systems should focus on protecting the file containing the list of authorized trading partners and their passwords. The controls you need for checking authorization include limiting access to the procedures for checking that authorization list when you receive a transaction. One way to get these controls is through capturing information such as user IDs, passwords, and date and time an action was taken. This information should be reported and reviewed for possible breach of authorization in your EDI control database. To ensure trading partner ID validity, you can rely on translation software packages and VANs/ISPs to validate trading partner IDs and reject and suspend unauthorized transmissions. The VAN or ISP and your translator should also verify the validity of a particular transaction set for the trading partner. You can also use your interface software layer to check further for authorization by validating the customer or supplier number. And, in your application software layer, you can verify the customer or supplier number again. To add security, some VANs and ISPs use tiered passwords and process traditional authentication methods. For example, in addition to an identification code, they can use a unique password that can be encrypted for further security.

Transactions Are Recorded

In a traditional computer application, the classic batch total addresses the control objective of recording transactions. In an EDI environment, the programs must record each transaction when it is initiated. To assure that all transactions are recorded in an EDI application, you can build application controls into the four levels of software (communications, translation, interface, and applications) shown in the EDI software pyramid. The best practice is to establish the control in each of the four levels when the transaction is initiated, but this is not always necessary. It is usually sufficient to establish this control only on the interface software level, depending on the auditor's requirement.

The VAN, ISP, or communications software should validate successful transmissions. If you want to establish control on the interface level only, the interface software can automatically create batches of data from a transmission and sort these batches by document type. You can then match the resulting batches of document types with a similar report from the VAN/ISP. VANs generate batch control numbers that you can reconcile with entries in the EDI control database to assure that all transactions are recorded.

After the data travels through the application software, traditional edit reports (once you've modified them to do the reconciliation) can reconcile the batched data to the VAN, ISP, and/or communications log reports. Your communications software can record successful transmission of electronic messages and should log that information to the EDI control database. Most communications protocols use algorithms to predetermine values for a check digit for detecting noise or loss of signal in transmission, which might alter the data. Use of such algorithms is recommended.

As proof that transactions have been recorded, an EDI environment uses functional acknowledgments (FA) extensively. An FA is a notification of receipt of a document (it is important to note that it is not acknowledgment or acceptance of the contents of a document). Translation software should generate FAs automatically.

Transactions Are Recorded in a Timely Fashion

Auditors require you to record transactions in a timely fashion. Because various trading partners may have different notions of what is timely, you should define this issue with each and document that understanding in your legal agreement. For example, for each partner, you need to know when you assume liability or ownership of products.

In a traditional paper environment, liability does not exist until the goods are shipped or received (depending on trading partner agreements) and the shipping terms specified in the purchase order are fulfilled and agreed to in an acknowledgment. To avoid misunderstandings of what is timely, you must track the status of transactions in an EDI control database. The EDI control database may record a liability when the database is updated with receipt information captured at the company's receiving department, or the liability might exist when the customer receives an electronic shipping notice from its supplier or an electronic manifest from a freight company.

In addition, the VAN, ISP, or communications software should provide transmission reports to verify the date and time an EDI document was received, when it was placed in the trading partner's mailbox, and when the trading partner retrieved the document. (If you use direct communications links instead of a VAN or ISP, you can produce similar reporting.) Also, you can set up the interface and application software layers to capture date and time information for evidence that a business document was recorded in a timely fashion.

Transactions Are Valued Properly

When you receive an EDI invoice from your supplier, you can design control programs to compare invoice prices with purchase order prices. Auditors require proof of proper valuation of transactions, and this is one way EDI can ensure that.

For example, trading partners can send priced and extended electronic invoices that the application software can log to the EDI control database and record in the general ledger. The controls that ensure all transactions are recorded will help determine proper valuation when the auditor performs a comparison to the purchase order price. The auditor can identify the procedures for checking the price in the purchase order and invoice and can review the aging of incomplete transactions or reconciliations of complete transaction portfolios. The reconciliations might list only exceptions. Transactions that satisfy these reconciliations may be passed on for recording in the appropriate account.

As trading partners mature in their relationships, they are able to avoid exchanging redundant information. For example, a shipping notice or receiving information might replace an electronic invoice. In this case, access controls and authorization to change the prices associated with the trading partner's products are the primary form of assurance that the transactions are properly valued.

When the buyer and seller agree to this approach and grant the access, the seller can send periodic electronic price catalogs that the customer can use to update its price list. The customer and seller's access and authorization software as well as the auditor must review and control authorization for processing these periodic price catalogs.

The interface software is an ideal place to edit pricing data because if it is wrong, you can correct this data before integrating it with the application database. For instance, if you receive an invoice without the line item detail pricing, the software can retrieve purchase order pricing from the application database for reconciliation and can reject discrepancies.

Transactions Are Posted

EDI eliminates the monthly statements on paper that verify posting. The advantage of not having monthly statements is that trading partners do not have to wait for an artificial monthly period; they can acknowledge amounts on a transaction-by-transaction basis when economic events, such as production or business cycles, occur. However, you must find another way to ensure posting.

Transactions Are Summarized

Another audit requirement is that you must summarize transactions. The EDI control database can contain control tables that reconcile a file of complete transaction portfolios with the general ledger accounts to which they were posted. In an EDI environment, it is unlikely that manually prepared batch totals will exist to provide control totals to ensure proper summarization. Therefore, the interface software is often designed to prepare batches of like documents from a transmission batch and summarize selected information. An example would be a summary of purchase orders from a specific trading partner. Additionally, you can modify your application software to perform similar functions. Similar reports can be run to compare key totals with the VAN, ISP, or communications software.

Transactions Are Classified

Auditors require you to classify your transactions as, for example, inventory, fixed asset, or expense. Traditionally, to classify a transaction, a clerk hand writes appropriate general ledger numbers on a paper invoice for entry into the application files. Classification of an EDI transaction can be based on the nature of the product. Or, association with a vendor, a part number, or the initial electronic purchase order can determine whether a transaction is classified as inventory, fixed asset, or expense. You can modify existing application software to classify an electronic transaction set, or you can write interface software to perform the data classification. If you want to minimize manual review of the data, it is important to remember that you will need elaborate cross-referencing of part numbers and related general ledger numbers or of vendor numbers and related general ledger numbers. Then you can review exceptions resulting from anything that was not automatically classified for general ledger posting.

The control tables mentioned previously are an example of a means of automatic reconciliation. Such tables can ensure that transactions are posted to general and subsidiary ledgers. Also, you can have the application software automatically reconcile a batch of transactions with the posted accounts.

Transactions Are Complete

EDI standards mandate several procedures to ensure that EDI documents are sent and received in their entirety. These procedures include evidence from the VAN control report (or ISP, if they offer one), from the communications software, and from the translation software.

VAN control reports provide transmission information for batches (mailbags) of data sent and received. VANs also report EDI documents that were not retrieved by the trading partner.

The communications software can provide evidence of successful transmission of data. For example, this software can show proof of successful transmission and date and time.

The translation software is a key place to provide evidence of transaction completion. Components of translation software — ISA/IEA, GS/GE, ST/SE, and FAs — provide evidence of completion (see Chapter 3 for more information about these components).

Transactions Are Accurate

Before translation of EDI data to your corporate format and before mapping to the applications files occurs, you must check the accuracy of data sent and received to make sure you don't send someone an inaccurate order or invoice.

The translation software can perform syntax checks against the standards to ensure the existence of mandatory, valid, and properly sequenced data. You can also perform accuracy checks within the standard EDI document. X12 transaction sets include a CTT segment that allows transmission of the total number of line items and a hash total for a specific element in a transaction set. You can set up the translation software to automatically calculate the hash total of an element (for example, the total purchase order dollars) in the transaction set. This calculation confirms the accuracy of the order.

The FA can provide evidence of data inaccuracy by identifying the name and location of the segment and element in error. Error types identified include invalid codes and missing mandatory codes. The FA can also identify transaction sets that are accepted, accepted with errors, and rejected.

The interface software can perform additional accuracy checks. You can edit reasonableness checks and value ranges before the data is applied to the database.

GENERAL CONTROLS

General controls are non-application specific and include access, authorization, program development/modifications, and backup/disaster recovery. Used with application controls, general controls in a paperless environment add assurance that data is correct, complete, and secure.

Access

It is critical that you control all forms of access to computer systems in an EDI environment. Uncontrolled access to these systems can expose a company to establishment of unintended commitments to its customers and vendors that could easily be voided. Only well-trained and trusted personnel should be authorized to verify orders because you want to be sure you are filling an order that was intended for you, not for your competitor. People with access to EDI data need to know that if they receive a purchase order, they must make sure their company can fill it and agree to its terms and conditions before sending an acknowledgment. Once you send the acknowledgment, you have committed to supplying the customer.

To avoid problems with unauthorized access, consider designating personnel independent of computer and accounting departments to maintain access software.

Authorization

You must exercise the same comprehensive controls for trading partner authorization that you apply to access. Authentication is a technique that uses software to create an ID for the sender. The receiver must be able to read and verify the ID so the receiver can assure authorization and access to specific functions in the EDI environment.

Program Development/Modifications

In a sophisticated EDI environment, applications can make key decisions, such as paying a supplier by matching materials receipt with the ASN. This capability makes it critical that you thoroughly test all application modifications and enhancements and that you append additional controls to ensure data integrity.

Backup

You need to have highly reliable backup procedures now that there are no paper backups that can be pulled out of filing cabinets. If you are comfortable with your current backup procedures and frequency, you can continue. But you should review and confirm your backup policies before engaging in EDI activity. EDI data should be backed up at every point where there is opportunity for loss, misplacement, or modification of data. The data should therefore be backed up immediately after receipt (raw standard EDI data). You should also back up the data following translation and before populating the interface files. Again, the data should be backed up after it has run through the interface programs and before integration with the applications files. This will provide the proper trail to determine where data may have been affected as it travels through the software layers.

In addition to backing up EDI data files, it is important to keep backups of transaction maps and trading partner profiles. If you ever have to go back and revisit old data, you must be able to run it through the same maps and profiles it traveled through previously to re-create a specific outcome.

To further tighten backups, you may consider using microfiche or computer output to laser disk (COLD) storage. COLD is a rapid medium for capturing and retrieving data. Finally, make sure you back up communications logs and data.

Disaster Recovery

Increased dependence on computer systems for operations and financial records justifies appropriate control considerations for protecting a company's ability to continue its daily business operations. Off-site storage, hot and cold backup sites, and testing of recovery and backup procedures should be critical and regular practices in an EDI environment. In addition to your own backup and recovery procedures, you must ensure that your VAN or ISP has similar plans and procedures in place. Does your VAN/ISP use a hot site or cold site for recovery? Make sure you are aware of and comfortable with your provider's data retention policies as well. What is their online data retention for data that has been retrieved and data that has never been retrieved? What is their off-line data retention policy? Do they perform their own backups or outsource to a third party? Your VAN or ISP contract should include a confidentiality clause, a clause that states unauthorized access will be prevented and reported to you, a liability definition for timely and complete message delivery, a backup policy, and a schedule of interconnection with other VANs or ISPs.

CONCLUSION

EDI can improve the effectiveness and efficiency of the audit process by giving auditors more information, more reliable information, and quicker access to it than in a paper environment. Auditors performing attest procedures (verifying the accuracy of the books) need a good understanding of computers and EDI technical ability because EDI adds complexity and sophistication to computerized accounting systems. It requires a detailed understanding of the flow of transactions throughout the computer portion of the accounting and operational applications in order to evaluate application and general controls to substantiate evidential matter.

EDI changes business relationships by eliminating purchase orders and invoices and replacing them with new business procedures. As a result, companies depend more on their computer applications for operating and controlling their business. Companies need to be much more protective of electronic data because there is no paper backup with EDI. This new environment will require new forms of evidential matter, such as electronic data from an ASN, that you can use to apply powerful and extensive substantive procedures performed by computer-assisted audit techniques.

By including the proper audit controls in your EDI implementation, you protect yourself from potential auditing problems. But audit controls are not the only protection you need to think about in an EDI environment.

Chapter 10

EDI Control Areas

In the previous chapter, we discussed the need for controls. In this chapter, we look at where in the EDI software pyramid you might implement controls to provide the most effective, maintainable system.

With the increased dependence on data accuracy, organizations need data controls more than ever. To complicate matters, this data is captured and traded electronically using EDI transaction sets. But EDI actually provides a greater degree of accuracy than traditional paper equivalents. Controls are available in many different areas of an EDI environment, including in the application software, interface software, translation software, and communications software areas.

APPLICATION SOFTWARE

To ensure the integrity of EDI data systems, we should minimize changes to the application software. Changes we may need to make include file structure changes, data field additions/changes, and dual system changes. It is best to accommodate any special EDI needs outside this software area and keep it as "vanilla" as possible. But because some changes are inevitable, a sound change-management system is required to make sure all changes to the software are maintained and documented properly. This will help to ensure that any changes you make to the application software will also be considered for the interface software. For example, if your application software is modified to include enhanced or different editing of purchase orders, then the corresponding interface software must be modified to perform the same.

INTERFACE SOFTWARE

The interface software is a perfect opportunity area for capturing key control data. Because interface software is often custom-developed, it can be used to accommodate special EDI requirements that can be kept outside the application software area. Some key control data that should be logged within this software layer includes the document trace number (for example, the purchase order number), the record count of the interface file, the trading partner internal ID number, and the microfiche log number (if microfiche is used).

TRANSLATION SOFTWARE

One of the key areas of control is within the translation software area. Some controls are built in and mandated by the standards, while others are provided as an added benefit by the translation software. Built-in controls include the envelope layers (ISA/IEA, GS/GE, ST/SE) and functional acknowledgments, which provide evidence of transaction completion.

Electronic Envelope Controls

Figure 10.1 illustrates the envelope layers.

FIGURE 10.1
Interchange Envelope Structure

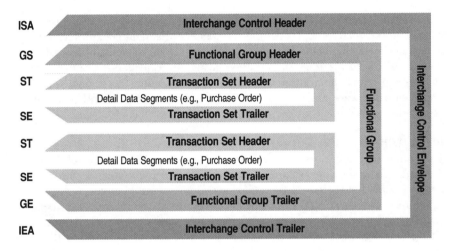

The interchange control header and trailer (ISA/IEA segments) include a sequential control number. Your translation software can track and report missing, duplicate, or out-of-sequence control numbers. The control numbers in the ISA and IEA segments must match (see Figure 10.2). If not, there is an indication of a problem in the completeness or accuracy of the transaction set. The trailer segment (IEA) captures the total number of functional groups in the transmission, so you can verify that transactions are complete and sent and received in full. Each transaction set is also stamped with date and time information.

FIGURE 10.2
Interchange Control Header and Trailer

Notes	ASC X12 Format
Interchange Control Header	ISA*00*0000000000*01*PASSWORDME*01*123456789*bbbbbb*987654321*bbbbbb*890714* 2210*U*00204* 000000008 *0*P/L: N/L
Functional Group Header	GS*IN*012345678*087654321*900509*2210*12345*X*002040 N/L
Transaction Set Header	ST*810*12345001N/L BIG*900713*1001*900625*P989320 N/L N1*BT*ACME DISTRIBUTING COMPANYN/L N3*P.O.BOX 33327 N/L N4*ANYTOWN*NJ*44509 N/L N1*ST*THE CORNER STORE N/L N3*601 FIRST STREET N/L N4*CROSSROADS*MI*48106 N/L N1*SE*SMITH CORPORATIONN/L N3*900 EASY STREETN/L N4*BIG CITY*NJ*15455N/L PER*AD*C.D.JONES*TE*618558230 N/L ITD*01*3*2**10 N/L IT1**3*CA*12.75**VC*6900 N/L IT1**12*EA*.475**VC*P450 N/L IT1**4*EA*.94**VC*1640YN/L IT1**1*DZ*3.4**VC*1507N/L TDS*5111N/L CAD*M****CONSOLIDATED TRUCKN/L
Hash Totals	CTT*4*20N/L
Transaction Set Trailer	SE*21*12345001N/L
Functional Group Trailer	GE*1*12345N/L
Interchange Control Trailer	IEA* 1 *00000008 N/L

The functional group header and trailer (GS/GE segments) include another sequential control number that must match (see Figure 10.3). The trailer (GE) automatically captures the total number of transaction sets in the functional group, providing proof of completeness.

FIGURE 10.3
Functional Group Header and Trailer

Notes	ASC X12 Format
Interchange Control Header	ISA*00*0000000000*01*PASSWORDME*01*123456789*bbbbbb*987654321*bbbbbb*890714*2210*U*00204*000000008*0*P/L:N/L
Functional Group Header	GS*IN*012345678*087654321*900509*2210*12345*X*002040 N/L
Transaction Set Header	ST*810*12345001N/L
	BIG*900713*1001*900625*P989320 N/L
	N1*BT*ACME DISTRIBUTING COMPANYN/L
	N3*P.O.BOX 33327N/L
	N4*ANYTOWN*NJ*44509 N/L
	N1*ST*THE CORNER STORE N/L
	N3*601 FIRST STREET N/L
	N4*CROSSROADS*MI*48106 N/L
	N1*SE*SMITH CORPORATIONN/L
	N3*900 EASY STREETN/L
	N4*BIG CITY*NJ*15455N/L
	PER*AD*C.D.JONES*TE*618558230 N/L
	ITD*01*3*2**10N/L
	IT1**3*CA*12.75**VC*6900 N/L
	IT1**12*EA*.475**VC*P450 N/L
	IT1**4*EA*.94**VC*1640YN/L
	IT1**1*DZ*3.4**VC*1507N/L
	TDS*5111N/L
	CAD*M****CONSOLIDATED TRUCKN/L
Hash Totals	CTT*4*20N/L
Transaction Set Trailer	SE*21*12345001N/L
Functional Group Trailer	GE*1*12345N/L
Interchange Control Trailer	IEA*1*00000008 N/L

The transaction set header and trailer (ST/SE segments) provide added evidence of completeness with another sequential control number that must match (see Figure 10.4). The trailer segment (SE) of the transaction maintains a count of the total number of segments (including the ST and SE segments).

FIGURE 10.4
Transaction Set Header and Trailer

Notes	ASC X12 Format
Interchange Control Header	ISA*00*0000000000*01*PASSWORDME*01*123456789*bbbbbb*987654321*bbbbbb*890714* 2210*U*00204*000000008*0*P/L:N/L
Functional Group Header	GS*IN*012345678*087654321*900509*2210*12345*X*002040 N/L
Transaction Set Header	ST*810*12345001N/L BIG*900713*1001*900625*P989320 N/L N1*BT*ACME DISTRIBUTING COMPANYN/L N3*P.O.BOX 33327 N/L N4*ANYTOWN*NJ*44509 N/L N1*ST*THE CORNER STORE N/L N3*601 FIRST STREET N/L N4*CROSSROADS*MI*48106 N/L N1*SE*SMITH CORPORATIONN/L N3*900 EASY STREETN/L N4*BIG CITY*NJ*15455N/L PER*AD*C.D.JONES*TE*618558230 N/L ITD*01*3*2**10 N/L IT1**3*CA*12.75**VC*6900 N/L IT1**12*EA*.475**VC*P450 N/L IT1**4*EA*.94**VC*1640YN/L IT1**1*DZ*3.4**VC*1507N/L TDS*5111N/L CAD*M****CONSOLIDATED TRUCK N/L
Hash Totals	CTT*4*20N/L
Transaction Set Trailer	SE*21*12345001N/L
Functional Group Trailer	GE*1*12345 N/L
Interchange Control Trailer	IEA*1*00000008 N/L

The transaction set can also calculate hash totals in the CTT segment. The CTT allows the transmission of the total number of line items and a hash total for a specific element in a transaction set. You can set up the translation software to automatically calculate the hash total of an element (for example, the total purchase order dollars) in the transaction set (see Figure 10.5). This calculation confirms the accuracy of the order.

FIGURE 10.5
Calculating Hash Totals

Notes	ASC X12 Format
Interchange Control Header	ISA*00*0000000000*01*PASSWORDME*01*123456789*bbbbbb*987654321*bbbbbb*890714* 2210*U*00204*000000008*0*P/L:N/L
Functional Group Header	GS*IN*012345678*087654321*900509*2210*12345*X*002040 N/L
Transaction Set Header	ST*810*12345001N/L
	BIG*900713*1001*900625*P989320 N/L
	N1*BT*ACME DISTRIBUTING COMPANYN/L
	N3*P.O.BOX 33327 N/L
	N4*ANYTOWN*NJ*44509 N/L
	N1*ST*THE CORNER STORE N/L
	N3*601 FIRST STREET N/L
	N4*CROSSROADS*MI*48106 N/L
	N1*SE*SMITH CORPORATIONN/L
	N3*900 EASY STREETN/L
	N4*BIG CITY*NJ*15455N/L
	PER*AD*C.D.JONES*TE*618558230 N/L
	ITD*01*3*2**10N/L
	IT1**3*CA*12.75**VC*6900 N/L
	IT1**12*EA*.475**VC*P450 N/L
	IT1**4*EA*.94**VC*1640YN/L
	IT1**1*DZ*3.4**VC*1507N/L
	TDS*5111N/L
	CAD*M****CONSOLIDATED TRUCK N/L
Hash Totals	CTT*4*20N/L
Transaction Set Trailer	SE*21*12345001N/L
Function Group Trailer	GE*1*12345 N/L
Interchange Control Trailer	IEA*1*00000008 N/L

Functional Acknowledgments (FAs)

Our daily business processing depends on the accurate and timely receipt of our business transactions, but we cannot completely rely on the VAN or the ISP to deliver our electronic messages. The postal service does not guarantee on-time delivery of mail; neither does the VAN or the ISP. The only sure way to know that your business partner received what you sent them is by means of an acknowledgment.

FAs are used to acknowledge receipt of EDI business documents. Although they do not acknowledge receipt of the *contents* of the documents, the simple acknowledgment of receipt can help avoid potentially paralyzing results.

The translation software can automatically generate functional acknowledgments to provide evidence of the receipt of a transmission. Once the FA is received, you must reconcile it with the outgoing or incoming transmissions they verify.

In addition to acknowledgment of receipt, the FA can provide evidence of data inaccuracy by identifying the name and location of the segment and element in error. Error types identified include invalid codes and missing mandatory codes. The FA can also identify transaction sets that are accepted, accepted with errors, and rejected.

Although FAs are dynamically generated, require no manual intervention, and cost next to nothing to transmit, many companies still don't use them; many that do, use them improperly.

Most vendor translators offer FA reconciliation. Using the reconciliation features properly can make a big difference to the certainty of your EDI environment.

Reconciliation Detail

FAs can be reconciled at three levels of detail: functional group, transaction level, and segment/element detail. You can set up FAs to acknowledge receipt of a functional group of transaction sets such as POs or invoices (AK1, AK9 segment level). The FA can also acknowledge receipt of a specific transaction set (AK2, AK5 segment level). More important, the FA can acknowledge whether a received transaction set encountered problems. The FA can acknowledge that it received a transaction set, but that errors were noted. It can point to the specific element (AK3) and segment (AK4) and tell you exactly what it did not like. Figure 10.6 is an example of an FA.

FIGURE 10.6
X12 Functional Acknowledgment

```
ISA*00* *00* *01*SNDRID*01*RCVRID*YYMMDD*HHMM*U*00200*000000100*0*P@GS*FA*
123456789*987654321*901012*0828*208284674*X*002003
ST*997*208384674
```

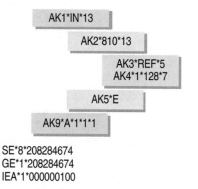

```
AK1*IN*13
    AK2*810*13
        AK3*REF*5
        AK4*1*128*7
    AK5*E
AK9*A*1*1*1
```

```
SE*8*208284674
GE*1*208284674
IEA*1*000000100
```

Error Codes
A = Accepted
E = Accepted but errors were noted
R = Rejected

Many companies who perform FA reconciliation don't realize that they must look deeper for relevant and critical details. Some translation software packages reconcile FAs with the associated transactions but fail to point out if the transaction was in error and whether it can be processed. For the FA reconciliation to be of value, not only must you send/receive it, but you must reconcile it. Once reconciled, you must check to see how the recipient acknowledged receipt of your documents: accepted, accepted with errors, or rejected.

Reconciliation Business Requirements

The criteria used to reconcile a functional acknowledgment can differ by trading partner and transaction set. Your translation software should allow you the flexibility to set up FA reconciliation by a number of factors, including by trading partner, transaction set, and date.

You should set up your system to notify you of unreconciled documents, which can indicate non-receipt, late receipt, or receipt in error. Some transactions are time critical so, for example, your requirement for FA reconciliation for advance ship notices (ASNs) may be within 12 hours, while your tolerance for invoice reconciliation may be 24 hours. Your requirements may differ for each trading partner. So your translator should have the flexibility to set up each trading partner and document to be reconciled within a given suspense period.

You should be aware that if you produce FA reconciliation reports to alert you of problems and late notices but have no one responsible for monitoring them regularly, you have again defeated the purpose of this transaction.

Other Translation Software Controls

EDI Tables

Within the translation software, you usually have the ability to set up cross-reference tables, which are used to cross reference your part number with that of the customer or ship-to location numbers. You must establish procedures to synchronize these EDI tables with the same or similar tables in your application software and well as with your trading partner.

Rejected/Improper Transactions

You should establish procedures to follow in the event that you receive improper transactions. Improper transactions include those with errors, those not established for the specific trading partner, or those not established or mapped at all. The procedures you define should establish key criteria, such as the procedures that must be followed when a transaction set is rejected, who is authorized and the actions they are allowed to take (delete the document, reroute it, etc.), the acceptable timeframes to resolve the issue, and the procedures that must be followed to prevent duplicate processing. Finally, it is important to monitor recurring errors. Errors that are repeated can demand a lot of administrative time be reviewed and acted on, but more importantly, they may indicate attempts at security breach.

Data Edits

The translator should be used to ensure that EDI data complies with the standards and is properly written to the files. Numeric data should be tested for blanks or zeroes, for alphanumeric data, and for appropriate right justification.

Trading Partner Maintenance

The translator lets you establish unique criteria used to trade each transaction set with each trading partner. There should be established procedures that ensure accuracy and consistency in maintaining the trading partner profile tables. Clearly-defined rules should be established and followed to add new trading partners to the EDI system. These procedures should define the trading partner ID scheme used (DUNs number, federal tax ID number, etc.), the sender and receiver IDs used, the acknowledgment type requested, the acknowledgment suspense period, the standard version and release used for each transaction set, the contact name and telephone number, and a procedure to ensure synchronization of the trading partner master file and the VAN or ISP information regarding the same. Trading partner administration forms could be used to enforce that the above is followed.

Record Retention

Paper or electronic documents are required as forms of evidence from time to time. There are many opinions regarding the optimal retention period of records. Keep in mind that each business document may warrant a different retention period, and in the absence of backup records, each situation is judged based on a variety of factors including legal precedent and activity history. To avoid problems and disputes, you should comply with policies set forth with some or all of the following, depending on your specific needs and level of comfort.

- Corporate policies
- The Internal Revenue Service
- State tax laws
- The National Archives and Records Administration

Although you may have heard that records should be retained for seven years, there is no magic rule for an acceptable record retention period. The general rule of thumb is anywhere between seven and ten years.

Security and Authorization

Most commercial translators have some built-in security features; it is important to use the ones that are appropriate for your environment. For instance, you may allow different functions for different users: person A can set up and modify maps, person B can monitor incoming and outgoing communications logs, person C can physically make changes to data within a transaction set.

COMMUNICATIONS SOFTWARE

Communications software is another area that can be used for EDI controls. If you use a direct link or link to an ISP, you need to capture at least two key pieces of information: the date and time of transmission, and whether the communications session concluded successfully.

ISPs, relatively new to carrying EDI transactions, generally do not provide detailed audit reporting. There is usually no confirmation of receipt or date and time zone consistency. To ensure these capabilities, encryption and authentication become a must.

VANs offer a variety of control features and reporting that can further strengthen your control monitoring. Control information provided by VANs usually includes a batch number, a network (interchange) control number, the date and time the document is received by the VAN, the date and time the document is placed in the receiver's mailbox, the date and time the receiver picked up the document (and whether they did), and the date and time the EDI document was forwarded to another VAN or ISP for trading partners using a different provider than you.

VAN control reports offer a wide variety of useful tracking information as well. They include

- **Unretrieved documents.** A report listing documents you sent that were never retrieved from a trading partner's mailbox.

- **Monthly statistics**. A summary of transaction sets sent and received, including an entry for each communication session to help identify transmission failures. This report can also help verify that the number of records you sent is the same as what the network received.

- **Unacknowledged documents**. A report that provides a list of all transaction sets that were sent or received but were not acknowledged.

- **Document/trading partner summary**. A report that provides a summary of transactions sent and received as well as the total number of characters sent and received for a given period.

- **Receiver status**. A report providing the status of documents sent to you by trading partners; lists the documents awaiting retrieval in your mailbox, the documents you have already retrieved, and the documents in your mailbox that contain errors.

- **Sender status**. A report that reveals the status of documents you sent to the network provider. It lists the documents received by the network that have not yet been processed, the documents received by the network that have been placed in the trading partner's mailbox, the documents retrieved from the network by your trading partners, and the documents rejected by the network.

DOCUMENTATION

One of the most important tasks in a paperless environment is proper documentation. Documentation can be done electronically to avoid paper copies. Part of your EDI documentation involves the capture of key information, which should include

- **System documentation**. The list and layout of files used, the list and flow of programs used, the list of transaction sets, generated reported (automated and manual), list of trading partners, and a list of VANs and ISPs.

- **Procedures documentation.** The trading partner's specific business requirements and procedures to follow, a list of transaction sets, generated reports and what they are used for, transmission reports and what they should be monitored for, error handling routines (who, how, when, error severity), and backup policies and procedures for backing up data, maps, and trading partner profiles.

Chapter 11

EDI System Security

As in any environment that involves electronic exchange of business information, system security is a critical issue. With EDI, security is especially important because you are transferring sensitive and confidential data and information.

Many companies are using or considering using the Internet for EDI mail exchange, and new concerns about security are surfacing. When you use the Internet, no one guarantees confidentiality, proper delivery of messages — or that hackers will not attempt to decode your transmission.

With the increased use of the Internet and the Web, how can we continue to protect our privacy? What about the trading partner's privacy? Are EDI transactions traveling safely across these networks around the world? Are we increasing our liability risks?

Although using direct links, proprietary networks, and VANs has been fairly secure, the Internet poses a different threat. Private companies, consumers, and the government alike have a strong interest in privacy issues when exchanging EDI transactions via the Internet. Consumers question the security of sending personal information — their names, addresses, telephone numbers, and, in particular, credit card information. Companies are concerned about protecting credit card information as well as specific trading partner preferences. Competitor access to such information could be embarrassing and costly.

There are numerous liability issues revolving around the privacy of transactions such as purchase orders or inventory inquiries. But more importantly, there are electronic cash and credit card payments that must be secure. What level of security is sufficient and reasonable? VANs, ISPs, and telephone companies are not liable for consequential damages when messages are not delivered or are altered. Is anyone liable for anything?

SECURITY TECHNIQUES

As Figure 11.1 shows, to ensure proper security in a paperless environment, you need a means of authentication, such as an electronic signature. Your trading partner must have encryption capabilities so that you and your trading partners can code and decode transmissions. And you may need to provide physical key management. We discuss these security techniques below.

Authentication

You should use authentication methods such as machine authentication coding or electronic signatures to ensure the validity of the sender and receiver IDs. Authentication is a technique that assigns a value to each electronic node in a transmission. The receiver of the document must verify the authentication code to gain access to the data. For example, in Figure 11.1, Smith Manufacturing must verify the 9-byte authentication code (equivalent to an electronic signature) to be able to open the EDI document.

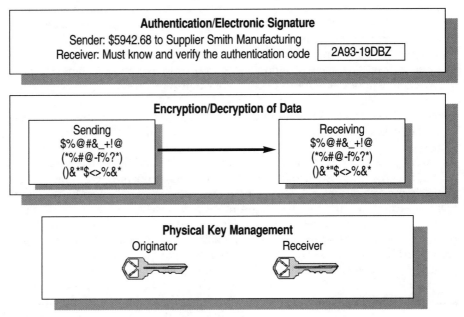

FIGURE 11.1
System Security

Authentication/Electronic Signature
Sender: $5942.68 to Supplier Smith Manufacturing
Receiver: Must know and verify the authentication code | 2A93-19DBZ |

Encryption/Decryption of Data

Sending
$%@#&_+!@
(*%#@-f%?*)
()&*"$<>%&*

Receiving
$%@#&_+!@
(*%#@-f%?*)
()&*"$<>%&*

Physical Key Management
Originator   Receiver

Authentication is used to:

- Verify the identity of the sender of the message to the intended recipient to prevent spoofing or impersonation

- Verify the integrity of the message by detecting changes, including transmission errors introduced between the sender and receiver

- Protect a unique message identifier that is used to detect attempts at insertion, deletion, or duplication of messages

ANSI X9.9 standards are used to compute a Message Authentication Code (MAC). The MAC is a cryptographically-derived hash total used to verify the authorized sender to the authorized receiver and protect the integrity of the data. The MAC protects all types of data, including numeric, text, and even punctuation. Once the data is authenticated, it should not be changed in any way.

Authentication can use a public-key or a private-key approach. With a public key, the code is made "public" to all authorized trading partners (or their devices), who must open messages using the valid key. With a private key, the sender and receiver must have the same key, but its use is restricted to those parties. The length of the private key determines its level of security.

Encryption

You should encrypt and decrypt data, as illustrated in Figure 11.1, to prevent hackers from interpreting sensitive information. Encryption ensures that if hackers do access the data, they find it unintelligible. Encryption of X12 messages can be performed using ANSI X9.23.

Use of the encryption option does not provide detection of accidental or deliberate alteration of messages. Authentication can be used for integrity, while encryption provides confidentiality of the same data. If encryption is used without authentication and an error occurs in transmission, the error may not be detected and the decrypted message may not be usable or processable.

Encryption normally increases the size of the message, so many encryption software packages perform data compression to offset this increase.

Key Management

You can use key management techniques to further ensure the authorization of the sender and receiver. Key management means that only specific individuals with a physical key are able to access the data and calculate the authentication code. An example of physical key management occurs every day in supermarkets. When a clerk makes an error, the supervisor must come to the register, insert a key, and enter a code before the clerk can resume.

SECURITY APPROACHES

There are two approaches to establishing security for EDI transaction sets, regardless of the communications vehicle used. One approach is to enclose the EDI document in security software layers. The other is to embed the security within the transaction set.

External Security

EDI documents that travel the Internet are treated as e-mail packets. E-mail has no privacy unless encrypted. A key consideration of Internet EDI is nonrepudiation. Nonrepudiation, an essential part of Internet EDI, is a self-contained acknowledgment that certifies that a message is from an authentic sender. Nonrepudiation can be used to ascertain whether data was sent or received. EDI transactions that must travel the Internet are good candidates for external security applications.

Embedded Security

Standard EDI transaction sets use the X12.58 security structure to provide the means to embed security within the transaction set itself. EDI transactions can be protected at either or both levels of functional groups and transaction sets. In other words, a single transaction set can be authenticated and encrypted. The functional group it resides in can also be authenticated and encrypted but does not have to be. You can authenticate alone, encrypt alone, or do both simultaneously. ANSI has developed standards to be used for encryption and authentication: the ANSI X3.92-1981, Data Encryption Algorithm; the ANSI X9.9-1986, Financial Institution Message Authentication; and the ANSI X9.23, Encryption of Wholesale Financial Messages. The X12.58 Security Structures allows use of these or other methods for encryption and authentication.

When imbedded in the X12 transaction set, the encryption and authentication information must be formatted to conform to X12 syntax and structure. Provisions for security data elements in the ISA (Interchange Control Header) is an alternative mechanism for supporting existing, password-oriented systems, and is not connected with the X12.58 standards. The greatest advantage of using this standard for EDI exchange is that, because X12 has blessed its use, it means that trading partners are adhering to the same standards for encryption and authentication.

The X12.58 embedded security provides the opportunity for authentication and encryption of EDI data. The business requirements addressed include

- Verification for the recipient of the security of the originator of a message
- Verification of data integrity (error detection, hash totals, control totals)
- Confidentiality of data
- Detection of duplication, insertion, modification, deletion, or impersonation

SECURITY CONSIDERATIONS

There are numerous security software packages available that offer encryption and authentication. Below we look at several key considerations in selecting the appropriate package for your company.

Support of Commercial and Government Algorithms

There are a lot of different standards for encrypting transactions, including RSA, DES, and DSS. Because both trading partners must use the same encryption standards, it is important that you determine which one most of your trading partners use. Make sure you can accommodate encryption needs of commercial businesses as well as government agencies.

User-to-User Security

This feature allows you to establish security by users, rather than by workstation. This is an important option, especially in networked computer environments.

Support of Multiple Environments

You may wish to use encryption on multiple operating environments (Windows 95/NT, OS/400, MVS). EDI documents can be encrypted on a platform other than the one used for mapping and translation. Therefore, depending on the platform used for encryption processing, your choice will help you to select the right vendor.

Automatic Generation/Distribution of Encryption Keys

To minimize manual processing, the encryption software should automatically generate and securely distribute public and private keys to appropriate users and trading partners.

Automatic Revocation of Certificates

The security software should have a built-in feature to automatically revoke unauthorized attempts at digital (electronic) signatures after a specific number of tries. This ensures that hackers who attempt to break the code will be stopped. The digital certificate will be locked following a predetermined number of failed attempts and new digital certificates will be issued, allowing EDI trading partners to resume normal business.

Automatic Signature Expiration

In addition to automatically revoking digital key certificates, it is more secure to change electronic signatures periodically. The software should have a feature that lets you establish an expiration date for each signature and for each trading partner.

Automatic Warning Before Signature Expiration

So that normal business is not disrupted, it is important that the software alerts users of approaching digital signature expirations and provide ample time for a new signature to be issued and distributed to the trading partner.

Data Compression

Because encrypting data adds to the file size, it is important to select a security package that performs data compression. This will help to reduce the size and transportation costs associated with encrypted data.

Transparency

Setting up and using security should be as transparent to the users as possible. You should be able to set it up and forget it.

Other Approaches

In addition to these security measures, you can increase security by taking the following steps:

- Use a VAN as an alternative to direct communications. VANs add a layer of security because they don't let your trading partners access your computer directly.
- If using the Internet, make sure you use standard encryption and authentication techniques.
- Set up the translation software properly. For example, use passwords and make sure you specify which documents are valid for a particular trading partner.
- Take full advantage of built-in security features offered by the standards and translation software packages.
- Perform edits and checks, such as confirming sender/receiver IDs, checking credit limits, and doing checks and balances if payments are automated in the interface and application software.

CONCLUSION

You must be careful about the setup environment and have proper procedures in place to increase the level of security in an EDI environment. There are a number of security threats to consider when using a public medium for transmitting EDI data, including data interception and manipulation, denial of service, ID interception, data misrouting, data duplication, and rejection.

Chapter 12

Testing, Certification, and Service Measurements

You will need to develop testing and certification policies to assist trading partners in establishing and following specific procedures in a structured framework for testing each EDI transaction set. The policy should include information about predicted implementation time frames, milestones, and test procedures.

Trading partners should use these policies to help them plan the rollout of their EDI implementation project. Following these guidelines will help ensure that, when fully implemented, your exchange of EDI transaction sets with your trading partners will be smoother and more successful and that all parties can achieve the objectives of automating business processes, reducing errors, and lowering costs.

REQUIREMENTS

The testing program for a transaction set should lead to a system that achieves a 98 percent overall production success rate. Of course, this rate cannot be achieved immediately, which is why a program of testing and certification is needed.

Throughout the test period, the trading partners must use the same transaction map and standard version. Testing may need to be restarted if either trading partner changes the document map or its version.

For the transaction to be successfully implemented, it must meet the following standards:

- You must be able to successfully retrieve or receive the transaction set from the VAN/ISP.

- The EDI translation software must be able to translate the transaction completely and without errors.

- The transaction must be properly edited or formatted in the interface software.

- The transaction must be properly integrated into the applications software.

- The trading partner must receive and reconcile functional acknowledgments with their corresponding transaction sets.

Unless the partners successfully complete the above steps, the transaction will be considered in error and will not generate usable production data. Below is a sample testing and implementation procedure.

TEST AND IMPLEMENTATION SCHEDULE

You should divide the test and implementation schedule into a series of periods based on the amount of time remaining before EDI is fully adopted. During each period, each trading partner may have different requirements and expectations.

The tests should occur in a parallel test environment, which means that, until the system is moved to a production environment, trading partners should transmit each transaction via EDI in addition to the traditional method (e.g., mail, fax). Once testing reaches the final parallel production date, trading partners can send only the EDI transaction and cease exchanging the traditional form.

Based on results from each testing round, the trading partners may decide to shorten or lengthen the following test schedule.

Phase 1 — Preproduction Parallel Testing

The first phase of testing should occur 6 to 8 weeks before the final parallel production date. Trading partners should use this phase to establish a base line and determine the initial success rate. Before this phase, there is no way to accurately estimate the percentage of transactions that will succeed, making it difficult to define success expectations.

During this phase, trading partners must closely coordinate their transmissions via telephone, fax, or e-mail. Before each transmission, the transmitting partner should notify the receiving partner of the upcoming transmission. Upon receipt (or nonreceipt), the receiving partner should promptly notify the transmitting partner of the transaction's results by telephone, fax, or e-mail. During this phase, the partners should base their actual production data on information transmitted by traditional means and use the EDI transaction only for comparison.

Phase 2 — Preproduction Parallel Testing

Phase 2 should occur 4 to 6 weeks before the final parallel production date. The transactions exchanged in this phase should be successful at least 50 percent of the time. Again, during this phase, trading partners must closely coordinate their transmissions via telephone, fax, or e-mail. Before each transmission, the transmitting partner should notify the receiving partner of the upcoming transmission. Upon receipt (or nonreceipt), the receiving partner should promptly notify the transmitting partner of the transaction's results by telephone, fax, or e-mail. In this phase, trading partners can still transmit actual business documents traditionally for comparison with their EDI equivalents.

Phase 3 — Preproduction Parallel Testing

Phase 3 should occur 3 to 4 weeks before the final parallel production date. The transactions exchanged in this phase should be successful at least 85 percent of the time. Because transmission error rates should be relatively low, trading partners need only inform each other when a transmission fails. During this phase, you should still base actual production data on information transmitted by traditional means.

Phase 4 — Preproduction Parallel Testing

Phase 4 should occur 2 to 3 weeks before the final parallel production date. The transactions received during this phase should be successful 98 percent of the time. Again, trading partners need only inform each other when a transmission fails. Failure notification should continue as well as discrepancy checking between EDI and the traditional business documents.

Phase 5 — Parallel Production

Phase 5 should occur sometime during the final 2 weeks before the final parallel production date. During this phase, transaction success should reach production levels of 98 percent. The trading partners should continue parallel data transmission, but beginning with this phase the parties will use the EDI transaction to create production data. Documents transmitted by traditional means can now be used randomly to confirm and check their EDI equivalents. When there is discrepancy, the receiver should contact the sender to determine the reason.

During this phase, trading partners should decide whether the system can support the production system based upon the success criteria identified earlier. If the system can support production, the trading partners can set a final parallel test date.

Phase 6 — Final Parallel Production Date

At the end of the agreed upon final test day, testing will end. The trading partners will cease traditional data transmission and rely solely on EDI transaction sets. No further discrepancy checking needs to occur. If discrepancies are noted, trading partners should contact one another immediately.

CERTIFICATION

Once the parties begin production at the production success rate, it is important to maintain it. If the parties fail to maintain that level for a period of at least two weeks, the parties should cease EDI production processing and begin a new testing cycle until they have resolved the problem. Additionally, if the trading partners adopt new versions of the EDI standards or implement a new transaction map during production, they must analyze the effects of such changes. In some cases, the changes may require new test procedures, although the time periods for each phase may be significantly reduced.

To determine whether the EDI transactions meet the desired success levels, trading partners must test a substantial number of transactions. To reach a sufficient number of test transactions, the trading partners should transmit approximately 20 to 150 separate EDI transaction sets during each test phase.

Because EDI transactions do not affect production data during test phases 1 through 4, you may need to include specific types and sizes of key information that will test certain variables (for example total dollars or quantities). Generating sufficient test data may also require extending the duration of test phases 5 and 6. During every transaction in test phases 1 and 2 — and when transactions fail in subsequent phases — both trading partners must be prepared to report the following:

- Actual data received
- Translation software error messages
- Communications error messages
- Integration error messages
- Applications errors
- Any other information the parties identify before beginning test phase 1

SERVICE MEASUREMENTS

In every organization, there is a specific department (IT, marketing systems support, customer service) that is responsible for maintaining the EDI environment and bringing up new transaction sets and new trading partners. In some cases, this responsibility is shared among various departments depending on the business use of the transaction set. Resources in departments responsible for EDI projects and activity should have measurable performance standards, which will let you establish goals and measure progress toward those goals. It is important for everyone to agree about the standard measurements before they are implemented. Imposing performance standards on unwilling personnel will create morale and service problems, so it is vital that all parties contribute to the development of the standards that affect them.

Table 12.1 lists some EDI-specific service areas and some suggested measurement levels. Goals can be set for technical tasks and business tasks.

TABLE 12.1
Measurement Criteria

Task	Suggested Time
Business	
Planned partner implementation	15 to 30 days
Planned new transaction implementation	15 to 45 days
Approval of EDI trading partner agreements	5 to 15 days
Follow-up on missing or overdue acknowledgments	Within 4 to 8 hours
Preliminary response to trading partner problems	Within 2 hours
Preliminary response to internal problems	Within 4 hours
Technical	
Availability of resource time for transaction set creation	98 percent per month
Follow-up on missing or suspended data	Within 4 hours
Time for transmittal of EDI transaction set after user creation	Within 2 hours
Resolution of trading partner problems	Within 2 to 3 days
Resolution of internal problems	Within 2 to 3 days
Help desk telephone support	Within 5 rings during business hours Within one hour during off hours
Successful uploading to VAN	98 percent of transactions successfully uploaded
Transaction processing from application system	Within 2 hours of creation by user
Transaction processing into application system	Within 2 hours of receipt from VAN/ISP 98 percent of incoming transactions successfully loaded following system testing
Audit report delivery and review	By the end of business day
Audit report follow up and action	By midday the next business day

Remember, these are simply guidelines to help you monitor your progress and success rate in your EDI program. It is not always possible to implement all the above, but it is a good idea to have these or similar goals established when you begin your EDI program and to follow up quarterly to ensure you are maximizing your investment.

Chapter 13

Legal Considerations

When companies do business with each other, they need to agree to the conditions (prices, delivery dates, etc.) that will apply for each transaction. Sometimes a handshake is all that signifies agreement about these conditions. Other times, the business partners draw up and sign a formal, legally binding contract. Often, preprinted forms that companies use to exchange business information serve as contracts. For example, the reverse side of a purchase order often contains the customer's terms and conditions. By accepting and filling the order, the supplier is agreeing to those terms and conditions.

The purpose of such agreements is to provide evidence in case of disagreements. But evidence (be it a contract or a purchase order) is useful only if it is enforceable. For example, a contract that is not signed is not enforceable.

In a paper environment, if customers do not receive goods from a supplier, they use a written, signed contract and/or a copy of the purchase order as enforceable evidence that an agreement existed. In an electronic relationship, such traditional forms of evidence do not exist. From a legal perspective, because there is no written agreement to the terms and conditions, there is no legal contract. So EDI users must find alternatives and ensure that these electronic documents are enforceable as evidence in a court of law.

Contracts have three fundamental elements: offer, acceptance, and consideration. Fortunately, EDI transactions map to these legal requirements through the communication of a transaction set (offer), an acknowledgment transaction set (acceptance), and remittance advice and electronic funds transfer for payment (consideration). This mapping is the basis for the EDI alternative to traditional forms of evidence that are valid in courts of law.

You can also protect your legal interests in an EDI relationship by agreeing to and signing a paper trading partner agreement before your EDI transactions begin. Such an agreement spells out the terms and conditions of the business relationship, and provides a legal basis for settling disputes.

EDI Evidence and Enforceability

In the U.S., the Uniform Commercial Code (UCC) defines rules, such as what constitutes a contract, what is evidence, and what is a signature for business transactions. According to the UCC, a contract for the sale of goods is not enforceable unless there is sufficient written proof of the business expectation between the trading parties, and all parties sign the contract. This means that it is the writing (for example, the terms and conditions printed on the back of the purchase order) that constitutes evidence of a contract. It also means that the second requirement, the signature, is met if and when the paper document is signed or stamped by the supplier.

The courts have been open to accepting letters, telegrams, and faxes as evidence of a contract. Whether e-mail or EDI documents will be accepted as well remains unanswered, which is why it is imperative to prepare and sign a paper trading partner agreement before establishing an EDI (or any other form of electronic trade) relationship with your trading partners. The trading partner agreement is a general contract that defines the electronic business relationship. Once the general agreement is made, you can append requirements and agreements, regarding individual transaction sets.

If, in addition to your trading partner agreement, you intend to use EDI documents as admissible evidence of a contractual relationship, you need to prove two issues: authenticity of contents and authenticity of transmission. The communications software, the EDI mail carrier (VAN or ISP), and EDI functional acknowledgments (FAs) are the major means of establishing these two types of authenticity.

Authenticity of contents of the documents must be proven. You must be able to show that the contents of the EDI document are complete and not tampered with, and that the sender and receiver of the document are in fact authorized to engage in EDI exchange.

Authenticity of transmission must be established. You must prove the creation and transmission of the document from point of origin through arrival at the recipient's computer. This includes proof of untampered flow of the EDI data through the communications network, whether or not VANs and ISPs were used.

VANs (and hopefully ISPs in the near future) can help furnish evidence for both issues because VANs provide users with a wide variety of control reports detailing EDI traffic. In addition, VANs can be summoned to provide neutral third-party evidence that EDI documents were sent and received. EDI FAs are often used as evidence of receipt. But you need to remember that FAs verify receipt of EDI documents, not receipt of the contents of the electronic envelopes. Better evidence is acknowledgment of the document's contents using a variety of EDI transaction sets. The best evidence is both acknowledgment of receipt and acknowledgment of receipt of contents.

CONTENTS OF THE TRADING PARTNER AGREEMENT

As noted earlier, when a company sends a paper purchase order to a supplier, the buyer's terms and conditions are printed on the order's reverse side. When the supplier fills the order, those terms and conditions are considered binding. However, in many cases, the supplier acknowledges the purchase order using another paper document, stating different terms and conditions. This practice of issuing counter terms and conditions is the origin of the term "the battle of the forms" because the courts are left to determine which terms and conditions are in effect. This type of trading tends to separate the needs of the customer and supplier.

In an EDI environment, you will eliminate such disagreements by negotiating and signing a trading partner agreement at the outset of any EDI relationship. Because the business needs of both parties are agreed to in writing, this type of trading brings customers and suppliers closer together and helps to avoid misunderstanding and disputes.

Terms and conditions, which define such matters as discounts, payment terms, and return policies, are key business issues companies must address when entering into a trading relationship. They define such matters as discounts, payment terms, and return policies. Whether you are in a paper or paperless environment, such issues must be addressed clearly and in writing for enforceability. Terms and conditions in an EDI relationship are ideally negotiated up front and included in the trading partner agreement to avoid, or at least minimize, lengthy and costly court battles. Exceptions are dealt with based on existence of an ongoing relationship.

In addition to addressing terms and conditions, EDI trading partner agreements should address issues such as what constitutes writing and signatures and the exact time that a legally binding EDI contract is formed. For example, does the purchase order become a legal contract when it is delivered to the supplier's mailbox at the VAN or when the supplier receives it in full on his or her computer?

Last, the trading partner agreement can specify the sequence of events that must take place in each transaction. For instance, when a purchase order is sent, it must be followed by an FA, then by a purchase order change, and concluded with another FA.

The trading partner agreement should also specify rules to cover issues such as mailbox float time. In other words, the agreement addresses how often and when VAN mailboxes should be checked. In addition, the agreement should specify the window of time within which an EDI document must be acknowledged to be valid. For example, if a supplier is required to acknowledge a customer's order within 24 hours and fails to do so, the customer can reserve the right to deem the purchase order canceled and place the order with another supplier.

The following list contains the most important items in a typical agreement. This should give you a starting point of what trading agreements should specify.

A trading partner agreement:

- Defines the nature and scope of trading partners' unique trading partnership relationship

- Helps overcome the shortcomings of the law and increases the enforceability of EDI transactions

- Provides a way to share the liabilities in communications errors or VAN or ISP problems
- Expresses the legal importance of implementation guides, forms, and other terms and conditions associated with EDI
- Clarifies that the trading partner agreement is to cover electronic information exchange, such as EDI and e-mail
- Clarifies that business issues for non-EDI related transactions must be addressed in other contracts
- Reduces confusion and misinterpretation of terms and conditions

The American Bar Association (ABA) has developed a draft trading partner agreement that you can use to model your own agreements. The ABA has developed a standard agreement for EDI transactions sets and another one for financial EDI transaction sets. The ABA model, which is available from your local ABA chapter, provides a generic but balanced approach to trading partner legal and control issues.

The Comprehensive Trading Partner Agreement

The comprehensive trading partner agreement should be based in part upon the standards recommended by the ABA. The primary section of the document should contain general principles regarding various EDI procedures. The document itself should not contain detailed information about specific EDI transaction sets; specific information should instead be contained in appendices (see Figure 13.1).

FIGURE 13.1
Electronic Data Flow

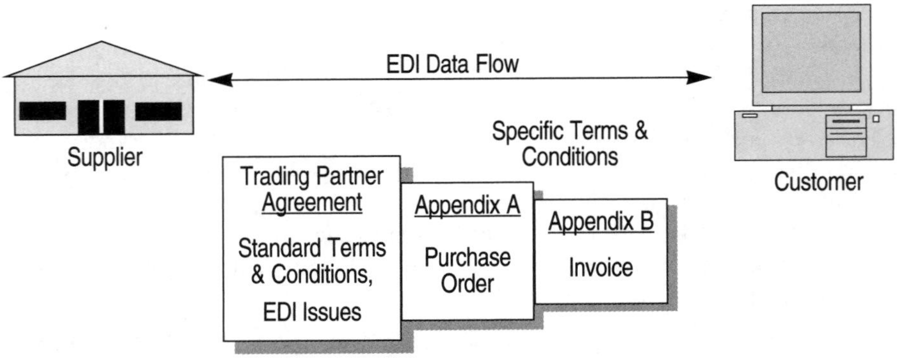

EDI partners using this format should execute a separate appendix for each EDI transaction set they will use. By using appendices to address transaction sets, you do not have to renegotiate the agreement every time a new transaction set is added. In addition, transaction-specific appendices let you define unique and different rules of trade for each. The document and its appendices are part of an integrated document and should not be used separately.

THE TRADE LETTER AGREEMENT

It is sometimes cost prohibitive for smaller companies to execute and negotiate trading partner agreements with all their customers and suppliers. As an alternative, such companies should at least negotiate and sign an *electronic trade letter*, which is an abbreviated version of the comprehensive trading partner agreement. This document generally addresses the terms and conditions but not other liabilities, such as communications responsibilities and document-specific issues. While not nearly as inclusive or detailed as the comprehensive agreement, the letter agreement does address many critical EDI contractual issues.

LIABILITY FOR CONSEQUENTIAL DAMAGES

Companies rely on VANs and ISPs to carry strategic and sometimes highly confidential data and often believe that the VAN or ISP is liable for consequential damages when EDI messages are not delivered properly and on time. It is incorrect to assume that companies share such liability with their third-party network providers. VANs and most ISPs require their customers to sign a lengthy contract that exempts the VAN or ISP from liability for consequential damages.

Telephone carriers are also exempt from liability for consequential damages. Years ago, a fire in a major Chicago suburb telephone station left telephone service unavailable to businesses and homes for several days. The courts did not hold the telephone company liable for consequential damages to local businesses. U.S. courts do not consider telephone carriers liable as long they have sufficient and reasonable means to assure that problems don't occur frequently and that if they do, they will be corrected within a reasonable amount of time.

If information carriers had to bear this level of liability, the cost of using VANs and ISPs would become prohibitive to EDI trading partners, forcing VANs and ISPs out of business and leaving EDI trading partners to use other means of message transfer. With the need to use direct communications links with trading partners, companies would have to develop their own means of audit and control (which would be very costly to smaller companies), and the EDI systems would be less standard and less reliable.

CONCLUSION

The legal considerations this chapter raises should be enough to point you in the right direction and protect you from the pitfall of neglecting to cover all the legal bases. Forewarned is forearmed.

Chapter 14

EDI Organization and Staffing

EDI brings new challenges, among them the need to have the proper owner-ship, resource infrastructure, and staff to manage the day-to-day requirements. Hiring the right resources, especially in a highly competitive market, is neces-sary to meet a growing demand from customers and suppliers to maintain existing EDI relationships and to nurture future growth. In addition to using existing resource skills, EDI and electronic commerce (EC) have created new positions in many organizations. The most notable is the external communica-tions officer (XCO). The XCO's primary focus is to assess and select the proper tools and technologies to streamline external business processes. This is a strategic role because the XCO not only monitors the current EDI and EC envi-ronment, but sets the future direction for business-to-business or consumer to business transaction processing.

OWNERSHIP

EDI has been the responsibility of many departments, from IT to customer ser-vice to marketing. Most companies begin their EDI project within the IT department because in many organizations EDI is viewed as a technical effort. Although often it is the CFO or the sales director who initiates EDI activity, it is passed to IT. IT has the right resources to make technology decisions and carry out the technical tasks, but that department is not well equipped in cus-tomer service or marketing skills.

EDI should be viewed as a competitive advantage and as a sales tool, as well as a solution that can change the way business is conducted. You should consider focusing EDI activity in the customer service or marketing areas. Cus-tomer service has the ability to leverage customer relationships to make EDI a more successful partnering project. Marketing has the tools to further leverage customer relations, but can also assist in promoting EDI and extending it beyond the first tier trading partners.

INFRASTRUCTURE

EDI ownership and staffing can be managed in several different ways.

Centralized

Figure 14.1 depicts the centralized model.

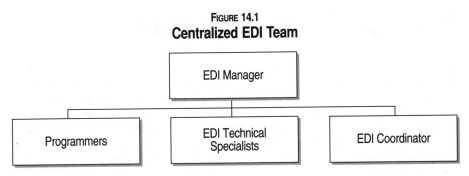

FIGURE 14.1
Centralized EDI Team

In a centralized model, EDI is owned and managed by a core of individuals in the same functional area. The advantages of this model include a central focus and a clear sense of direction for all EDI activity. Furthermore, the centralized model streamlines all EDI activity and ensures consistent decision-making and approach. It also clearly defines accountability and provides a career path for staff members, which means higher staff retention. Most importantly, the centralized team model establishes a single contact point for trading partners.

A disadvantage of this approach is that all resources may not be available within the same business area. This approach may also make it more difficult to perform cost allocation to different parts of the company. For example, the cost of EDI invoices may need to be allocated to the accounting department, while purchase order expenses affect the purchasing area or customer service. Another disadvantage of this model is that staff members tend to float between different business processes and transaction sets, and may not necessarily become experts.

Decentralized

Figure 14.2 depicts the decentralized model. In a decentralized model, EDI activity is managed by multiple groups within different functional areas of a company. Some companies have an EDI group within their purchasing group to handle procurement-related transaction sets and another EDI group within the transportation area for processing the freight bills and advance ship notices (ASNs). The advantages of this approach include a sense of autonomy for each functional area in the company because they can make their EDI decisions regardless of other departments' priorities. There is usually a strong sense of ownership because each department has a vested interest in the success of its EDI project. In this model, staff members tend to become focused experts because they narrow their focus on only a few transaction sets and business processes.

FIGURE 14.2
The Decentralized EDI Team

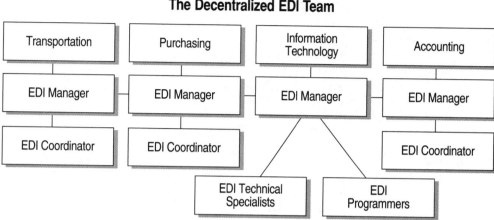

A disadvantage of this approach is that EDI prioritization is not done company-wide but by functional area. Since there is no central focus, there is no real sense of overall accountability and success for the company. Staff members may find their work redundant over time and may feel that their career growth is limited within their functional area, leading to higher staff turnover. In addition, information about EDI activity is scattered and there are multiple contact points for the trading partners.

Virtual Centralized

Figure 14.3 depicts the virtual centralized model.

FIGURE 14.3
The Virtual Centralized EDI Team

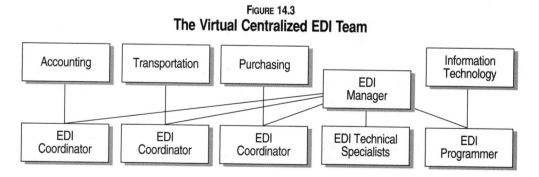

In a virtual centralized model, EDI activity is centralized and managed by a single group of individuals, but those staff members need not reside within the same department or functional area. Staff members from various departments therefore become virtual members of the EDI team. Advantages of this model include the fact that because departments provide their own resource, they feel a strong sense of autonomy and ownership and feel that they have a voice in the overall direction and decision-making process. This approach provides a central repository of all EDI activity and allows for company-wide prioritization. This model generally does not require organizational changes and makes it fairly simple to allocate EDI-related expenses. A disadvantage of this model is that there may be multiple contact points for trading partners unless the group can agree to a central point among them. A concern that is usually raised with this approach is that often the department that voices their opinion more strongly or appears to be more powerful tends to be given priority. Of course, in this model, if the EDI manager is associated with a "neutral" department, (s)he can help enforce company-wide priorities more effectively.

Regardless of overall ownership and staffing model, it is important for EDI to be business driven rather than treated as a technical implementation effort.

STAFFING

Whether implementing EDI for the first time or enhancing your existing setup, it is important to establish an EDI team, a core group of individuals who can carry out the activities outlined in the EDI plan. The primary role of the team is to establish and maintain EDI relationships, provide system maintenance, work with audit and legal staff, and provide ongoing education. In addition, team members can participate in user groups, standards organizations, and strategic rollout of EDI to additional business applications and trading partners. Figure 14.4 is a representation of an EDI team.

It is important to appoint representatives from all functional departments to serve on the EDI team. All functional areas in an organization may be affected by EDI implementation. Therefore input from each is valuable to ensure the feasibility of EDI application and prioritization. In addition, wide participation can result in a stronger sense of ownership and coordination within the company.

Although many of the roles may start as a part-time commitment, they can lead to full-time work, with some roles requiring multiple resources. Your specific requirements depend on the number of trading partners, transaction sets, and technologies used; the degree of legacy application integration; and future needs. The personnel you may need for your EDI team includes a manager, coordinator, marketing specialist, development project leader, EDI specialist, business systems analysts, and analyst/programmers. You will also need occasional support from legal, marketing, and other business areas. The functions of several of these roles can often be carried out by one individual.

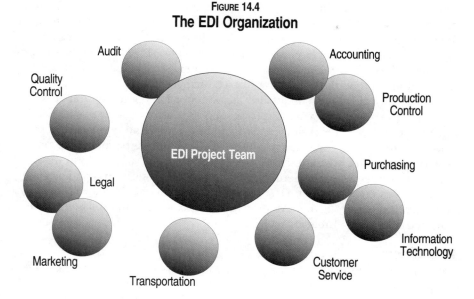

FIGURE 14.4
The EDI Organization

The primary reasons for establishing an EDI group are to:

• Establish and maintain EDI trading relationships

• Establish and maintain documents maps

• Develop and maintain legacy system integration

• Provide system maintenance

• Educate the internal and trading partner personnel

The EDI group's ongoing responsibilities should include electronic transmission of all business documents and completion of the pilot project and documentation of its results to determine the feasibility and measure the benefits of EDI. In addition this group is responsible for

• continued rollout to additional trading partners

• coordinating IT efforts to execute application projects that support EDI capabilities

• maintaining and monitoring existing trading partners

• maintaining EDI standards changes

• participating in standards organizations and user groups

In addition to an EDI manager and coordinator, the EDI organization must include personnel from all functional departments in the company. At least one functional expert (or key individual from each functional department) should support this organization by providing advice and input and executing necessary tasks. This is important for two reasons. First, as we've discussed, all functional areas in an organization may be affected by EDI implementation, so input from each is valuable to ensure the feasibility of EDI application and prioritization. Second, participation of every functional area results in increased cooperation and coordination within the company.

The EDI organization should also include members of the customer service and IT groups to provide part-time support. Customer service staff will provide EDI support for customers and vendors, answering questions about transmission problems, rejected transmissions, and trading partner setup problems or changes. In addition, customer service members may perform the tasks of trading partner setup, triggering transactions for transmission, and answering miscellaneous questions. The IT support staff generally handles the day-to-day operational aspects of EDI, such as technical resolution of transmission problems and rejected transmissions.

TEAM MEMBERS

The personnel you may need for your EDI team include a manager, EDI coordinator, marketing specialist, business systems analyst, development project leader, EDI specialist, and analyst/programmers. Let's look at the tasks each of these team members typically performs in EDI implementation. Then we can examine their job descriptions.

The *EDI manager* is the liaison between upper management and the EDI group. This individual must have solid knowledge of the business, an in-depth understanding of corporate objectives and direction, and strong experience with a variety of technologies, especially EDI and the Internet. This person will provide management perspective to the implementation of EDI throughout the entire organization and assist the EDI team in obtaining upper management commitment, funding, and necessary resources. For instance, this person should determine whether EDI will save the company money or whether EDI is a lower priority than something else, such as bar coding.

The *EDI coordinator* can act as the main interface between your company and your trading partners in the rollout of the EDI program. The coordinator must have hands-on experience with EDI so that (s)he can oversee everything during implementation. The EDI coordinator will be responsible for developing a solid program for EDI rollout, which means (s)he should attend standards organization meetings, conduct seminars for potential EDI trading partners, and act as consultant to all members of the EDI team. The coordinator should manage trading partner rollout, review project status, and identify achieved benefits. (S)he should manage the day-to-day operation of the EDI capability through other departments and initiate requests for system enhancements.

The *EDI marketing specialist* must have a solid marketing background. An understanding of EDI is desirable; however, a crucial skill this individual must have is the ability to sell the advantages of EDI to management. Another objective is to assist in promotion of EDI among your trading partners. (S)he can do this by developing short- and long-term strategies for EDI rollout, developing marketing material, identifying and participating in seminars and exhibits to create greater visibility of your EDI program, and meeting with the sales staff to identify and prioritize customer/supplier base for contact.

EDI business systems analysts specialize in a specific application and its EDI interface for each functional area in the company. These individuals must have an understanding of EDI and, more important, a solid knowledge of the internal application systems to effectively analyze and design proper interfaces between EDI data and corporate applications. In small- to medium-sized organizations, often one or two individuals have sufficient knowledge of all business applications of their organization and may fill this role. They assist in the development of EDI interface design and program specifications and participate in preparation and execution of system test plans.

The *EDI development project leader* must have a solid background in project management and is responsible for developing and managing the EDI project. (S)he should develop a plan, monitor system development and maintenance activity and assign resources, interact with the EDI coordinator to determine staffing requirements, track and report project status, participate in preparation and execution of test plans, and prepare program specifications. (S)he will act as interface between the internal EDI staff and EDI trading partners. This individual is responsible for the development of a proven plan for successful EDI implementation for trading partners as well as internally. EDI experience is not absolutely necessary, but is desirable.

The *EDI specialist* must have strong interpersonal skills and be able to effectively perform technical tasks, including data mapping and trading partner profile setup. This individual must be effective in resolving trading partners' technical EDI problems. In addition, this person is responsible for setting up and maintaining communications (direct, through a VAN or ISP), as well as maintaining a quality control program, providing security and backup, and ensuring disaster recovery.

The *EDI analyst/programmers* play a key role in the initial and ongoing development efforts required to accommodate electronic exchange of documents. These individuals will be responsible for designing, coding, and testing of EDI interface software, as well as performing modifications required to existing application systems due to changes in business procedures resulting from EDI.

Job Descriptions

The next several pages contain job descriptions for key EDI team members.

EDI Manager

Qualifications

- Six to eight years of general management experience with IT or other functional departments
- Knowledge of IT concepts. Solid understanding of key EC technologies such as EDI and bar coding and their impact in a business environment
- Must understand and be able to apply re-engineering concepts
- Strong written and verbal communications skills
- Strong interpersonal skills and good rapport with upper management

General Responsibilities

- Manages the entire EDI implementation effort as it relates to other projects
- Acts as liaison between the EDI team and corporate executives
- Ensures that EDI is used as a tool to achieve enterprise-wide critical success factors.

Specific Responsibilities and Activities

- Develops and manages strategic plan for EDI
- Participates in EDI team meetings
- Secures management commitment
- Obtains funding and resources
- Performs benchmarking for EDI
- Reports on EDI implementation and its benefits to upper management
- Identifies other EC technologies to integrate with EDI
- Develops and assists in the rollout of business process re-engineering projects

EDI Coordinator

Qualifications

- Four to six years of project management experience
- Direct experience with users and/or customer service
- Knowledge of IT concepts and capabilities and control functions related to above applications
- Solid understanding of EDI and its business applicability
- Strong project administration skills
- Strong written, verbal, and interpersonal skills

General Responsibilities

- Ensures, coordinates, and manages the successful implementation of EDI
- Works with the other members of the corporate EDI groups to plan and coordinate the implementation of EDI
- Provides liaison function between corporate EDI team and any other EDI groups within the company
- Represents his/her company at various standards organizations
- Responsible for internal EDI training and education
- Responsible for holding EDI seminars for trading partners

Specific Responsibilities and Activities

- Prepares and conducts trading partner surveys
- Participates in standards development organizations
- Participates in VAN, ISP, and translation software user groups
- Monitors daily tasks and implementation progress
- Manages the rollout of EDI to additional trading partners after completion of the pilot project
- Meets regularly with EDI manager to review progress on EDI implementation and benefits achieved
- Conducts EDI status meetings with representatives from user departments
- Coordinates customer service, marketing, and IT department activities to achieve EDI goals and objectives
- Manages the day-to-day operation of the EDI capability through other departments
- Manages internal and external EDI education and training
- Initiates requests for IT to make system and/or program changes
- Obtains, reviews, and exchanges trading partner agreements and routes to corporate counsel
- Obtains, reviews, and exchanges EDI implementation guides with trading partners

EDI Marketing Specialist

Qualifications

- Five to ten years of marketing experience
- Direct customer contact experience
- Knowledge of IT concepts and capabilities
- Basic understanding of EDI and its business applicability
- Strong sales skills
- Strong written and verbal communications skills
- Strong interpersonal skills

General Responsibilities

- Develops a short- and long-term market strategy for the successful implementation of EDI for you and your trading partners
- Provides liaison function between the EDI team and marketing and sales departments
- Responsible for internal EDI education of the marketing and sales teams

Specific Responsibilities and Activities

- Develops short- and long-term strategies for EDI rollout to your trading partners
- Develops marketing material
- Identifies and participates in seminars and exhibits to create greater visibility of your commitment to EDI
- Meets periodically with marketing team to identify and prioritize customer/ supplier base for contact
- Directs customer contact to market EDI
- Manages marketing team's EDI education
- Serves as liaison between potential EDI trading partners and the EDI coordinator to perform modifications and enhancements to the EDI setup

EDI Business Systems Analyst

Qualifications

- Four to six years of experience in systems and programming
- Customer contact experience
- Working knowledge of information technology concepts and capabilities
- Basic understanding of communications concepts
- Effective oral and written communication skills
- Some operating system and programming language experience a must
- Exposure to EDI a plus
- Ability to assume responsibility
- Strong business analytical skills
- Strong interpersonal skills

General Responsibilities

- Performs analysis of functional business areas to determine applicability and extent of systems development work
- Possesses ability to work with automated tools to document systems design and track project progress
- Prepares program specifications in accordance with company methodology

Specific Responsibilities and Activities

- Reviews and recommends EDI applications in specific functional areas of the company
- Prepares documentation for each project life cycle phase in accordance with your methodology and standards
- Interacts with the EDI development project leader to determine effective means of automating business functions through EDI, and identifies project scope
- Participates in preparation and execution of system test plans
- Prepares program specifications in accordance with your methodology and standards
- Plans and monitors system development and maintenance activity and assigned personnel to ensure effective development effort within scheduled target dates

EDI Development Project Leader

Qualifications

- Six to eight years of experience in systems and programming
- Minimum of one year of project administration experience
- Customer contact experience
- Basic understanding of communications concepts
- Strong verbal, written, and interpersonal skills
- Some operating system and programming language experience a must
- Exposure to EDI a plus
- Ability to direct others and exercise judgment in decision-making
- Strong business analytical skills

General Responsibilities

- Develops and supervises project teams in successful implementation of projects
- Acts as key interface with users
- Ultimately responsible for the entire design and development and testing tasks
- Works with EDI coordinator to ensure successful implementation of EDI with trading partners

Plans projects using automated tools and manages assigned staff

- Interacts heavily with customers to find technical solutions to EDI implementation, resolves problems, and documents results for analysis
- Performs analysis of functional business areas to determine EDI applicability and extent of systems development work

Specific Responsibilities and Activities

- Prepares and maintains project plan, tracks budgeted versus actuals
- Plans and monitors system development, maintenance activity, and assigned personnel
- Prepares documentation for project life cycle phase in accordance with your methodology and standards
- Interacts with EDI trading partners to determine implementation and education efforts required, identify implementation scope, and track and report project status
- Participates in preparation and execution of test plans
- Designs interface software
- Prepares program specifications
- Designs audit and control procedures
- Develops backup and recovery procedures

EDI Specialist

Qualifications

- Three to four years of experience in systems and programming
- Working knowledge of EDI translation software packages
- Solid understanding of EDI standards
- Expertise in data mapping
- General knowledge of communications standards
- Experience with VANs, ISPs, and Internet security packages

General Responsibilities

- Performs data mapping, mailbox setup, communications, and security setups
- Receives EDI data and ensures successful integration of data to interface and application files and to trading partner mailboxes
- Develops and ensures that sufficient audit and control procedures are in place

Specific Responsibilities and Activities

- Maps EDI transaction sets in translation software
- Creates and maintains trading partner profiles in translation software
- Establishes authentication and encryption, if necessary
- Communicates trading partner-specific technical issues to development project leader
- Establishes and maintains mailboxes on VAN(s)
- Establishes connections through the Internet
- Incorporates audit and control procedures within trading partner profiles, transaction set maps, and interface files

EDI Analyst/Programmer

Qualifications

- Three to four years of experience in systems and programming
- Working knowledge of IT concepts and capabilities
- Basic understanding of communications concepts
- Effective oral and written communication skills
- Hands-on programming language and operating systems experience a must
- Ability to work with limited supervision

General Responsibilities

- Codes, tests, and implements programs
- Provides documentation
- Prepares program specifications in accordance with company methodology

Specific Responsibilities and Activities

- Codes, tests, implements, and provides production support of programs according to design specifications, system or parallel test plans
- Prepares system documentation in accordance with your methodology and standards
- Interacts with business systems analyst to identify project scope and to track and report project status
- Works with EDI Specialist to ensure mapped EDI data is correctly integrated with applications systems
- Participates in preparation and execution of system test plans
- Prepares program specifications in accordance with your methodology and standards
- Constructs interface programs and modifies existing applications software
- Prepares programs and routines for audit and control
- Runs backup and recovery procedures

CONCLUSION

In addition to the above roles and responsibilities, there are two other critical needs for every EDI organization. First, you should obtain the services of a Certified Records Manager (CRM), who can prepare and maintain policies for managing electronic records. The CRM will help to ensure that proper electronic records are kept for the right length of time and in the proper format (COLD, tape, microfiche). Legal advice is also highly recommended for contract management as new trading partners and processes are automated.

Finally, you should find and maintain an EDI champion at your company. The champion is an executive-level manager who believes in EDI and its benefits and can help to sell it to other corporate executives. Your EDI champion is the most effective means of getting upper management exposure, with which comes funding and approval for your plans. The champion should help to put together a steering committee consisting of executives who can help to set objectives that are in line with the overall corporate business plan.

Chapter 15

Implementation Strategy

To have a successful long-term solution, you need to have an implementation strategy and a project plan in place before you begin. To determine the best EDI solution for your environment, you should perform three activities: a business process evaluation of your organization, a business partner review, and a technology assessment.

BUSINESS PROCESS EVALUATION

In a business process evaluation, you should perform an internal study of your key business processes. Your focus should be on identifying inter-organizational business processes — those between your company and your trading partners. You should develop a list of questions to be used in interviewing key personnel from each functional area of the company. The results of the interview process should be documented in a process flow diagram, identifying business activity, type of data and information exchanged, sources used (such as telephone, e-mail, fax, EDI), and the volumes and frequency of data exchange. This is your *current model*. Now you are prepared to develop a preliminary EDI model identifying the business processes that can most benefit from automation. However, it is premature to develop a plan based on your needs evaluation alone.

BUSINESS PARTNER REVIEW

EDI requires that companies work together very closely as they automate their procedures, so it is critical to communicate openly and clearly with your trading partners. A first step is to conduct a general survey of select suppliers or customers. Selection of this group can be done based on a number of different factors. You can consider the volume of transactions and data, the dollar value of the transactions, or the time criticality of the business processes. The survey should address technical EDI questions, but also focus on business issues. Questions you should ask include the trading partner's current EDI environment makeup:

- How long they have been involved with EDI?
- Which transaction sets are in place?
- How many trading partners are actively trading?
- What is the size and extent of their EDI project?

In addition, you need to know future commitments, as well as how well integrated the EDI applications are. Answers to these questions will allow you to select the most appropriate trading partners to ally with.

The choice of trading partners is very important. A trading partner's degree of willingness, readiness, commitment, resources, and experience are critical factors to consider. To determine the best choice of trading partners and to build the EDI plan, you must solicit, interview, and meet with the potential candidates. Based on the input from this activity, you can confidently select and prioritize the EDI application areas and other technologies to use, and develop the tactical plan. This step provides some insight into the next step, technology assessment.

TECHNOLOGY ASSESSMENT

The two previous two steps are designed to identify business procedures and trading partners that are good EDI prospects. During a technology assessment, you must determine which processes are most suitable for automation, based on a match between your internal needs and the ability and readiness of your trading partners.

This three-step process is important to help develop an EDI strategy. Along with your choice of trading partners, business processes to automate, and transactions and technologies to use, you should identify budget and resource requirements, an implementation timeline, and a rollout plan. Remember, EDI may not be a good choice for everything. You should focus on the processes that are the most paper intensive, labor intensive, time critical, and those with the highest potential for backlog.

PLANNING

When implementing EDI, you must be prepared to deal with technical, cultural, and procedural issues specific to your company. The technology side of EDI is not terribly difficult to implement. But, on the whole, EDI implementation and rollout to trading partners are difficult tasks because EDI affects many internal procedures and external relations and, as a business strategy, requires long-term commitment.

As we've seen in previous chapters, to deal with both sides of EDI, it is very important to develop a long-term EDI plan up front. Such a plan requires that you assess and secure management commitment, understand and use the company's organizational structure, obtain and provide EDI education, perform cost/benefit analysis, and create a plan for the implementation effort. The "Developing an EDI Strategy" checklist on page 173 leads you through the steps involved for developing an EDI plan.

Your EDI implementation plan should include your objectives for the project based on the results of an external and an internal survey, and should list the benefits you expect. The approach outlined in your plan should be to implement EDI in phases: select a few trading partners and documents, try out some transmissions, and make sure everything works before you go live with EDI.

Developing an EDI Strategy

✔	Task	Target Date	Notes
	Assess and secure management commitment		
	Understand and use organizational structure		
	Obtain EDI education		
	Perform cost/benefit analysis		
	Create project plan		
	State objectives		
	Define phased approach		
	Internal survey		
	External survey		
	Budget requirements		
	Resource requirements		
	Trading partner selection		
	Document selection		
	Standards selection		
	Hardware evaluation		
	Software evaluation		
	VAN/ISP evaluation		
	Pilot		
	Perform operational evaluation		
	Implement EDI		
	Rollout to trading partners		

The plan should include the selection and prioritization of trading partners, a business process application, a technology blueprint, other IT-related issues such as computer hardware and software decisions, and a pilot program.

Once the pilot is completed, it is important to measure its effectiveness and success. This will lead into the next phase of any EDI program: trading partner rollout. Remember that once an EDI relationship is established and working well, it is fairly cost effective to replicate it with other trading partners. The technology investment is already there, the benefits have accrued, and the bugs have been worked out. To obtain maximum value from this investment, you should develop a trading partner rollout strategy and an aggressive marketing and education campaign to entice other customers and suppliers to enter into an electronic commerce relationship with you.

The plan should also cover budget and resource requirements as well as trading partner, document, and standards selection. You should also plan for software, communication, and hardware evaluation. Finally, you can plan your pilot EDI project, including who your test-period trading partners will be, which documents you'll try out with them, what your test period will be, and how long you will continue to rely on paper backup before committing to electronic documents. Then you can perform an operational evaluation to review current procedures. Only with such preparation should you tackle implementation and trading partner rollout.

IMPLEMENTATION ISSUES

When you have mapped the information flow and identified and prioritized areas for EDI implementation, with proper planning and the cooperation of management and others in the organization, the EDI implementation should be successful. The implementation issues necessary to get your EDI solution up and running include upgrading/purchasing hardware and software, meeting with trading partners, exchanging legal trading partner agreements, and implementation guides, establishing EDI links, and conducting a pilot project. Let's look briefly at the specifics involved with each of these implementation issues.

Hardware

Before implementing EDI, you need to have all the applicable hardware up and running. You may have to add hardware or upgrade existing hardware to deal with the new volumes of processing EDI will require. In addition, EDI requires acquisition and installation of communications hardware, such as modems and communications ports.

Software

You must install translation and communications software. Application software may require modifications, and you must develop interface software.

Meeting with Trading Partners

Meeting with your selected trading partners is an important step towards a mutual understanding of technical and operational requirements in an EDI relationship. You must ensure your operations are aligned with theirs if, for example, you expect a response to your request for quote within a certain time frame.

Exchanging Legal Agreements

Exchanging and signing a trading partner agreement before commencing the electronic relationship is essential because, in case of dispute, the documents that constitute a contract in a paper environment are no longer available with EDI.

Exchanging Implementation Guides

Implementation guides define in detail technical requirements for document maps and are required to set up the translation software package to establish the trading partner relationship.

Establishing EDI Links

To exchange EDI documents, you must set up the trading partners in the translation software package and possibly flag them in the applications software to specify in the customer or vendor master that this is an EDI trading partner. Then you must establish the communications link, whether through a direct line, a VAN, or an ISP.

Conducting a Pilot Project

Before you go live with EDI, you need a pilot project to make sure everything is working correctly. In this pilot project, you use a few transaction sets to exchange EDI documents with selected trading partners in a controlled environment. During the first phase of the pilot, you do parallel testing — you transmit actual EDI documents and also send the traditional paper or fax copy it is replacing. This lets you and your trading partner compare the two sources of data to ensure that the EDI information is accurate.

Trading partners determine the duration of the parallel test period based on their level of comfort. Typical duration of the parallel test ranges from two weeks to three months. After the parallel period is over, you can do live, paperless EDI. Soon you'll be adding new trading partners to your EDI setup.

Trading Partner Rollout

Once EDI is implemented, you must expand its use among your trading partners to ensure its success and increase its payback. The more trading partners you have, the less expensive EDI is per trading partner.

To attract new trading partners, many companies develop EDI-specific marketing brochures or include their EDI capabilities in their marketing materials. Most companies develop an EDI implementation guide and distribute it to potential EDI trading partners. Other ways of attracting trading partners include conducting free seminars for vendors and customers, attending EDI conferences, or even setting up a booth at exhibits. Finally, attendance and participation in standards development meetings is a key to attracting trading partners because you meet people who already have an interest in EDI.

IMPLEMENTATION: BUSINESS STEPS

In a complex process such as EDI implementation, you need to make sure you're taking all the business as well as technical steps necessary to reach the goal. Use the "Business Steps" checklist on pages 177–178 to ensure that you don't overlook any important business steps.

IMPLEMENTATION: TECHNICAL STEPS

Sometimes we lose touch with the step-by-step processes we have to follow to ensure proper implementation of EDI. The "Technical Steps" checklist on page 179 should assist in identifying and following the technical tasks required to implement EDI. Note that you have to perform some tasks simultaneously.

Business Steps

✔	Description	Target Date
	Review operational procedures to identify potential EDI applications	
	Survey trading partners to determine EDI capabilities and interest	
	Review survey results	
	Select and prioritize prospective trading partners	
	Select and prioritize transaction sets	
	Select trading partners and documents for the pilot project	
	Select appropriate standards	
	Acquire standards manuals	
	Join standards organization	
	Send letter to trading partners with	
	Explanation of benefits of EDI link with you	
	Brief overview of planned project with time lines	
	Listing of investment requirements (budgets, resources)	
	Assign/Identify key program-management roles in your company	
	EDI champion (upper-management person)	
	EDI business manager	
	EDI marketing manager	
	Technical manager	
	EDI coordinator	
	Assign/Identify key program-management roles in trading partner's company	
	Business sponsor	
	Technical coordinator	
	EDI coordinator	

Business Steps ... *CONTINUED*		
✔	**Description**	**Target Date**
	Draft internal awareness program	
	Education sessions	
	EDI white paper	
	Draft trading partner seminar program	
	EDI seminars	
	EDI implementation guide	
	Prepare internal EDI business plan	
	Outline your EDI plan	
	Define detailed trading partner implementation steps	
	Develop trading partner agreement and/or electronic trade letter	
	Contact and facilitate vendor selection process for trading partners	
	Translation software vendor	
	VAN or ISP	
	Coordinate trading partner seminar activities	
	Arrange seminar logistics	
	Draft and send invitation	
	Conduct seminar	
	Distribute EDI implementation guide	
	Exchange implementation guide with trading partners	
	Exchange trading partner agreements	
	Follow up with seminar attendees	
	Implement EDI with new trading partners	
	Begin parallel test of paper/EDI transmission	
	Begin live status (paperless)	
	Evaluate program/perform benchmark	
	Plan next phase of EDI growth	

Technical Steps

✔	Description	Target Date
	Select and install translation software.	
	Select and connect with VANs/ISPs or establish direct communications links.	
	Define first pilot to test two or three transaction sets with two or three trading partners, from start to finish.	
	Define technical requirements.	
	Review trading partner document maps.	
	Design/develop maps.	
	Design interface files where the EDI data will reside.	
	Write documentation (procedural and technical).	
	Review internal record layouts (to accommodate EDI data, sometimes these layouts must be changed or added to).	
	Review selected documents to determine how application systems are affected.	
	Review standards.	
	Review operating environment to make sure that there are not capacity issues and that EDI procedures can be run at certain times without interfering with other jobs.	
	Begin mapping on the translation software, design specifications, and interface file coding.	
	Begin first pilot. Define transactions with trading partners in order of implementation by categorizing them as priority 1, 2, and 3. The first pilot includes priority 1 transaction sets with a few trading partners; The second pilot includes priority 2 transaction sets with the same 2 or 3 trading partners as pilot 1 or with priority 1 transaction sets with priority 2 trading partners.	
	Complete first pilot program and evaluate/start second pilot project.	
	Complete second pilot program and evaluate/start third pilot project.	

GOING LIVE

The step-by-step action plan below provides a guideline for establishing trading partner relations for exchanging EDI documents.

Action Plan for Establishing Trading Partner Relations		
Step	**✔**	**Task**
1		Representatives from both companies meet to discuss EDI plans and evaluate the feasibility of an EDI relationship. Participants identify and prioritize EDI documents to be exchanged, providing target implementation dates.
2		Your trading partners send you their trading partner profile identifying their current EDI environment, including transaction sets, means of communications, and standards used.
3		All parties sign the trading partner agreement and return it to the EDI coordinator.
4		Programmers exchange technical EDI information. This information will include a detailed explanation of how each company maps the selected documents.
5		Prepare the hardware and software systems for EDI exchange,, by setting up EDI in the auto job scheduler or hooking up the modem,, for example.
6		Begin the test phase. You have to test communications to ensure proper transmission to the selected VAN/ISP. On receipt, the VAN (if using a VAN) verifies the format and data of the initial document. A paper copy of the document is exchanged for manual verification.
7		A parallel status is now in effect. During the parallel phase, you continue to exchange a paper copy of the electronically exchanged document to confirm the accuracy of the electronic equivalent. Both trading partners must feel comfortable with the EDI document before moving to live status. Unless special circumstances are identified,, you can expect to exchange the paper copy of the document for a parallel period of between three weeks and three months.
8		When the paper copy is eliminated, the status is considered live.

SETTING UP AN EDI TRADING PARTNER

Establishing a new trading partner is a multistep process involving paper documentation, application configuration, business and transaction set analysis, and negotiation. The list of steps you can follow to successfully establish a new trading partner is on page 181.

Action Plan for Setting Up a Trading Partner		
Step	**✔**	**Task**
1		Identify the trading partner.
		What is their corporate identity?
		What type of relationship do you currently have with them?
		Who are the preliminary contact people?
2		Gather trading partner specifications.
		What are the ship to/ship from/bill to addresses?
		Determine whether your internal product numbers and the trading partner's match; if not create a cross-reference list.
		Determine identification numbers (DUNS number, tax ID, etc.)
3		Begin technical analysis.
		Analyze mapping between your EDI transaction set and the trading partner's.
		Use gap analysis to determine whether EDI set will fulfill business needs.
4		Conduct communication analysis.
		How will the partners confirm transmissions?
		When will the partners transmit transaction sets?
5		Begin creating transaction maps.
		Determine whether to use generic or trading partner specific maps.
		Modify existing maps; create new maps.
6		Sign trading partner agreement and agree upon testing and certification policies.
7		Make application changes.
8		Set up partner in EDI translator.
9		Set up partner in application system.
10		If necessary, register partner with VAN/ISP.
		Determine whether interconnect will be needed.
11		Exchange test data scripts with trading partner.
12		Begin testing with trading partner according to testing and certification procedures.
13		Move to production within testing and certification process guidelines.
		Enable production EDI maps into application system.
14		End testing.

Conclusion

That's all there is to it. These steps take you through a complete EDI implementation.

EDI is not just a technology, but a powerful tool that you can wield to streamline business procedures and save costs, simultaneously. A planned EDI implementation will ensure long-term successful use of EDI and will serve strategic business interests.

Chapter 16

The Future of EDI

Although EDI has been around for more than 25 years, its use continues to grow, with implementation efforts having leveled off somewhat. EDI has made its way into every industry, affecting every business function, encompassing the world. Many companies have been using EDI for some time but are finding new and innovative ways of incorporating it into other areas of their business and across their entire trading channel. No longer just a way to exchange purchase orders and invoices, EDI is used to submit insurance claims and to apply for bank loans. EDI is replacing — and more important, it is eliminating — paper documents as well as unnecessary business procedures.

For many years, e-mail was viewed as a means to eliminate paper. Although e-mail is an electronic exchange of information, it is not standard data and does not allow computers to interpret and act on business information, and requires human intervention. With the expansion of e-mail communication standards into the area of EDI, companies can not only exchange text-based information, but they can also send formatted, standard EDI documents, as well as binary text that contains such things as engineering drawings.

EDI is among leading-edge technologies that are moving the business world toward an environment of electronic commerce. Electronic commerce is a business environment where technology streamlines commercial information exchange and improves the efficiency of people and processes. For example, by adopting EDI and bar coding, retailers have found an innovative way to gather and exchange consumer information quickly and accurately. This information has brought the consumer the ability to do one-stop shopping. The right products — available at the right time for the best price — are a major key to the success of retailers. EDI, bar coding, and the close trading partnership the retailers have established with their suppliers have made that goal possible.

The same concepts and technologies that have been the catalysts for change within companies as they have moved to automate the majority of their internal operations can be applied to inter-company relationships. It only makes sense to use the most cost-effective resources available to us. The costs of labor, postage, and paper have consistently risen over the years, while the relative cost of computers and communications has dropped. Therefore, it makes sense to reduce our people and paper expenses and exploit the more efficient computers and technologies available to us today.

Everyone strives for higher customer satisfaction because it translates into customer loyalty. Loyalty depends on a good product, reasonable prices, and quick turnaround. Although personal relationships between key management at customer and supplier companies used to determine customer loyalty, today, loyalty depends much more on the hard facts. Loyalty does not shift quickly because a new supplier offers a lower price. When companies engage in electronic commerce, their businesses become tightly integrated and there is a great deal of dependence and trust between them. Today, customer loyalty can be secured with electronic commerce, not just the personal relationships.

The Internet is perhaps the biggest reason for a renewed enthusiasm in EDI. If nothing else, there is new interest in EDI as companies that found it too expensive are viewing the Internet as a much cheaper solution to send and receive business transactions. In the next several years, the Internet will probably become the dominant medium for EDI transactions. It will open up opportunities for smaller companies to do EDI and electronic commerce.

EDI is more affordable than ever before. Some Web-based solutions start as low as $25 for enrollment, with monthly fees of $65 for up to 30 transactions. Each additional transaction costs only $1.50 more. With costs so low, solutions so readily available and easy to use, we can expect to see a proliferation in the use of EDI, particularly among smaller companies.

The other important trend sweeping organizations around the world is the integration of EDI with other technologies. Although EDI and bar coding have been successfully integrated and used for years, companies have begun using EDI with other EC tools such as computer telephony integration (CTI), image processing, workflow automation, smart cards, and automated ID equipment. The trend is to extend the EDI investment by integrating it with other technologies in an effort to further streamline business procedures and eliminate manual intervention as much as possible.

The implementation of EDI technology can save time and money and improve the quality of data, but it is the strategic applications of EDI that truly benefit organizations. EDI as a strategic tool can improve business procedures and can, in fact, eliminate business procedures that do not add any value. EDI brings companies closer together as they define their responsibilities to each other and create a win/win business environment.

Appendix A

The Evolution of EDI Standards

The evolution of EDI standards has followed parallel paths wherever it has occurred. Development starts when individual businesses create their own standards as a way to facilitate the exchange of business information and to improve cost-effectiveness within a particular industry, such as automobile manufacturing. Then, as more and more businesses and industries become involved with EDI, the need for all-encompassing standards for a country and then for a continent is recognized and acted upon. Finally, EDI users have seen the need for global standards, and today's efforts are focused on creating and implementing such standards.

In the course of this process, national and international standards organizations have come into being to oversee standards development. Each national, regional, and international organization has its own set of standards, a terminology to describe those standards, and procedures for implementing them. However, today, many of these organizations are working together to consolidate standards development and implementation procedures and to create one standard for the whole world.

Original EDI standards development began with several independent definition efforts. In the early 1970s, the first standards started to emerge in North America and Europe.

To be able to exchange data in a standard format, early EDI trading partners developed proprietary standards for their own transactions. For example, companies in the transportation industry began developing their own proprietary standards in the late 1960s so that each company could exchange electronic business documents with its customers and suppliers.

In the early 1970s, companies in certain industries realized they were all doing business with many of the same trading partners and recognized that it made good sense to use a common set of standards within their particular industry. Industry groups began to develop their own standards. For example, the public warehousing industry developed Warehouse Information Network Standards (WINS), and the grocery industry developed Uniform Communications Standard (UCS).

Private industries began to push standards as a means of moving data quickly and cheaply. In the 1970s, the now-defunct Transportation Data Coordinating Committee (TDCC) standards became prevalent in the United States. Simultaneously, the United Nations Guidelines on Trade Data Interchange (GTDI) standards became popular in Europe.

As these standards were maturing, several other EDI standards began to emerge. In the early 1980s, national standards evolved to serve multiple industry types within the same country. The United States adopted the American National Standards Institute (ANSI) Accredited Standards Committee (ASC) X12 standards, and the United Kingdom adopted the Trading Data Communications Standard (TRADACOMS) and the Organization for Data Exchange through Tele-Transmission in Europe (ODETTE).

ANSI is a nonprofit organization founded in 1918 to oversee the standards development process in the U.S. ASC X12 is the group ANSI chartered in 1979 to develop standards for EDI. The standards that ASC X12 developed are also named X12. The Data Interchange Standards Association (DISA) is the secretariat or administrative arm of ASC X12. DISA processes memberships, manages finances, supports and tracks the standards development work, responds to EDI user questions, and holds an annual conference and exhibit.

TRADACOMS and ODETTE evolved from the GTDI standards of the early 1970s but grew apart from their parent standards over time. These two major EDI standards are still in use in Europe. TRADACOMS, which includes more than 20 documents across a wide variety of industries, is commonly used in the United Kingdom. The Article Number Association (ANA), the association that introduced bar coding in U.K. supermarkets, developed TRADACOMS in 1982. ODETTE is the automotive standard that companies such as Ford, Rover, and Peugeot developed in the mid-1980s. Auto manufacturers and suppliers from eight European countries use ODETTE.

EDI national standards development in the U.S. followed a path similar to the U.K.'s. When ANSI ASC developed the X12 standards, they were initially aligned with TDCC standards but became incompatible with them due to differences in continuing development and maintenance. By the time the X12 "generic" standards were developed, many U.S. industry groups had established their own standards. There were major differences in the syntax and structure of the standards, and to resolve them, volunteers involved in the standards development process formed the Joint Electronic Data Interchange (JEDI) committee. As result, TDCC, UCS, WINS, and X12 standards today use a common dictionary, syntax rules, and basic structure. In addition, all industry-specific standards are considered subsets of X12 and have been aligned to work with translation software packages without much effort.

As certain standards became prevalent on a given continent, continental standards were formalized. For example, in North America, ASC X12 became the continental standard, and in Europe, EDI for Administration, Commerce, and Transport (EDIFACT) became the standard. A number of years ago, the Commite Europeen de Normalisation (CEN), a Brussels-based organization of 18 national standards bodies in Europe, endorsed EDIFACT as an international standard. Because CEN endorsement implies acceptance of a standard by all member countries, EDIFACT is the only recognized EDI standard within Western Europe.

For this reason, the ANA has moved TRADACOMS and ODETTE toward compatibility with UN/EDIFACT.

Europe's approach to EDI standards has been a little different from that of the United States. European governments have been much more active in standards development than the U.S. government. In addition, most European trade is international and is characterized by the use of various transportation modes. Accordingly, EDI standards development has required more participation from the governments of several nations, and the transportation industry has been the focus of development. By contrast, in the U.S., the early development of standards focused on the procurement cycle because most trade is domestic, and government involvement was not a priority.

To facilitate trade through the use of standard documents, such as customs documents, the U.S. and Europe took the lead in the late 1980s in developing international standards to exchange information among all nations. Today, the most widely accepted international standard is UN/EDIFACT.

After World War II, European countries, Canada, and the U.S. formed the United Nations Economic Commission for Europe (UN/ECE) to deal with general trade issues. Other countries, such as Japan, Australia, and Hong Kong, were added as observatory participants. In the 1970s, the UN/ECE was commissioned to develop international EDI standards. For more than 10 years, the United Nations Working Party on Facilitation of International Trade Procedures, an organization within the UN/ECE, has been involved in developing standards to facilitate international trade and improve its cost-effectiveness.

UN/EDIFACT is the set of international EDI standards developed under UN/ECE auspices. Many countries support UN/EDIFACT, and the International Standards Organization (ISO) has endorsed its development and cooperates in many facets of EDI and syntax development and approval with the UN under a Memorandum of Understanding (MoU) between UN/ECE, ISO, and the International Electotechnical Commission (IEC) .

ASC X12 Organization and Standards Development Process

In North America, the ANSI ASC's X12 committee is composed of volunteers from a variety of private industries as well as from government agencies. The X12 committee holds tri-annual, week-long meetings, at which subcommittees work on developing standards for a specific functional area, such as purchasing, transportation, and finance. Each subcommittee can break down its workload further by defining responsibilities for task groups. Tasks groups and subcommittees often hold interim meetings to make progress on their large workloads.

There are already many standards in existence that facilitate electronic commerce. But any individual or business can propose development of a new standard or propose changes (including additions) to existing standards. All such proposals must achieve approval by the ASC X12 subcommittee that will have long-term responsibility for the final standard (new or revised). The proposals must be technically evaluated and approved by the Technical Assessment Sub-committee and voted on by the ASC X12 membership. Any comments received during vote must be addressed by the responsible subcommittee with a concerted effort to resolve any disapprovals. At any step during these processes the original submission may be modified or even withdrawn in favor of using a different approach as ASC X12 members work with the submitter to accommodate the business requirement. The ASC X12 Procedures Review Board (PRB) will procedurally review the proposed standard or change to a standard before it goes for vote. If procedures have not been followed, the proposed new standard or change to an existing standard will not be allowed to be voted on by ASC X12 members until procedures have been followed. After the ASC X12 voting process, the subcommittee determines whether it wants the proposed standard or change to be published. If so, the PRB again procedurally reviews the proposed standard or change before allowing it to be published.

The X12 standards are revised and published several times a year. New draft standards are issued every year, with ANSI's formal approval of the standards to occur every three to four years. Draft standards are ready for use. All the revisions that result from the X12 meetings are published and distributed to ANSI ASC members who may wish to use them. During the next three or four years, as drafts are heavily used, they are corrected and enhanced. Then, when a draft looks good, ANSI formally approves it.

A six-digit number identifies each version and release of ASC X12. For example, the number 00V0RS might identify a standard. In this case, V is the version number and indicates ANSI approval. R is the release number and indicates the annual X12 issuance. S is the subrelease number and indicates the tri-annual X12 issuance.

Not all EDI users are up to the latest approved version and release of the X12 standards. Companies will continue to use the old ones for some time. In fact, most previously approved versions and releases are currently in use across the world, because issuance of X12 releases and approval of new versions by ANSI do not mean that previous versions are obsolete. Specific releases and versions are not compatible with previous or future versions and releases, so when you set up a transaction set in the translation software, you must specify the standard, version, and release used.

UN/EDIFACT ORGANIZATION AND STANDARDS DEVELOPMENT PROCESS

The development of UN/EDIFACT standards has been similar to the process for ANSI ASC standards. The UN/ECE includes several *working parties,* one of which is responsible for various tasks specifically focused on trade. For example, Working Party 4 (WP.4) of the UN/ECE facilitates international trade procedures, including EDI.

WP.4 includes two expert groups. Group of Experts 1 (GE.1) is responsible for data elements and automatic data interchange. Group of Experts 2

(GE.2) is responsible for procedures and documentation and for standardizing paper documents used internationally. Under the WP.4 structure six regional rapporteurs (expert advisors) were approved. The rapporteurs and their support groups, which include government and private sector participants, are responsible for technical development and maintenance of the standards within their region or jurisdiction. The rapporteurs and their support teams meet twice a year in a Joint Rapporteurs Team meeting to update the UN/EDIFACT standards, and report their results to GE.1 for approval. The rapporteur regions include Pan America, Western Europe, Eastern Europe, Asia, Australia/New Zealand, and Africa.

According to the jurisdictional principle, participation was open to all countries within the defined jurisdiction but had to be through a structure that included at least two countries. Use of the rapporteur system allowed UN/EDIFACT to be developed quickly and to grow in areas outside of the member states where countries on their own would not have been able to develop EDI.

The UN/EDIFACT Standards Development Process

UN/EDIFACT transaction sets are called *messages*. Messages considered suitable for implementation are known as United Nations Standard Messages (UNSM). Messages in Development (MiD) are not included in published directories but are published by the UN as an official document for information only.

Under the Rapporteur's regional structure, the Pan American EDIFACT Board (PAEB) has been the focal point for transmission of North and South American Data Maintenance Requests to the UN/ECE and other participating regions.

The CEFACT

Until March of 1997, the UN/ECE WP.4 was responsible for the registration and maintenance of UNSMs and other supporting material. Following a two-year re-engineering process, a more streamlined structure was formed, known as The Centre for the Facilitation of Procedures and Practices for Administration, Commerce and Trade (CEFACT). At this time, the WP.4 was dissolved.

The CEFACT is planning a migration to move the technical work from the concept of UN/EDIFACT Rapporteur teams to empowered technical bodies (working groups) under CEFACT. This allows the separation of technical development from policy making and will convey a lot more power to the technical bodies. Technical decisions can be made and implemented by the bodies who will report their activities to the CEFACT rather than submitting recommendations for approval.

CEFACT provides a framework for flexibility by allowing a more open environment. Within the empowered technical bodies, participants are considered experts in their own right and not representatives for a country or region. This framework allows for an unlimited number of experts. It is expected that

CEFACT technical groups will be a combination of experts from national, regional, and international organizations.

Because the CEFACT member organizations can participate on a national basis or by cooperating with other member nations in retaining a regional structure, the U.S. has elected to participate through its national EDI standards body, the ANSI ASC X12 committee. The CEFACT Head of Delegation for the U.S. has granted ASC X12 non-exclusive authority to appoint U.S. experts who will participate in several of the newly formed working groups. The Pan American EDIFACT Board disbanded in April 1998, and X12 will assume responsibility for the necessary functions of UN/EDIFACT development.

The newly formed group, which will focus on the development of UN/EDIFACT standards, is known as the UN/EDIFACT Working Group (EWG). The purpose of the EWG is to:

- Develop and maintain UN/EDIFACT
- Provide the tools and administrative support required for UN/EDIFACT development
- Develop and maintain guidelines and proposals that support harmonized UN/EDIFACT implementations
- Promote the global use of UN/EDIFACT

Appendix B

Year 2000 Considerations

Reprinted with permission from NEWS/400, Issue no. 212, March 1998.

ISSUES FOR E-COMMERCE

Many organizations have focused their Year 2000 (Y2K) efforts around internal applications but haven't taken external data as seriously as they should. However, even if your systems are Year 2000 compliant, you can't rely on your trading partners to have the same readiness. You have no control over when, how, or *whether* your trading partners will address Y2K issues — making total compliance nearly impossible.

Your company may receive EC data via a variety of gateways and formats. It's important to consider and address the potential for noncompliant dates in all of these. Although EDI is a major component of your concern, you must resolve issues with other data sources, such as the Web, too.

Web-transmitted data is usually integrated with back-end applications, so you should carefully consider the integration programs, as well as the Web-based form that may be capturing the information. It may be fine to use the date on which a user accesses the Web site as the default century for data such as order-entry date. But the century for other data, such as expected shipment date, delivery date, or cancel-by date, shouldn't simply be defaulted. To make your Web form easier to use, you can make a series of assumptions, display a suggested century value to the user, and ask for verification. Once date data is entered, your integration and application programs must do further evaluation and validation. If you use a vendor-developed Web product, ask the vendor what migration plans it has for accommodating future Y2K data and converting existing systems.

EDI compliance is a bit more complex because we use standards defined by various organizations to determine how transaction data is exchanged. The standards have been moving toward total compliance for some time. In X12 versions above 3010, the DTM segment allows for the century as an optional element. Unfortunately, an optional century means that trading partners can easily ignore this element. X12 version 4010, published in December 1997, is fully compliant, allowing for an eight-digit date field. However, the existence of this version doesn't imply that older standards versions will change to add the century.

Another factor to keep in mind is that EDI translation software vendors sometimes take as long as six months to bring up the latest release of standards, leaving version 4010 to be unavailable until mid-1998 in many cases.

We shouldn't expect everyone to immediately upgrade to the new Year 2000–compliant version, so it's questionable how soon we can really rely on the standards themselves to monitor and enforce the century designator.

WHAT TO DO

One important resource that can help you address your Year 2000 situation is your translation software vendor. You should familiarize yourself with the vendor's procedures and policies regarding this issue. Ask when the translation software will support X12 version 4010. Find out whether the vendor provides routines for converting six-digit date fields to eight-digit fields. In addition, make your own assessment of alternatives. Check to see whether your translator allows for sufficient logic processing to calculate the century. Find out whether the reports the translator provides (e.g., in the communications log) are mis-sorted. This information will let you plan around your translator's inadequacies and provide feedback to the vendor for future software revisions and upgrades.

Two other places where dates can be made to comply are the application software and the EDI interface software. Most Year 2000 projects adequately address the changes necessary to application software. You should make sure your interface software is modified or enhanced as well. This could mean that you have to append a century field to the interface files and start to capture that data now. You can make this change independently of any application file and translator changes. Keep in mind that application or interface software that has been converted for the year 2000 may have problems if it receives non-compliant data through EDI.

It's absolutely critical to treat EDI and Year 2000 issues as something that must be resolved with trading partners. Plan *together* to ensure a consistent approach within a common timetable. In addition to your translation software vendor, you should contact your current trading partners, VANs, and ISPs to get an idea of their plans and time frames for specific activities. Prepare a proposal to resolve the issues for each transaction set and each trading partner, and be sure to send this document to your trading partners and refine it to meet *their* goals and timetables. Once you and your trading partners and vendors have coordinated activities, you can prepare an internal schedule for EDI translation and interface software upgrades, creating new maps, converting existing maps, and testing with the VANs or ISPs or via your direct communications links.

The key considerations for your EDI environment and Year 2000 compliance include the following:

- Assume 60 percent noncompliance among your trading partners in the year 2000; planning for this supposition will ensure you are well prepared.

- Remember that standards versions with some level compliance do not require the century field as a mandatory field.

- Synchronize your migration plan with your trading partners (each organization will have a different time frame that may impact your schedule).

- Know that you may need to convert some maps, while modifications to other maps will suffice.

- Be aware that your translation software vendor may provide migration tools for compliance.

- Remember that if you receive forecast data (e.g., the forecast transactions sent to automotive suppliers one year in advance), your deadline for being Year 2000 compliant may be January 1999 or sooner.

If your EDI system is not yet fully compliant, consider implementing the steps in the checklist on page 194.

Remember that even if your systems are 100 percent compliant, you cannot rely on external data to be the same. You should seriously consider amending existing trading partner agreements to address noncompliance liabilities. If you don't have a trading partner agreement in place, consider creating some type of written agreement to address Y2K issues.

The consequences of not being Year 2000 compliant can be severe for an EC environment. The absence of accurate date information can impact shipment and delivery schedules, payment orders (funds transfers), and archival of data for audit and control purposes. Unresolved Year 2000 issues can lead to critical problems or delays in business activity and ultimately cost your company a lot of time and money. Plan now to protect your customers and your business.

	EDI Checklist for the Year 2000
✔	**Action**
	Assign responsibility to an IT resource.
	Develop a plan for identifying and dealing with noncompliant trading partners.
	Conduct a trading partner survey.
	Identify all EDI systems throughout your company.
	Build an inventory of application interface programs.
	Develop an inventory of all transaction sets, trading partners using each, and target dates.
	Identify all maps actively traded, including their version and release.
	Collect all trading partner agreements.
	Evaluate the impact of Year 2000 on your application interface programs and files.
	Conduct analysis and validation with VANs and ISPs.
	Develop a joint plan with each trading partner. The joint plan includes an implementation plan, estimates and a trading partner–specific "cookbook" on how and when any Year 2000 issues will be resolved. The implementation Plan should estimate timetables and budget/resource requirements.
	Develop an implementation plan and estimates.
	Identify resource requirements.
	Develop a trading partner–specific "cookbook" on how and when the issue will be resolved.
	Send a copy of the cookbook to each trading partner and obtain agreement.
	Design and develop or modify maps and programs for compliance.
	Migrate trading partners to the new maps.

Appendix C

EC Information Sources

ABCD Microcomputer Industry Association
(703) 780-9839

Accredited Standards Committee X12 (ASC X12)
(703) 548-7005

ACXIOM (Direct Marketing)
(501) 336-1160

Advertising Industry Electronic Data
Interchange Group (AIEDIG)
(212) 664-6040

Aerospace Industry Association
(202) 371-8400

Air Conditioning & Refrigeration Institute (ARI)
(703) 524-8800

Air Conditioning & Refrigeration Wholesalers
(ARW)
(561) 338-3495

Air Distribution Institute (ADI)
(708) 449-2933

Air Transport Association of America
(202) 626-4128

Alcohol Beverage Industry (ABI) EDI Group
c/o National Alcohol Beverage Control
Association (NABCA)
(703) 578-4200

Alliance for Telecom Industry Solutions (ATS)
(202) 628-6380

The Aluminum Association
(202) 862-5100

American Apparel Contractors Association
(AACA)
(404) 843-3171

American Apparel Manufacturers Association
(AAMA)
(800) 520-2262

American Association of Collegiate Registrars
& Admissions Officers (AACRAO)
(202) 293-9161

American Association of Port Authorities
(703) 684-5700

American Bankers Association (ABA)
(202) 663-5000

American Bar Association (ABA)
(312) 988-5000

American Crop Protection Association
(202) 296-1585

American Electronics Association (AEA)
(408) 987-4200

American Forest & Paper Association
(202) 463-2700

American Furniture Manufacturers Association
(AFMA)
(910) 884-5000

American Garment Council (AGC)
(404) 843-3171

American Gas Association (AGA)
(703) 841-8400

American Hardware Manufacturers Association
(847) 605-1025

American Health Information Management
Association (AHIMA)
(312) 787-2672

American Iron & Steel Institute
(202) 452-7100

American Medical Informatics Association (AMIA)
(301) 657-1291

American National Standards Institute (ANSI)
(212) 642-4900

American Petroleum Institute (API)
(202) 682-8517

American Production & Inventory Control
Society (APICS)
(800) 444-2742

American Society for Industrial Security (ASIS)
(703) 522-5800

American Supply Association (ASA)
(215) 822-6880

American Supply & Machinery Manufacturers
Association, Inc. (ASMMA)
(216) 241-7333

American Textile Manufacturers Institute (ATM)
(202) 862-0500

American Trucking Association/Management
Systems Council (ATA/MSC)
(703) 838-1721

American Warehouse Association (AWA)
(847) 292-1891

American Wood Council
(202) 463-2700

Association for EC Professionals Int'l (AECPI)
(813) 835-0870

Association for Electronic HC Transactions
(AEHCT)
(202) 244-6450

Association for Information Technology
Professionals (AITP)
(847) 825-8124

Association for Information & Imaging
Management (AIIM)
(301) 587-8202

Association of American Railroads (AAR)
(202) 639-5544

Association of Home Appliance Manufacturers
(312) 984-5800

Association of Records Managers &
Administrators Int'l (ARMA)
(913) 341-3808

Automated Imaging Association
(313) 994-6088 x17

Automatic ID Manufacturers USA (AIM USA)
(412) 963-8588

Automotive Industries Association (AIA)
(215) 822-6880

Automotive Industry Action Group (AIAG)
(248) 358-9799

Book Industry Study Group
(212) 929-1393

Business Products Industry Association (BPIA)
(800) 542-6672

Chemical Industry Data eXchange, Inc (CIDX)
(609) 393-7088

Collision Industry EC Association
(313) 699-0097

Computing Technology Industry Association
(COMPTIA)
(703) 780-9899

Construction Industry Action Group (CIAG)
(713) 676-3011

Container EDI Council (CEDIC)
(415) 398-2120

Copper & Brass Fabricators Council, Inc.
(202) 833-8575

Council of Chief State School Officers (CCSSO)
(202) 336-7054

Council for Electronic Rev Communication
Advancement (CERCA)
(703) 684-0128

Council of Fleet Specialists (CFS)
(816) 421-2600

Council of Logistics Management
(630) 574-0985

Crafted with Pride in USA Council Inc.
(212) 819-4397

Data Interchange Standards Association (DISA)
(703) 548-7005

DOD Logmars Program
(717) 895-7146

Ductile Iron Pipe Research Association (DIPRA)
(215) 822-6880

Electronic Commerce Council of Canada
(416) 510-8039 x268

EDI Coalition of Associations EDICA
(410) 263-1014

EDI for Administration, Commerce, and
Transport (EDIFACT)
(703) 548-7005

Electronic Commerce Association
(613) 592-9141

Electronic Commerce Center
(860) 612-0590

Electronic Commerce World Institute
(514) 288-6355

Electronic Funds Transfer Association (EFTA)
(703) 435-9800

Electronic Industries Association (EIA)
(703) 907-7500

Electronic Messaging Association (EMA)
(703) 524-5550

Electronics Industry Data Exchange
Association (EIDX)
(909) 781-5216

Environment and Safety Data Exchange (ESDX)
(415) 324-4424

Environmental Protection Agency (EPA)
(202) 360-2706

Federation of Tax Administrators (FTA)
(202) 624-5894

Fluid Power Distributors Association
(609) 424-8998

Food Distributors Int'l (formerly National
American Wholesale Grocers Association)
(703) 532-9400

Food Marketing Institute (FMI)
(202) 452-8444

Footwear Industries of American (FIA)
(202) 336-5449

Freddie Mac (Federal Home Loan Mortgage
Corporation)
(703) 760-2000

Gas Appliance Manufacturers Association
(GAMA)
(215) 822-6880

Gas Industry Standards Board (GISB)
(713) 757-4175

Graphic Communications Association (GCA)
(703) 519-8173

Grocery Manufacturers of America Inc. (GMA)
(202) 337-9400

Health Industry Business Communications
Council (HIBCC)
(602) 381-1091

Health Industry Distributors Association (HIDA)
(703) 549-4432

Health Industry Manufacturers Association
(202) 783-8700

Healthcare EDI Coalition
(501) 661-9408

Home Infusion EDI Coalition (HIEC)
(602) 381-1092

IBFI-Int'l Association for Document &
Information Management Solutions
(703) 841-9191

Industrial Safety Equipment Association
(703) 525-1695

Information Systems Security Association Inc.
(ISSA)
(847) 657-6746

Information Technology Industry Council (ITIC)
(202) 737-8888

Integrated Business Communications Alliance
(IBCA) (formerly Industry Bar Code Alliance)
(215) 822-6880

International Food Manufacturers Association
(IFMA)
(312) 540-4400

International Food Service Distributors
Association (FDI)
(703) 532-9400

International Sanitary Supply Association (ISSA)
(215) 822-6880

International Society of Logistics (SOLE)
(301) 459-8446

International Standards Organization (ISO)
(703) 548-7005

Manufacturing Execution Systems Association
International (MESA)
(412) 781-9511

Miami-Dade Community College (Education)
(305) 237-2102

Mortgage Bankers Association of America (MBAA)
(202) 861-6500

Motor & Equipment Manufacturers Association (MEMA)
(919) 549-4800

National Association General Merchandise Representatives (NAGMR)
(312) 644-6610

National Association of Aluminum Distributors
(215) 564-3484

National Association of Credit Management (NACM)
(410) 740-5560

National Association of Electrical Distributors (NAED)
(203) 761-4900 X4905

National Association of Floor Covering Distributors
(312) 644-6610

National Association of Manufacturers (NAM)
(202) 637-3186

National Association of Purchasing Management (NAPM)
(602) 752-6276

National Association of Retail Dealers of America
(303) 758-7796

National Association of Sign Supply Distributors
(215) 822-6880

National Association of Sporting Goods Wholesalers (NASGW)
(312) 565-0233

National Automated Clearing House Association (NACHA)
(703) 834-2350

National Computer Security Association (NCSA)
(717) 241-3410

National Customs Brokers & Forwarders Association (NCBFAA)
(212) 432-0050

National Electrical Manufacturers Association (NEMA)
(703) 841-3292

National Electronics Distributors Association (NEDA)
(312) 558-9114

National Energy Services Association (NESA) (formerly NGTA-National Gas Transportation Association)
(713) 939-9200

National Fluid Power Association (NFPA)
(215) 822-6880

National Industrial Transportation League (NITL)
(703) 524-5011

National Institute of Standards & Technology (NIST)
(301) 975-3634

National Insulation Association (NIA)
(215) 822-6880

National Mining Association
(202) 463-2603

National Paper Trade Association (NPTA)
(516) 829-3070

National Retail Federation (NRF)
(202) 783-7971

National Sporting Goods Association (NSGA)
(847) 439-4000

National Welding Supply Association (NWSA)
(215) 564-3484

National Wholesale Druggist Association (NWDA)
(703) 787-0000

New England ACH Association (NEACH)
617-338-6370

North American Graphic Arts Suppliers Association (NAGASA)
(202) 328-8441

North American Heating Refrigeration & AC Wholesalers (NHRAW)
(614) 488-1835

North American Logistics Association (NALA)
(847) 292-1891

Ohio University Center for Auto ID
(614) 593-1452

Optical Industry Association (OMA)
(904) 247-9286

Optical Product Code Council (OPCC)
(703) 237-8433

Pan American EDIFACT Board (PAEB)
(703) 548-7005

Petroleum Equipment Institute (PEI)
(918) 494-9696

Petroleum Industry Data Exchange (PIDX)
(818) 505-2284

Pharmaceutical Manufacturers Association
(PharMA)
(202) 835-3400

Plumbing Manufacturers Institute (PMI)
(630) 858-9172

Power Transmission Distributors Association
(PTDA)
(847) 825-2000

Product Code Council of Canada (PCCC)
(416) 510-8039

Rail Industry Group of National Association of
Purchasing Management (NAPM)
(913) 295-5946

RAPID Inc.-Responsible Agricultural Product &
Information Distribution
(202) 293-1234

Recording Industry Association of America
(RIAA)
(202) 775-0101

Serial Industry Systems Advisory Committee
(212) 929-1393

Smart Card Forum
(703) 610-9023

Society of Manufacturing Engineers (SME)
(313) 271-1500

Specialty Steel of the US
(202) 342-8400

Specialty Tools & Fasteners Distributors
Association (STAFDA)
(215) 822-6880

Telecommunications Industry Forum (TCIF)
(202) 434-8842

Textile Apparel Linkage Council
(214) 631-8326

Textile, Apparel, Sundries and Findings
Linkage Council
(703) 524-1864

Textile Care Allied Trades Association (TCATA)
(215) 822-6880

Treasury Management Association (TMA)
(301) 907-2862

Treasury Management Association of Canada
(416) 367-8501

Uniform Code Council (UCG)
(937) 435-3870

Uniform Communication Standard (UCS)
(937) 435-3870

Utility Industry Group (UIG)
(404) 526-2456

Voluntary Inter-Industry Commerce Standards
Committee (VICS)
(202) 626-8171

Warehouse Industry Standard (WINS)
(937) 435-3870

Warehousing Education & Research Council
(630) 990-0001

Washington School Information Processing
Center (WSIPC) (Educational Institution)
(425) 349-3870

Workgroup for EDI (WEDI)
(703) 391-2716

Xplor International
(310) 373-3633

EDI Publication Information

Buyers Guide AIAG2
Automotive Industry Action Group
6200 Lahser Road Ste 200
Southfield, MI 48034
(248) 358-3570
Annual publication
Price $20

Electronic Commerce World
Electronic Commerce:
Management and Technology Integration
EC World, Inc.
2021 Coolidge Street
Hollywood, FL 33020-2400
(305) 925-5900
ecworld@ix.netcom.com
Monthly publication
Annual subscription $45

EDI Yellow Pages
Comprehensive list of national EDI users and vendors.
EDI, Spread the Word!
13805 Wooded Creek Dr. Ste 100
Dallas, TX 75234
(972) 243-3456
Annual publication
Price $99

Who's Who of EDI
EDI, Spread the Word!
13805 Wooded Creek Dr. Ste 100
Dallas, TX 75234
(972) 243-3456
Annual publication
Price $227 (includes EDI Yellow Pages)

EDI Yellow Pages International: Business Partner Directory
Directory of 45,000 EDI vendors and companies doing EDI, listed by industry.
EDI, Spread the Word!
13805 Wooded Creek Dr. Ste 100
Dallas, TX 75234
(972) 243-3456
Annual publication
Price $99

E-COMM
A "how to" approach for corporate and technical managers.
14407 Big Basin Way
Saratoga, CA 95070
(408) 867-6300
http://www.ecmedica.com
Monthly publication
Price $40

EDI Forum
PO Box 710
Oak Park, IL 60303
Quarterly publication
Price $250

EDI Insider
Material for EC, EDI, and the healthcare industry.
Washington Publishing Company
806 W. Diamond Ave. Ste 400
Gaithersburg, MD 20878
(800) 972-4334
Bimonthly publication
Annual subscription $495

Phillips Business Information
Client Services
1201 Seven Locks Road, Ste 300
Potomac, MD 20854
(800) 777-5006
clientservices.pbi@phillips.com

Bank Automation News
News of banking and electronic commerce.
Biweekly publication/25 issues
Annual subscription $595

Card News
Coverage of the transaction card market, including card associations, bank and non-bank issuers, acquirers, and card vendors. Covers security issues, new card programs, co-branding and other marketing strategies, and online Internet application.
Biweekly publication/25 issues
Annual subscription $695

Corporate EFT Report

Covers corporate electronic funds transfer operations; reviews financial EDI and EFT, new payment technologies, federal regulations and standards, and ACH.
Biweekly publication/25 issues
Annual subscription $595

Credit Risk Management Report

Offers effective strategies for consumer credit programs, trends and developments in risk management, legislation, risk-related Internet issues that are affecting all areas of collections, and credit operations. Reviews strategic analyses of retail, bank card, installment, and legal credit issues, legal and legislative updates, and online services. Directed toward managers and executives in the consumer lending market.
Biweekly publication/25 issues
Annual subscription $595

CTI

Business advisory focusing solely on the issues, topics, and happenings in computer telephony. Includes in-depth market analysis, financial snapshots of industry players, product comparisons, marketplace trends, and round table discussions with industry leaders.
Biweekly publication/25 issues
Annual subscription $497

Document Imaging Report

Designed to bring you updates, competitive deployment strategies, the latest alliances, and new products in today's imaging marketplace; offers valid solutions to installing or upgrading imaging systems, as well as recognizing workflow issues.
Biweekly publication/25 issues
Annual subscription $597

EDI News

Covers concise coverage and valuable analysis of EDI adoption and implementation issues, the latest developments and trends in consumer EDI, Internet vs. VANs, EDIFACT, X12 and authentication/certification. Provides complete details on product technology, standards development, deployment strategies, and new products.
Biweekly publication/25 issues
Annual subscription $597

EFT Report

Covers in-depth analyses of the electronic payments industry. The inside story on how new retail delivery solutions provide convenience and access to consumers while opening new markets to the industry. A good source of the latest news about ATMs, security, privacy, EBT, POS, and smart cards.
Biweekly publication/25 issues
Annual subscription $595

Electronic Commerce News

Offers key suggestions for developing strategic EC business plans. Brings you the news and analysis of EC technologies and components so you'll know what tools work. Reviews how to integrate EC technologies into the marketing, sales, distribution, and purchasing process.
Weekly publication/50 issues
Annual subscription $697

Electronic Messaging News

Discusses expert industry analyses, as well as updates on new messaging hardware and software. Reviews groupware, EC, and workflow applications and how they can impact messaging.
Biweekly publication/25 issues
Annual subscription $597

Financial Services Report

Offers comprehensive reporting on new policies for credit scoring, innovative applications of platform technology, solutions in the back office that deliver high-value transactions to the front office, intelligence on Federal Reserve activities, bank investment opportunities, marketing strategies, mergers and acquisitions, and new technologies.
Biweekly publication/25 issues
Annual subscription $895

Item Processing Report

Covers the check and remittance processing marketplace, discussing new technologies and trends in image processing, OCR, check truncation, electronic check presentment, and more. Publishes tips and techniques from industry experts, strategic intelligence for real-world applications, and the problems incurred when selecting, using, or upgrading systems.
Biweekly publication/25 issues
Annual subscription $595

Optical Memory News
A source of information about the optical storage industry; covers the newest developments in mass storage applications, presented in an easy-to-follow, concise format, and delivers a myriad of network opportunities, product reviews, and trend analyses.
Biweekly publication/25 issues
Annual subscription $597

Retail Delivery Systems News
For the retail banking executive responsible for strategic direction; provides solutions to problems involving new products, technologies, and applications. Topics include smart cards, Internet banking, home banking, market research, and industry news.
Biweekly publication/25 issues
Annual subscription $595

Voice Technology & Services News
Covers the $3.5 billion voice processing industry, reviewing the players and business opportunities. Includes regular updates on applications, emerging technologies, standards development, marketing trends, vendor profiles, case studies, and more.
Biweekly publication/25 issues
Annual subscription $597

Uniform Code Council, Inc.
8163 Old Yankee Street, Ste J
Dayton, OH 45458
(937) 435-3870
http://www.uc-council.org

The following four directories are free for members and $50.00 for non-members:

Uniform Code Council Network Providers Directory
Details EDI network providers, including services and the communication protocols and speeds they support.

Uniform Code Council Software Providers Directory
Details EDI software suppliers with a brief synopsis of their services and of the EDI standards they support and the hardware for which it has been written.

EDI Software Directory
Directory of EDI software services and vendors

Network Providers Directories
Directory of EDI third-party network providers

American Bar Association
750 N. Lake Shore Drive
Chicago, IL 60611
(312) 988-5522
info@abanet.org

Commercial Use of EDI
Annual Publication
Price $40

Digital Signature Guidelines
The Guidelines explain digital signature technology in simple terms, examining how this technology can be applied as a computer-based alternative to traditional signatures; are designed to assist anyone involved in online transactions that need to be secure and authentically signed.
Price $34.95

Model Electronic Payments and Commentary (for Domestic Credit Transfers)
Model agreement with commentary and introduction for lawyers and business persons involved with electronic payments.
Price $9.95

Model Trading Partner Agreement and Commentary
Model agreement to be used as a draft in the custom development of trading partner agreements.
Price $39.95

Glossary

AIAG — Automotive Industry Action Group. This group defines the automotive EDI standards by the same name.

AIR — Air freight standards.

ANA — Article Number Association; the association that introduced bar coding in U.K. supermarkets and developed TRADACOMS.

ANSI — American National Standards Institute. Parent organization of ASC X12. The group is the recognized coordinator and clearing house for information on U.S., and in some cases Canadian, national standards. Also serves as the North American representative to ISO (International Standards Organization).

ASC — Accredited Standards Committee of ANSI; develops and maintains U.S. generic standards (X12) for Electronic Data Interchange.

Authentication — A method for ensuring that the sender and receiver of electronic messages are valid and authorized. Authentication is a technique that assigns a value to each electronic node in a transmission. The receiver of the document must verify the authentication code to gain access to the data.

Automated Data Capture — Includes bar coding and radio frequency devices; used to automatically capture and use information to improve the timeliness and quality of data and to provide users with the ability to manage and track transactions.

Bandwidth — The capacity of a communications medium for carrying data.

CEFACT — Centre for the Facilitation of Procedures and Practices for Administration, Commerce, and Trade. A group formed to plan a migration to move the technical work from the concept of UN/EDIFACT Rapporteur teams to empowered technical bodies (working groups) under CEFACT.

CEN — Commite Europeen de Normalisation; a Brussels-based organization of 18 national standards bodies in Europe.

Code — Numeric or alphanumeric representations of text for exchanging commonly used information. Codes are like building blocks that create transaction sets or messages. Some elements in a transaction set require the use of valid codes. For example, valid codes to identify sender and receiver IDs and DUNS (Dun and Bradstreet) number, Federal tax ID number, and telephone number.

COLD — Computer output to laser disc; a way to store images and text on a laser disc. COLD storage and retrieval of data is extremely efficient. Used for image-based documents and other things including EDI.

Collaborative Technologies — A set of tools used to allow intra- and inter-organizational exchange and disbursement of key business information. E-mail can be viewed as a collaborative tool.

Communications Protocol — The method by which two computers coordinate their communications. Bisynchronous and MNP are two examples.

Compliance Monitoring — A check done by the VAN/third party network or the translation software to ensure the data being exchanged is in the correct format for the standard being used.

Composite Element — Using one element, with sub-element breakdown to define two closely related data fields. For example, rather than use two elements to define sender ID and ID type, you use one element and break it down into two subelements of sender ID and ID type.

Control Segments — Segments containing identifying characteristics for each part of a transmission (i.e., control headers/trailers, functional group headers/trailers, transaction set headers/trailers, etc.).

Control Structure — The beginning and ending (header and trailer) segments for entities in electronic data interchange.

CTI — Computer telephony integration; use of telephone and networks to automatically integrate data captured via the telephone into the computer applications.

CRP — Continuous replenishment program; a business strategy that allows the supplier to replace stock at its customer's locations (stores or distribution centers) based on predefined safety stock levels. CRP means the customer does not place purchase orders with the customer.

Data Element Dictionary — A dictionary of all data elements used by a standard format. The dictionary describes each element of a segment. Elements may be used in more than one segment. Segments may be used in more than one transaction set or more than one industry.

Data Mirroring — Copying or mirroring data from a main or host computer to a backup machine.

Data Segment — See *Segment.*

Data Segment Sequence — The sequence of data segments in a document or message. It may occur in any of the following three areas of the message:

- Heading Area: A data segment occurring in this area refers to the entire message.

- Detail Area: A data segment occurring in this area refers to the detail information only and will override any similar specification in the header area.

- Summary Area: Only segments containing total or control information may occur in the summary area, e.g., invoice total, overall discount. A specific data segment type may occur in more than one area.

Document — A transaction set or message.

Document Turnaround — A turnaround document is one that is sent to confirm or acknowledge the detail that a trading partner may have sent via a transaction set. The turnaround document is set up to be generated automatically.

DSD — Direct store delivery; a business operation where the supplier delivers the products directly to its customer's retail stores rather than to their distribution center. DSD is generally used for products that have a limited shelf life (milk, bread).

DSTU — Draft Standard for Trial Use; a pre-release of standards prior to ANSI approval and is released for publication and use.

EC — Electronic commerce; use of integrated technologies to streamline external business procedures in order to facilitate trade. EC technologies include EDI, Internet, Electronic Document Management, Smart Cards, Automated Data Capture, among others.

ECR — Efficient consumer response; a business strategy adopted by the grocery industry. QR means trading partners use technology to effectively managed the flow of business data in an effort to have the right product at the right time and for the right price.

ECS — Electronic customer support is the ability to provide online electronic support to customer inquiries.

EDIA — See *TDCC.*

EFT — Electronic funds transfer; the bank-to-bank exchange of standard EDI transaction sets for transferring funds.

EHCR — Efficient healthcare consumer response; a business strategy adopted by the healthcare industry. QR means trading partners use technology to effectively managed the flow of business data in an effort to have the right product and services at the right time and for the right price.

EDI — Electronic data interchange; the computer-to-computer communication of business documents using standard data formats. Standard formats ensure that different companies can exchange business data without modifying their computer systems. EFT (electronic funds transfer) is the financial equivalent of EDI.

EDIFACT — EDI for Administration, Commerce and Transport; a set of standards designed for international EDI. UN/EDIFACT messages are developed under the auspices of Working Party 4, an international trade facilitation committee of the United Nations Economic Commission for Europe.

EDI Standard/Format — A format for transmitting business documents between business entities in a non-proprietary environment. Various groups have developed standards, such as ANSI and TDDC.

E-Form — Electronic form.

Electronic Commerce — See *EC.*

Electronic Document Management (EDM) — The capture, storage, and retrieval of electronic images of documents.

Electronic Envelope — An electronic envelope consists of codes that mark the boundaries of electronic documents. The electronic envelope contains the document. To transmit EDI transaction sets to trading partners, you must enclose the transaction sets in electronic envelopes.

Electronic Mailbox — A repository of information belonging to a single user. The mailbox makes it unnecessary for the user to provide dedicated hardware for the purpose of awaiting incoming calls. It also provides consolidation of EDI transactions, allowing the user to send to multiple receivers in a single session.

Electronic Signature — See *Authentication.*

Element — One of more characters that represent numeric or alphanumeric fields of data. A related group of elements makes up a segment.

Element Separator — A special character used to separate elements in a segment. The suggested character is a special control character called an RS or record separator.

Encryption — The scrambling of data at each end of a transmission to prevent in-transit readability. Data is encrypted at the sending end and decrypted on the receiving end through use of a predetermined algorithm and unique key. Encryption is done for information privacy and security.

ERS — Evaluated receipt settlement; a business strategy that allows the customer to pay its supplier based on matching the material received with the advance ship notice. ERS means that the supplier does not send its customer an invoice.

Extranet — A Web-based system with limited, authorized access to trading partners.

Financial EDI — The exchange of financial EDI transaction sets corporate to corporate, but not corporate to bank. Typical transactions include lockbox and remittance advice.

Flat File — A fixed field, fixed record-length application data file.

Front-End Processor — A communications computer associated with a host computer. It can perform line control, message handling, code conversion, and functions such as control of special-purpose terminals.

FTP — File transfer protocol; a way to update (delete, rename, move, and copy) files at a server. People who create Web pages use FTP to get their files to the server where they will be accessed.

Functional Acknowledgment — The electronic acknowledgment to indicate the results of transmission of electronic documents.

Functional Group — A group of like documents (e.g., a group of purchase orders).

Gateway — The interconnection between VANs, allowing transmission of electronic documents across multiple VANs.

GEIS — GE Information Services.

Generic Mapping — Generic mapping requires a study of multiple maps before you can design a single generic transaction set. Generic mapping means you try to fit multiple trading partners' requirements for a transaction set into one.

GTDI — The United Nations GTDI (Guidelines on Trade Data Interchange) standards became popular in Europe in the 1970s.

GUI — Graphical user interface.

Hardware — The physical equipment (computers, modems, printers) used in data processing.

Header — The segment that indicates the start of an entity that is to be transmitted. Headers are control structures.

Header Area — The Transaction Set Header Area contains preliminary information that pertains to the entire document, such as the date, company name, address, P.O. number, terms, etc.

HEDIC — Healthcare EDI Corporation; a non-profit organization that was formed in 1991 to provide EDI education and to assist in the roll-out of EDI among hospitals and their suppliers.

HIN — Health Industry Number; a unique number used to identify all healthcare entities.

HTTP — Hypertext Transfer Protocol; the set of rules for exchanging files (text, graphic images, sound, video, and other multimedia files) on the World Wide Web.

Hub — Usually a large corporations who established an EDI program and expects its trading partners or spokes to use it.

ICR — Intelligent character recognition; an image technology that reads and captures an image of handwritten text. ICR works by extracting key features of a character and comparing them with its dictionary of features, further enhanced with some rules of grammar and language.

Imaging — The creation, storage, and retrieval of electronic copies of paper documents.

Interface Software — Also referred to as integration software, interface software is software that is used to integrate EDI data with the applications.

Interchange — The exchange of information between one company and another. A set of documents sent from one sender to one receiver at one time.

Interchange Control — A layer around an electronic envelope that contains information regarding the control numbers, sender and receiver IDs, and other relevant information.

Interconnection — The ability of VANs to connect to one another for EDI mail exchange.

Interface — The connection between items of equipment and/or software.

Interface Software — User application software that extracts data from business application files and makes it available to the translation software.

Internet — A public network of networks connected around the world using TCP/IP communications protocols. The Internet was born over 20 years ago by the department of defense, but is today used by all. It is not owned or managed by anyone.

Intranet — An internal implementation of Internet technologies, using standard Web browsers, Web servers, and TCP/IP communications. Generally used for publishing internal documents.

ISO — International Standards Organization; endorses the development of international standards, including UN/EDIFACT.

ISP — Internet service provider.

IT — Information technology.

JIT — Just in time manufacturing; a business strategy adopted by the manufacturing industry. JIT means trading partners use technology to effectively managed the flow of business data in an effort to manufacture the right product at the right time and for the right price.

Key Management — A security technique that allows only specific individuals with a physical key to access the data and calculate the authentication code.

Loop — A repetition of a segment or a group of segments.

MAC — Message authentication coding; a cryptographically derived hash total used to verify the authorized sender to the authorized receiver and protect the integrity of the data.

Mailbag — An EDI term meaning an electronic manila envelope that contains batches of EDI mail.

Mailbox — See *Electronic Mailbox*.

Mailslot — A subset of a mailbox. An electronic mailbox may contain numerous mailslots that can be set up to capture various trading partners or transaction sets.

Mapping — The process of converting a proprietary file to standard and vice versa.

Message — The collection of data, organized in segments, exchanged to convey meaning between partners engaged in EDI, also called document or transaction.

Message Authentication Coding — See *MAC.*

MICR — Magnetic ink character recognition; a type of printed writing that can be read by special imaging products.

MIME — Multi-purpose Internet Mail Extension; a standard envelope protocol that carries e-mail messages.

MOTOR — Trucking industry freight standards.

OCEAN — Ocean freight standards.

OCM — Organizational change management; a business strategy to help educate and prepare and organization for procedural and cultural changes that are about to happen.

OCR — Optical character recognition; an image technology that reads and captures an image of printed text. OCR works by matching image patterns with a dictionary of character templates. Once a close match is made, the scanner creates the ASCII equivalent of the character and stores it.

ODETTE — Organization for Data Exchange through Tele-Transmission in Europe; French standards that were defined for EDI exchange, primarily used in the automotive industry.

OEM — Original equipment manufacturer.

Paper-clipping — The ability to send non-standard data, such as a CAD/CAM drawing or spreadsheets, with a standard transaction set. You can paper-clip the two and send them together.

PAEB — The Pan American EDIFACT board; a standing task group of ASC that represents the position of the Pan American area on the UN/EDIFACT standards.

Private Key — In authentication, using a private key, the sender and receiver must have the same key, but its use is private only to those parties. The length of the private key determines its level of security.

Private Network — A communications network set up using existing phone lines or dedicated VAN phone lines and/or system.

Proprietary Standards — A set of standards used between organizations involved in exchanging electronic transactions. Proprietary standards are only available to a company and those they wish to exchange transactions with and is unique to their environment. Use of proprietary standards is no longer endorsed.

Public Key — In authentication, using a public key, the code is made "public" to all authorized trading partners (or their devices), who must open the message using the valid key.

Public Standards — A set of standards used between organizations for the exchange of standard business documents. Public standards are available to anyone interested in EDI exchange.

QR — Quick response is a business strategy adopted by the retail industry. QR means trading partners use technology to effectively managed the flow of business data in an effort to manufacture the right product at the right time and for the right price.

Segment — Unit of information in a transaction set. A segment can be used in multiple transaction sets or multiple times in the same transaction set. It is composed of elements and is analogous to a record.

SKU — Stock keeping unit; a unit designator to uniquely identify a product. Used in numerous industries.

Smart Cards — Magnetic cards that contain a microprocessor chip. Thousands of bits of data can be stored on a smart card and the data can be downloaded when making contact with the card reader; but more importantly, computations can be performed. Basically contained in a credit card size computer is the card's operating system, files, and algorithms. Smart cards can be used for payment, authorization, identification, and much more.

SMTP — Simple mail transfer protocol; a TCP/IP protocol governing electronic mail transmission and reception.

Spoke — Usually a small or medium size company which does EDI with a larger trading partner, or hub.

Standard Format — The basic agreed-upon format for an EDI document. Each transaction set or message format will look the same.

Statute of Frauds — A set of rules defined by the UCC to define and help administer business transactions and trade in the US.

Subelement — See *Composite Element*.

Subset — A subset of a national standard for ease-of-use within one industry. The subset usually indicates only those segments, elements, and code values needed by the industry. Also usually contains explanatory remarks.

Swipe Card — Magnetic cards store small units of data and allow card readers to read information from them. Swipe cards include credit/debit cards and access key cards.

Syntax — The collection of data formation rules for and EDI transaction set, much as grammar defines formation rules in a natural language.

TCP/IP — Transmission control protocol/Internet protocol, a communication protocol, used for Internet access.

TDCC — Transportation Data Coordinating Committee; used to be the secretariat for UCS, VICS, WINS, MOTOR, OCEAN, RAIL, and other standards with ANSI ASC X12. It was renamed EDIA and is no longer around.

Telephony — See *Computer Telephony Integration.*

Trading Partner — In the broad sense, any company doing business. A company that sends a purchase order and the company that receives it are each others' trading partners. The term is often used in a more specific sense to refer to companies sending and receiving documents via EDI.

Trading Partner Profile — Specific information that is used to uniquely identify an EDI trading partner. This information is usually maintained in the translation software.

Trading Partner Specific Mapping — Mapping the trading partner's exact segment and element requirements, with the idea that the map is used only for that one trading partner.

TRADACOMS — Trading Data Communications Standards; British standards defined for EDI exchange that was primarily used in the automotive industry.

Trailer — The ending segment of a set of segments. The trailer is a control structure.

Transaction Packeting — Automatic (out of translation software) grouping of like transactions to the same partner for the purposes of minimizing phone costs and the amount of work required to distribute transactions to business partners.

Transaction Set — The record formats for the data sent/received in a business transaction.

Transaction Set ID — A numeric or alphanumeric representation that identifies a transaction set. For instance, the transaction set ID 850 identifies a purchase order in X12.

Translation Software — Software that translates a flat file into a standard format and vice versa for transmission to a business partner via EDI.

UCC — Uniform Code Council; a U.S. organization that defines rules, such as what constitutes a contract, what is evidence, and what is a signature for business transactions.

UCS — Uniform communications standards; used in the grocery industry.

UPC — Universal product code; a unit designator that uniquely identifies a product.

UPN — Universal product number; a unique number to identify all healthcare products.

UN/ECE — After World War II, Western and Eastern European countries, Canada, and the United States formed the UN/ECE (United Nations Economic Commission for Europe) to deal with general trade issues. Other countries, such as Japan, Australia, and Hong Kong, were added as observatory participants. In the 1970s, the UN/ECE was commissioned to develop international EDI standards.

VAN — Value added network. VANs add value to the communication environment by allowing multiple computer types, modems, and transmission speeds to access the VAN electronic mailbox. Based on EDI control data, they will automatically place the EDI documents into the correct business partner mailbox.

VAN Interconnect — See *Interconnection.*

VICS — Voluntary Inter-Industry Communications Standards (used for general merchandising).

VMI — Vendor-managed inventory; a business strategy that allows the supplier to directly manage its customer's inventory levels at stores and distribution centers. The vendors is able to do that based on point of sale and usage information the customer sends. This gives the supplier the necessary information to know when and how much stock needs to be replenished, effectively managing the customer's inventory levels.

Web — See *World Wide Web.*

WINS — Warehouse Inventory Standards.

Workgroup Technologies — See *Collaborative Technologies.*

World Wide Web — A graphical subset of the Internet. Initially used for publishing marketing information, but becoming a tool to allow companies to conduct electronic commerce activities.

Workflow Automation — The automation of information processing. Traditionally, workflow has referred to automating internal procedures, but with electronic commerce, workflow applies to the management of external and internal information flow.

WWW — See *World Wide Web.*

X.400 — An international standard developed in 1984 to accommodate store-and-forward messaging for e-mail.

X.435 — A subset of X.400 designed to carry EDI messages.

X12 Standards — Generic EDI standards designed to allow a company to exchange data with any other company, regardless of industry. X12 standards are set by Accredited Standards Committee X12, whose work is approved by the American National Standards Institute. Accordingly, X12 standards are often called the ANSI X12 standards.

XCO — The External Communications Officer's primary focus is to assess and select the proper tools and technologies to streamline external business processes. This is a strategic role as the XCO not only monitors the current EDI and EC environment, but must set the future direction for business to business or consumer to business transaction processing.

Index

New Books in the 29th Street Press Library

THE AS/400 EXPERT: READY-TO-RUN RPG/400 TECHNIQUES

By Julian Monypenny and Roger Pence

As the first book in The AS/400 Expert series, *Ready-to-Run RPG/400 Techniques* provides a variety of RPG templates, subroutines, and copy modules, sprinkled with evangelical advice, to help you write robust and effective RPG/400 programs. The code building blocks are provided on an accompanying CD-ROM. 203 pages.

DDS PROGRAMMING FOR DISPLAY & PRINTER FILES, SECOND EDITION

By James Coolbaugh

Updated through OS/400 V4R3, the second edition offers a thorough, straightforward explanation of how to use DDS to program display files and printer files. A companion CD-ROM includes all the DDS, RPG, and CL source code presented in the book. 429 pages.

OPNQRYF BY EXAMPLE

By Mike Dawson and Mike Manto

Drawing from real-life, real-job experiences, the authors explain the basics and the intricacies of OPNQRYF with lots of examples to make you productive quickly. An appendix provides the UPDQRYF (Update Query File) command — a powerful addition to AS/400 and System/38 file update capabilities. 216 pages.

RAPID REVIEW STUDY GUIDES

Series Editor: Mike Pastore

Our Rapid Review Study Guides give you pre- and post-assessments to measure your progress, exam preparation tips, vocabulary drills, hands-on activities, and sample quiz questions on CD and in the book. Current titles include *Networking Essentials, Windows 95, System Management Server 1.2, Windows NT 4.0 Server, TCP/IP for Microsoft Windows NT 4.0, Windows NT 4.0 Workstation, Internet Information Server 4.0,* and *Windows NT 4.0 Server in the Enterprise.*

SQL/400 BY EXAMPLE

By James Coolbaugh

SQL/400 by Example includes everything from SQL syntax and rules to the specifics of embedding SQL within an RPG program. For novice SQL users, this book features plenty of introductory-level text and examples. For experienced AS/400 programmers, *SQL/400 by Example* offers a number of specific examples that will help you increase your understanding of SQL concepts and improve your programming skills. 204 pages.

TCP/IP AND THE AS/400

By Michael Ryan

TCP/IP and the AS/400 provides background for AS/400 professionals to understand the capabilities of TCP/IP, its strengths and weaknesses, and how to configure and administer the TCP/IP protocol stack on the AS/400. It shows TCP/IP gurus on other types of systems how to configure and manage the AS/400 TCP/IP capabilities. 362 pages.

WINDOWS NT MAGAZINE INSTANT SOLUTIONS:
TROUBLESHOOTING IIS 4.0 AND VISUAL INTERDEV 6.0

By Ken Spencer
Series Editor: Sean Daily

In the first of our Instant Solutions series of books, Ken Spencer takes knowledge selected from his development and system management experiences and from teaching and condenses it for you. In a handy problem/solution format, he includes tips for installing IIS and Visual InterDev, tips for optimizing IIS performance, tips for troubleshooting IIS and Visual InterDev security, and more. 168 pages.